W9-BUH-318

A LECTOR'S GUIDE

To The Episcopal Lectionary

by

Frank J. Mulligan

A LECTOR'S GUIDE

Copyright © 1986 by Frank J. Mulligan.
All rights reserved.
ISBN 0-9618112-0-X

FOREWORD

The Lectionary Committee of St. Mark's Church, Wichita, Kansas, was delighted to receive the manuscript of "A Lector's Guide to the Episcopal Eucharistic Lectionary," with the author's request that we consider it for publication.

Our Bishop, the Right Reverend Richard F. Grein, and many others, believe that the performance of the Liturgy of the Word is an area of our public worship in need of attention. The Guide addresses that need in brief, easy-to-grasp fashion. Designed by its author out of long experience in helping people deliver the Word with maximum effectiveness, its faithful use by those privileged to speak in the voice of the Spirit will, we feel, mark it as a gift to the Church.

We also believe that in addition to the enhancement of the public reading of the Word, the Guide can act as an effective basis for Bible study.

As we offer "A Lector's Guide" to the Church, we pray that the presence of Christ in the Word will be a richer experience for all who use the insights shared by the author.

The Rev. Robert W. Harvey, Rector,
St. Mark's Episcopal Church
Wichita, Kansas

Epiphany, 1987

AUTHOR'S PREFACE

The gathering and setting down of these encouragements for our Lectors and Lay Readers, who pass on to us the Word of Life, was a labor born of love for the message of the Spirit. I am especially grateful to the Pastoral Staff of Christ Church Cranbrook, Bloomfield Hills, Michigan, with whose approval this guide was first used, and to the Staff of the Cathedral of St. Paul in Detroit, whose interest has kept the project alive. Without these people there would be no guide.

Equally indispensable were the many insights gained from a long acquaintance with the Jerome Biblical Commentary, some of which are paraphrased here.

I pray that it will be of service to all whose preparation and delivery of the Word benefit from its recommendations.

The Author.

INTRODUCTION

Yes — as the rain and the snow come down from the heavens, and do not return without watering the earth . . . so the Word that goes from my mouth does not return to me empty, without carrying out my will and succeeding in what it was sent to do.

Isaiah 55:10-11

As our people listen to our presentation of God's Word, they are especially open to the message which, through our lips, will be passed on to them. The transmission of the Word is an event they look forward to, because there are important questions to be asked, if the Lord's words to Isaiah are to be fulfilled.

Our hearers may well ask, "How can we deal with the problems we must face this week? What has the Lord to tell us? What does the commemoration of this event in our Savior's life mean to us?"

We need the reality of the Word of the Lord. We need to know, to feel, that the Bible story we hear is real, nourishing, relevant to our lives. At a wedding, we think of our responsibility to love all human beings. Will that love be exemplified in the presentation of the readings? When we gather at a funeral service to give a loved one back to God, will the reading ease our own fear of death? We need the reassurance of the Word, as it speaks of the fullness of life available in our every circumstance.

As Lectors and Lay Readers, we are the transmitters of that Word. Our voice, our inflections, our very manner with the sacred Book, will nuance the reception of the Spirit of God for our hearers.

The purpose of this guide is to assist in the understanding, both by us and by those who listen to us, of the Word we announce to them. It is intended neither as a scholarly exegesis of the Scriptures, nor, in itself, as an aid to prayer and meditation. It contains simply an outline of the general sense of the passages assigned, in all three cycles, A, B and C, for the Sunday readings, along with suggestions about our vocal presentation of the text.

Except as occasionally noted, the Bible text used herein is the Revised Standard Version, most commonly read in Episcopal parishes.

For the sake of space, we have omitted three categories of readings:

1. The optional texts suggested in the Lectionary of the Book of Common Prayer;

2. The parenthetical verses which suggest the extension of a reading;
3. Special occasion readings, suited to the needs of a particular celebration for a community.

Every one of the sacred writers — most of them unknown to us — burned with a passion to share their reflections on the human condition and on our relationship to the mystery of God. They were eagles of the Spirit — consumed with a vision, shouting with joy, sobbing with distress, sorry for their sins, angry with idolatry, impatient with infidelity, rapt with the nearness of the One they knew not, whose loving presence they felt so keenly. And the profusion of songs, the poetry, the dramas, the revelations which flowed from their hearts, is all "inspired by God and profitable for teaching, for reproof, for correction, and for training in righteousness (2 Tim. 3:16-17)." It can be read and re-read time and again privately, with much personal benefit.

But the printed word travels in dried ink across a cold and lifeless page. The Bible at our lectern needs the human voice to transmit it, to infuse it with life, to bring home to those who hear it the immediacy that its messages had when the authors took pen in hand.

When we take our place at the lectern and open the Bible to read, then, we are no less than actors and actresses — storytellers, like the people of old. We strive to re-create, through their lines writ so long ago, the atmosphere of the day they were first set down.

Herein lies a demanding challenge. The most difficult lesson for a reader of the Word to learn is that the orderly system of commas, semicolons and periods in the pages of a book rarely applies to our presentations. That system was designed for columns of type on a page, to separate one idea from another, just as the Bible's chapters usually encompass one train of thought. As our human voice invests God's Word with life and breath, no longer will the commas, semicolons and periods dictate the tone of the sacred text. As readers, we observe the rules of oral punctuation, of which the following three are of prime importance.

The first rule we call the "mental period," at which we drop our voice, either to isolate a thought, to conclude it or emphasize it. For example, in the eleventh chapter of Matthew's Gospel, Jesus asks the Pharisees, "Why then did you go out? To see a prophet? Yes, I tell you, and more than a prophet." We never fail to drop the voice after "more;" the word and its sense leap out at us. We *know* John the Baptist was more than a prophet. Yet there is no period after "more." Our knowledge of the language puts it there.

Another rule of oral punctuation is the de-emphasizing of the word "said," or "saying." Most of the time this is the least important word in a sentence. It is merely a connecting link between the speaker in the text and the words uttered. It means nothing beyond that. Sometimes we will read a sentence like, "and the Lord spoke to Moses, saying, 'I will give you a land of milk and honey,'" or some such phrase. We drop the voice after "Moses," picking it up immediately for the important following words, which represent what the Lord said and to whom he spoke them. If someone spoke, it follows that something was said. There is no reason at all to stress the word "saying."

The third important rule is the knowledge of when to pause. It is the finest skill a reader can have. A slight pause after each sentence, sometimes more than once during a sentence, helps the thought to sink in and gives the listeners time to reflect on it, enabling them to follow the passage more intelligently. Pauses also mark transitions — from a narrative to a quotation, or a change in the situation being described.

To set down all the rules of oral punctuation would consume too many pages, and distract from the purpose of this guide. Most of the principles of good reading will be exemplified in the suggestions offered. But there is no substitute for the reader's gradual accumulation of experience, a knowledge of the sense of the passage, and careful study of the assignment before its public presentation.

We conclude our introduction with some fundamental principles of the art of reading the Word of the Lord.

1. No reader will be effective without preparation. You ought to know what book of the Bible you are reading from, and what the idea of the passage is. Read over your assignment — and its context — enough to find some meaning for yourself in it.

2. Your reading is nothing more than sound unless it comes from your personal prayer life experience. Thinking about how today's assigned text fits into your life will be the best single way to make your words carry conviction.

3. The people's attention must be on the reading, not the reader. The reader is a herald. The Bible's focus is on the Word, nothing else.

4. Practise reading your assignment aloud. Tape it; hear yourself. Try varying speeds. Vary the stresses until it makes sense to you. Read it aloud to someone else.

5. At the lectern, control the volume of your voice so that you speak each word clearly, with special attention to sentence endings.

6. You can never read too loudly. Most churches have good sound systems, but there are continual rustlings and noises in the congregation. The people in the last row need to hear you too. A word here about reading loudly: we never shout; we just read with more intensity. When a proclamation, as on feasts of great joy, is in order, we

ought never to be afraid to raise our voices. We have been trained, perhaps too well, as children, that speaking loudly in church is disturbing to others, a show of bad manners. Not so with the Word. We are proclaimers. We have put away the things of a child.

7. Force yourself to be slow and deliberate, never hurried. Let no one have a problem understanding or following you.

8. Maintain as much eye contact as you can with your hearers. Don't let the lectern or the book block your view of them, or theirs of you. If you are short of stature, ask those responsible to find a box for you to stand on.

9. Stand relaxed, with good posture. If you make a mistake, correct it and move right along.

10. Keep your scheduled appointment. We depend on you very much.

Frank J. Mulligan
Cathedral Church of St. Paul
Detroit, Michigan

About the author —

Frank Mulligan, a resident of Detroit, has spent his adult life in ordained pastoral ministry and in the sharing of his faith in national periodicals on pastoral, scriptural and spiritual themes. Formerly Director of Lay Readers at Christ Church Cranbrook, Bloomfield Hills, Michigan, he is a parishioner and Lay Reader at the Cathedral Church of St. Paul in Detroit. He is presently engaged in a Doctor of Ministry program at the Institute for Advanced Pastoral Studies in Detroit.

Year A

FIRST SUNDAY IN ADVENT

Suggested theme for today's readings —
The call of the Lord is fundamentally a call to newness of life.

Isaiah 2:1-5

General sense —

We begin the new Church year with Isaiah's prophetic vision of the gathering of the nations. The ancient idea of the mountain of God as their goal evokes deeply expectant soundings in all of us, as we celebrate once more the holy season of Advent.

This is the first of eight successive readings from this visionary of our destiny, extending through the Third Sunday after Christmas.

For your reading —

These hope-filled lines constitute a proclamation, especially as they stand out in striking contrast to the deplorable conditions described in Chapter 1.

Read with the strong conviction you share with all Christians that our hopes for peace and justice will be answered, at least in ourselves, with the coming of the Lord.

Verse 5 is to be read as a prayer response to the marvelous insights of the first four verses. Pause before you read it; then, as you make eye contact with your hearers, pray with them for a holy preparation for Christmas.

Romans 13:8-14

General sense —

In pursuit of the unity befitting a gathering of Christians, all must strive for individual goodness. There is a demand for charity in these lines, followed by motivation based on the nearness of the last days. We conclude with an appeal that being one with Christ will progressively wean us from the desire to sin.

For your reading —

Once again, as with Isaiah, we are summoned to renewed effort in our earthly struggles, as we prepare for the coming of the Lord.

Verses 8 through 10 review some of the principles of charity as it applies to everyday life. Read these lines carefully, with frequent pauses, stressing particularly verse 10, the total primacy of love.

11

In the final four verses the Apostle urges, as he does so often elsewhere, the nearness of the end of the world as the overriding reason for a life of virtue. These thoughts lend themselves to a stronger tone on your part; their relevance to our own lives still applies today.

Matthew 24:37-44

General sense —

The call to newness of life, common to all three readings today, appears again here, in the person and words of Jesus. Our destiny, he reminds us, will be revealed in the midst of our ordinary circumstances, unannounced to us.

For your reading —

This warning is more informative than it is ominous, so that too severe a tone in your voice does not seem to reflect the aim of Jesus. Deliver his message for what it proposes to be: a caution about what all of us know in our bones to be true — we do not die when we plan to, but when the Lord decides to take us. No need to speak sternly here at all.

SECOND SUNDAY IN ADVENT

Suggested theme for today's readings —
The strength of our hope lies in our striving for peace and justice.

Isaiah 11:1-10

General sense —

These lines describe no individual but the ideal king from the line of David. His charismatic gifts will make his reign one of peace and justice, standing as a signal that the whole world will share in his salvation.

For your reading —

In these lines are embodied our hopes for all the Advents of our lives. Read them as if you were announcing tidings of great joy, the charter of deliverance for an oppressed people — which of course you *are* reading, since the hope of great things sustains us all still.

Let your voice be clear and joyful. There are two natural pauses: before verse 6 and after verse 8. Those three verses describe the effect of an ideal world even on the animal kingdom.

The two final verses, 9 and 10, are the summit of the prophet's hope. Read them a bit more slowly and strongly, as you conclude on a note of optimism.

Romans 15:4-13

General sense —

Isaiah's theme of joyful Advent hope finds an echo here, as

Paul reminds the Church at Rome of the age-old encouragements of Scripture.

For your reading —
No particular verse stands out here. Verse 8 seems to be a bit stronger, but the whole passage hangs together so well as a hymn of hope and a summary of the causes of our expectations, that it would best be read in one tone of encouragement, similarly to the previous reading today from Isaiah.

Matthew 3:1-12

General sense —
Every Advent we pay tribute to this giant of Christ, John the Baptist, whose fire chars our half-hearted resolves as he proclaims the coming of the all-pure One into our midst.

The message of hope continues to be the theme of today's readings, as John cries out for justice and announces the kingdom to come.

For your reading —
John's sternness in verses 2 and 3 should be reflected in your voice. Let your mind return to your hearers in verse 4, as the narrative resumes and you address them directly.

At verse 7 the sternness comes back, all the way to the end of the passage. There is some easing in verse 11, as John promises to serve toward reconciliation, but the thrust of the message is taken up again, so that the reading can be described as a call for our attention, as we expect the Lord's coming.

A word about raising your voice: there is never a reason to shout. A moderate elevation of the voice, added to a slowing of the pace, is very effective in conveying a message with firmness and strength.

THIRD SUNDAY IN ADVENT

Suggested theme for today's readings —
All of our daily struggles are signs of the Kingdom of God growing within us.

Isaiah 35:1-10

General sense —
This outburst of confident joy is typical of our Advent readings. Isaiah comes close to envisioning another Exodus. He pictures the people gaining sight, hearing and strength as they march through the "wilderness and dry land." The blossoming desert, now graced by the Holy Way, is their happy passage back to Zion — or, figuratively, back to the way of the Lord.

For your reading —
These lines amount to a proclamation, so vivid is their imagery and so joyfully confident is their tone.

There are such clearly defined images, tumbling forth so rapidly, that it is not an easy passage to deliver. Almost every phrase strikes the eye of the mind with an image which would surely be stressed in other readings. Go slowly.

The last few words of verse 9 are the climax of the prophecy. "The redeemed," brought from exile, ransomed from bondage, are the chosen of God and the object of his final mercy. Only they — accent here the word "redeemed" — shall walk the Holy Way.

Verse 10 resounds with the echoes of the Exodus, as it looks forward to the Incarnation. Read it quietly. The Lord will come for all of us.

James 5:7-10

General sense —

James gently urges us to the patience of Advent, looking, as did Isaiah, to the coming of the Lord. It may strike us as odd that Jesus' name does not occur here as an example of suffering and patience. This epistle, however, is not specifically Christian in tone. It may have been a sermon or lesson given to a Jewish community, to whom the value and meaning of Christ's life would not have occurred at that point in history.

For your reading —

This loosely structured epistle has no outline or central theme, so that your reading needs no climax. Treat the passage as a short note on patience, suitable for the season, as well as an encouragement to fraternal charity.

Matthew 11:2-11

General sense —

Jesus personally authenticates the mission of John the Baptist, and in the same breath (verse 11) declares that John was only an announcer of even greater things to come.

John was looking for reassurance that Jesus was "he who is to come," perhaps because Jesus' preaching had not the fiery warnings of doom typical of the Baptist.

We are reminded of the coming of the true Kingdom today in verse 11.

For your reading —

You have been assigned to read a passage sparkling with contentious dialogue: the confrontation between the Precursor and the Messiah, the transition from the old to the new.

Enliven the conversation with the frequent modulations demanded by the text.

In verse 11 slow your pace, so that the emphatic tone of Jesus shows through as it should.

FOURTH SUNDAY IN ADVENT

Suggested theme for today's readings —

The center of our life is the listening for the coming of the Savior.

Isaiah 7:10-17

General sense —

We take the significance of this passage from the Gospel of Matthew, who considered verse 14 to refer to the Incarnation.

Isaiah's words, debated since the dawn of Biblical scholarship, and never to be understood completely, contain the expression for a young marriageable woman, rather than the technical word for a virgin.

In the solemnity of this prophecy, however, added to the use of the name Immanuel, Isaiah's vision stretches far into a hope-filled future, when the ideal king will be a true sign of God's presence among his people.

For your reading —

The Lord suggest that Ahaz ask for a sign that he will not be deposed. Ahaz finds it unacceptable to so tempt the Lord, Whereupon God, through the prophet, provides the sign.

Your reading of this key prophecy demands the usual voice changes associated with conversation, and a slowing of your pace for the vision in verse 14.

Verse 17 is the prophet's view of things to come, and merits a special emphasis as you conclude.

Romans 1:1-7

General sense —

Today, as Christmas nears, the name and life of Jesus Christ are specifically invoked. We look forward anxiously to the coming of the Savior, "designated son of God," who will be given to us this week, as we celebrate another Incarnation of him "to whom we are called to belong."

For your reading —

Paul here reveals the machinery of the action of God our Father leading to the gift of his Son.

This brief passage is really an elongation of the greeting of peace we share every time we celebrate the Eucharist. Read it, then, with a happy, upbeat tone; then, in verse 7b, drop your voice after "grace," and after "peace." Make that greeting a devout and fervent one. End the single sentence which makes up this entire passage with total eye contact with your hearers.

Matthew 1:18-25

General sense —

Matthew quotes Isaiah's prophecy as referring directly to Jesus's birth, after instructing the Jews, for whom he wrote this

Gospel, how the birth of the Savior happened.

This is the only Gospel in which Joseph is featured — a good and righteous man, and an example of Old Testament holiness for the Jewish catechumens to hear and identify with.

For your reading —

You are a storyteller here, anticipating the joyous event of later this week.

Tell your story with simplicity and directness, not emphasizing unduly any one part, but adopting the quiet, hushed tones of the days immediately before Christmas, as we listen intently for any news of the coming of our Savior.

CHRISTMAS — FIRST SERVICE

Suggested theme for today's readings —
The mystery of the Nativity fulfills the expectancy of our Advents all year long.

Isaiah 9:2-4, 6-7

General sense —

These noble lines may have their roots in a ceremony of royal accession. The ideal King was hailed as an adopted Son of God, the promises of the eternal covenant with David were recalled, and, in verse 6, the titles were bestowed on him with the hope that he would live up to them.

This is a key Messianic passage, a natural choice for the early dawn of Christmas, when this first service is celebrated, as we pass through the shadows of Advent.

For your reading —

When you reflect on how quickly this new presence in our life has superseded the expectant emptiness of Advent, you will catch the exultant mood of this great announcement.

Lean strongly on all the "image" words: "great light" (2); "multiplied"(3); "increased its joy"(3); "rejoice"(3); "Joy at the harvest"(3) "broken"(4).

Now pause, and begin the great news, speaking more slowly and carefully. Drop your voice after "child;" the notion of "born" is not important here. That word is a routine part of any birth announcement.

It seems better, in the ensuing phrase, to accentuate "given" rather then "son," to mark the Lord's generosity here.

Four titles conclude the reading, to be enunciated one by one, all of which are clearly separated by the commas which mark them.

Titus 2:11-14

General sense —

These lines from Paul's letter to his legate in Crete outline, as did Isaiah's proclamation in our first reading, the theological significance of the feast we celebrate today. The design of God in our behalf reaches from the eternity we came from to the eternity we are destined for, as it joins the grace of God at one end to our hope of future glory in Christ at the other.

Verse 13 is perhaps the most eloquent of Paul's professions of belief in the divinity of Jesus.

For your reading —

The brief texts assigned to this early morning Christmas service fit the mood of the occasion, a reminder of the true source of our Christmas joy. You are to announce the most marvelous Word of all: we have been delivered, ransomed, forgiven. And we must govern our lives in accordance with that dignity.

Perhaps you would feel more comfortable omitting the word "men" in verse 11, either by substituting "people" for it, or by just letting the phrase end with "all."

The passage is clear enough to enable you to do your very best with it.

Luke 2:1-14

General sense —

The mystery of the Nativity, foretold by the prophet and remembered by Paul today, still confronts our pride and baffles our intellect with its utter simplicity. As in the telling of so many other Bible stories, the facts and details are almost totally sublimated to the meaning. It is a message of redemption, of a prophecy fulfilled.

The local government, Jesus' royal lineage, the angels of heaven, ourselves with whom he is pleased, and the lowly shepherds, all join in a five-level masterpiece of storytelling to certify the universality of God's redemption.

For your reading —

This is a difficult reading. We've all heard it so many times, yet it must be told once again today. How do you make it meaningful?

Since this is the first Christmas Gospel, normally read early in the morning, begin in a hushed tone of wonder. We are hearing the event almost as it is happening — live, as it were — before the more theological reflections of the later services today. (Or, if you will, before the choir and the trumpeters have arrived.)

Imagine yourself sitting in a quiet room with some friends. Pause before verse 6 for the climax of the story.

At verse 8 your tone rises, as others share the happening. At verse 13 the angels light the sky. Now the world knows. End your reading strongly as the mystery draws us all to its center.

CHRISTMAS — SECOND SERVICE

Suggested theme for today's readings —
Undeserved grace

Isaiah 62:6-7,10-12

General sense —
The liberator who would, by mere coincidence, end the Babylonian Exile, is on his way. Cyrus, King of Persia, will overrun the Babylonian army, in the process freeing their victims, the Israelites, who had been away from home these forty-nine years.

The sacred writer, crying, "Behold, your salvation comes" (verse 11), personifies the people's joyful anticipation, even as today we rejoice at the coming of our Savior.

For your reading —
Announce the glad tidings loudly and clearly in verses 6 and 7.

Verses 10 through 12 are even more graphic. Lean on the key phrases, such as "Prepare the way for the people (verse 10); and "build up, build up the highway (verse 10)."

The climax of the passage, especially "behold, your salvation comes," rings out through verses 11 and 12. Make these lines your strongest. Be sure that every hearer is aware of their significance for this wondrous season of Christmas.

Titus 3:4-7

General sense —
The author of this brief letter reminds us that any goodness of ours had nothing to do with the appearance of God our Savior, any more than the Hebrews earned their deliverance by Cyrus in our first reading. We are still the objects of his mercy and love in this New Covenant, through his Son Jesus and the grace of the Holy Spirit.

For your reading —
Treat this passage as the calm and practical reminder that it is, reading it slowly and carefully.

We need to hear these inspired words to enter into the quiet and humble atmosphere which pervades our early Christmas morning worship.

Luke 2:15-20

General sense —
The adoration of the shepherds brings the local community to the divine creche, as our Father provides for his Son the first neighborly welcome.

And the mystery deepens. Who were the others "who heard it" in verse 18? Why did everyone wonder? What were their thoughts? What did Mary ponder in her heart?

The secret of the Nativity eludes us every year. We will be back next Christmas to be drawn into this marvelous — and unearned — grace, again.

For your reading —

Read these mysterious lines rather reflectively. This is a good opportunity to pause a bit after each sentence, to let each detail sink in and be treasured. We want to keep the quiet glow of this night in our hearts, as Mary did, so that we never cease to wonder about what has happened here.

Read verse 19 as if you had just turned, amid all the excitement, and noticed Mary's face.

CHRISTMAS — THIRD SERVICE

Suggested theme for today's readings —
How the Word penetrates us
Isaiah 52:7-10

General sense —

Now, at this third celebration of Christmas, the good news comes to us through the figure of the runners who used to race across the mountain ridges, as they neared Jerusalem with the news of distant battles won.

Their shout is repeated by the watchmen on the city walls as the writer draws an analogy of how the Word of the Lord penetrates us.

For your reading —

One of the most difficult lessons for us to learn as lectors or lay readers is that it is OK to raise our voices when the reading demands it.

"To the ends of the earth," as the passage says today, we hear great choirs, symphony orchestras, bells of every description, from handbells to booming carillons, ringing out the joy of our deliverance. Why can we not raise our God-given voices to proclaim the fullness of these rapturous lines we are assigned to read today?

People are so distracted by worldly troubles of all kinds that we must call out the Good News to attract their attention, not only at Christmas but all the year around.

Hebrews 1:1-12

General sense —

If you were to sum up the significance of the coming of Jesus into our world, these lines would best grasp the universality of that event and its importance in the plan of God throughout the ages. It is as if we were to view Christmas through the eye of God himself, as our Father's love penetrates our being.

For your reading —
Verse 3a is an important one to stress: it places in perspective the origin and intended effect of Christ's coming.

Pause before verse 5, as you begin the masterful chain of Old Testament quotations attesting to pre-eminence of the Incarnation. Make sure your voice separates the quotations by the few words which introduce each one, like "or again," or the single word, "or," which begins verse 10.

Your voice should be both solemn and triumphant. The Old Testament words are God's own, speaking of his Son, in the mind of the writer. This is a reading to be proclaimed.

John 1:1-14

General sense —
For centuries, until the streamlining of the Roman liturgy in recent years, these verses were read as the "last Gospel" at every Mass, after the final blessing and dismissal.

All earthly reflections on the mystery of the Incarnation pale before this profoundly divine genealogy. As it identifies Jesus Christ with the Word of the eternal God, it simultaneously penetrates and sanctifies the world by identifying the Word with all that is transitory, mortal and imperfect — the flesh of humanity.

For your reading —
This hymn to the Incarnation is so far beyond our power to grasp that the reading of it barely does it justice. What we can do is what other readers have done before us: we announce it slowly, savoring each powerful line, passing it on bit by bit to our hearers, so that they can attempt to understand it, even as we struggle to do the same.

Pause before verse 6, where John is introduced. As his role dissolves into the Light, you are back into the meaning of Jesus' mission and of our own divine adoption through him.

End your reading with the magnificent climax of verse 14, as the light of Christ dissolves in turn into the glory of God the Father. Read this verse as strongly and clearly as you can. It sums up a theme of today's readings: the penetration of our lives by the Word of the Lord.

FIRST SUNDAY AFTER CHRISTMAS
Suggested theme for today's readings —
God reveals himself as he reveals his will for us.
Isaiah 61:10 – 62:3

General sense —
Probably the three most magical words in the world to our Iranian hostages back in January 1981 were, "We're going home!" Many centuries ago, after a long and bitter exile, the

sacred writer here envisions the return of Israel to her former dignity.

Unlike 1981, when the departure of a President signalled liberation, the prophet, living under a theocracy, instantly attributes all good things to God. He dwells not on victory or revenge but on the restoration of the glory of his people, by the will of a loving God.

For your reading —

This is one of those occasions when you must discipline yourself to speak out loudly. We are permeated with Christmas. The joy of the Church after the dark days of Advent is here released to the full, and it is right that, as heralds of the Word, we should reflect that atmosphere in our rendering of this splendid text.

The printed punctuation lends itself admirably to the theme of the reading, so that the only challenge to you remains the raising of your voice to the tone of a proclamation. There is no need to strain yourself by shouting. Let the power come from your midsection up through your vocal passages. After some practice with this at home you will find that this works quite well.

Galatians 3:23-25, 4:4-7

General sense —

The notion of faith versus the Law is a complex and elusive one, until we grasp the ancient Jewish idea of the Law's pre-eminence. One need only to skim through the early books like Leviticus to see the permeation of the rules into every detail of daily life as a guardian of morality.

But, as Paul says today in defending his gospel, with Christ's advent our faith makes us sons and daughters and heirs of God by our redemption. The Old Testament God of thunder and storm is in the Spirit's cry, "Our Father." The Christian is free. There is only one law left: the law of love, revealed in Jesus Christ.

For your reading —

The reading proceeds in a somewhat narrative tone, as Paul explains the supersession of the old Law by the new dispensation.

At verse 4 of chapter 4 the thesis nears its climax with the effects of our adoption. Your speed should slow down, to reflect the importance of our sonship (or daughtership). Lean on *"born under the Law,"* because that starts an action phrase: "to *redeem* those who were under the Law." The strongest word in verse 5 is "sons," our new status.

Lean on the final word of verse 6, too: "Father!" Finish with a pause after "son" in verse 7, to repeat the affirmation of our new dignity.

John 1:1-18

General sense —

The "General sense" portion of the page for the Third Service for Christmas holds here, and should be consulted. Verses 15 through 18 are added for this day, to offer the witness of John the Baptist, the superseding of the Law of Moses, and the complete revealing of the Old Testament hidden God in Jesus, according to God's saving will.

For your reading —

Verse 15 comes after a pause, as the Baptist is re-introduced. Raise your voice a bit to emulate his cry, in verse 15.

Verse 17 makes a strong contrast. A clear stop after "Moses" will make that evident to our hearers.

In verse 18, although no one has seen God, "he" has now made him known to us. "He" needs to be leaned on strongly as you conclude.

For verses 1-14, there are some reading suggestions in the comment on the Gospel for the Third Service at Christmas, which should be consulted.

SECOND SUNDAY AFTER CHRISTMAS

Suggested theme for today's readings —
Christ comes to us as our hope in the darknesses of life.
Jeremiah 31:7-14

General sense —

Jeremiah's vocation as a prophet was a difficult one. He witnessed the fall of a great empire, that of Assyria, and the rise of a greater one, Babylonia. And in the midst of these convulsions, the Israelite kingdom of Judah came to its downfall in the ruin of Jerusalem and in the Exile.

Yet he hopes, in today's passage, for Israel's conversion and her return to Palestine. Though that was not to be, the prophet's hope did not vanish — as ours does not either, no matter what happens.

For your reading —

We apply Jeremiah's triumphal proclamation to the presence of the Christ Child in our midst, and immediately it takes on a new and everlasting meaning.

There are no mood changes in this passage. Read it as if we were marching through the desert toward our holy city, (verse 8), with your voice raised in gladness.

Your principal effort must be to keep a positive, happy tone throughout. Notice how many groups you are addressing: the blind, the lame, the pregnant, the farmers, the girls, the young and old men, even the priests. Accent each group as they are named. This good news, as Jeremiah insists repeatedly, is for *all* the people.

Ephesians 1:3-6, 15-19a

General sense —

The happy noise of another Christmas is with us still. "The immeasurable greatness of his power in us who believe" is the cause of our joy. Out of the cold and darkness of the winter we are "blessed in Christ with every spiritual blessing." A smiling Paul greets us across the ages, and our Christmas celebrations are richer for it, whatever our personal darknesses may be.

For your reading —

Begin strongly with Paul's invocation of praise in verses 3 and 4.

At verse 5 we have another reason to be glad: we are now God's sons (and daughters too, of course, as soon as our Bible is modernized!). Let your voice soften a bit as this amazing change in the status of the believer is described.

Now pause again, as you begin verse 15. Paul takes a breath, and turns directly toward us. Read these last five verses more carefully, being very conscious of your eye contact with the people. Stress particularly the Apostle's identification of his faith with our own, as you finish trying to understand "the immeasurable greatness of his power in *us* who *believe*."

Matthew 2:13-15, 19-23

General sense —

The Holy Family in Egypt, their flight and return, is peculiar to the Gospel of Matthew alone, and like our first two readings, it is a momentary time of darkness mixed with hope. It appears nowhere in any other literature. It could be a symbolic presentation of Jesus' royal Messiahship and how the secular world fought against it. Three years would elapse before the world would claim him, in the agony of Holy Week.

For your reading —

The verses which tell of Herod carrying out his promise of verse 13 are skipped over here. You are presented with a quite straightforward account of this uprooting of a young family. Just let the story tell itself as you read.

The dream motif is a common vehicle of Old Testament revelation, used here by Matthew for the teaching manual for which he wrote his Gospel.

THE EPIPHANY

Suggested theme for today's readings —
The effects of the coming of Christ in us.

Isaiah 60:1-6,9

General sense —

Is the glory of the Lord wrapped around us, in this manifestation to the non-Jewish world we celebrate today? Or is it we, who by his presence within us radiate his light from ourselves?

We shall, says verse 5, "*be*" radiant; and all three of today's readings echo that quality and its natural corollary.

For your reading —

These glowing lines are indeed a proclamation, worthy of a permanent Sunday feast every year, as the command comes to acknowledge our dignity, to "rise and shine."

Read it, then, like a proclamation, in an upbeat and triumphant mode. No one verse seems to stand out over the others, so that you must sustain your tone throughout.

The last few words in verse 6 would be an excellent ending here; verse 9 seems anticlimactic. But it concludes your reading on a fitting and accurate note, deserving of your special emphasis: it is we who are glorified.

Ephesians 3:1-12

General sense —

Isaiah foretold the charismatic effect of a coming of the Lord: the reflection of him in us. Paul exemplifies that Spirit: he is the Lord's preacher, come what may, blessed with the gift of helping the world to understand the mystery of Christ.

For your reading —

Verse 4, after Paul's introduction, reveals the heart of his thesis: we have been made heirs of a divine promise. Render verses 4 through 6 as a keynote of the reading, strongly and emphatically.

The ensuing verses explain what it means that "God might now be made known." They climax as you conclude, in verse 12, with God's gifts of "boldness and confidence of access." This is your second place of emphasis, to give your hearers a memorable, and practical, thought for the day.

Matthew 2:1-12

General sense —

Before Paul but after Isaiah, we read now of one of the events at the climax of history: the manifestation of the Messiah to the world.

Whether the incident is poetry or legend or history does not matter. Our faith does not hang thereby. What is interesting is that at the center of this very Jewish story in a very Jewish Gospel stand three Gentiles, men of another clime and culture, bestowing on Jesus the symbolic gifts of gold for his kingship, incense for his divinity, and myrrh for his suffering.

For your reading —

Drop your voice after "Jerusalem" in verse 1. The word "saying" is to be glided through, because the words of the question in verse 2 are more important.

Use your storytelling skills throughout here. Few passages in the Bible lend themselves better than this smoothly flowing narration, in which not a word is wasted.

Pause briefly after "worshipped him" in verse 11, for a moment of reverence as the worlds of Jew and Gentile meet at last.

FIRST SUNDAY AFTER EPIPHANY

Suggested theme for today's readings —
Through his revealing of himself, God reshapes our world.

Isaiah 42:1-9

General sense —

From the Book of Consolation, this passage begins quietly with the Son of the Suffering Servant. The Suffering Servant is the ideal Servant of God, the perfect Israelite, who personifies the prophet's insight into the meaning of the nation's tribulations.

The Song ends with a hymn of praise to God's power to re-create the universe through his Word — a power we celebrate at the Epiphany, in the presence of the new Servant of God, Jesus Christ.

For your reading —

Read the first three verses calmly, after you have caught your hearers' attention with the opening verse. Drop your voice after "chosen," as the meaning moves from the qualities of the Servant to God's love for him.

After the usual pause on finishing verse 4, verse 5 begins a bit more loudly.

Verse 5 is an introduction to God's words, so that the strongest part of the reading is the last four verses, 6 through 9. Dropping your voice after nearly every phrase will give the words of the Lord the weight and dignity they deserve.

Read verse 8 strongly, as the Lord repeats his name, and maintain that tone until the end.

Acts 10:34-38

General sense —

Peter's statement, as this short passage opens, marks a breakthrough in Jewish thinking. The Israelites were by tradition a closed society, forbidden even to associate with outsiders, whom they considered pagans and sinners.

Peter suddenly understands that God's grace is universal, extended even to the Gentiles, as Isaiah, in our first reading, had foreseen long ago. That insight revolutionizes Peter's whole approach to his missionary work from this moment on.

How mysterious are the ways of God, that he who denied

Jesus three times is now given this pivotal insight, that God doesn't care what religion we belong to, if any, as long as we do "what is right and acceptable to him."

For your reading —
The Feast of the Epiphany, by which God manifested his son to the Gentiles in the person of the Magi, suits this reading to our celebration this week.

You have only a half-minute to bring this important message to your hearers. Make every second count, as you let the wonder and awe Peter must have felt come through in your voice.

Matthew 3:13-17

General sense —
Jesus, in an act of the most exquisite courtesy and humility, submits to a rite of repentance and confession of sin. "Righteousness is fulfilled" as this devout Jew practises the good and virtuous life. He sees himself here not as the royal conquering Messiah, but, reminiscent of Isaiah's phrase, as the Suffering Servant. There is no indication that anyone else at the scene witnessed either the baptism or the heavenly vision.

For your reading —
This is an important conversation, revealing, as seldom in the Gospels, how Jesus thought of himself.

Speak the words of Jesus in verse 15 with the gentleness of someone who asks no favors.

In verse 16 the tempo changes quickly, as the heavens open for our Father's endorsement. Drop your voice after "heaven" in verse 17. This is the key word because it is the source of the vision. The word "saying" is to be glided through as if it were not there. "This is my beloved son" is what matters.

SECOND SUNDAY AFTER EPIPHANY

Suggested theme for today's readings —
The presence of Jesus Christ in the world is the core and center of our Christian life.

Isaiah 49:1-7

General sense —
The prophet, discouraged by the fruitlessness of his ministry, receives from the Lord, in verse 6, an even wider responsibility: to speak to the entire world. The bold exchange in verses 3 and 4, after Isaiah has complained of being hidden away in an insignificant role, is typical of people who consult God with their service record, expecting that good things will happen to them.

This call to the Gentiles is one of many in the Old Testament which prefigured the manifestation of the infant Jesus to the Magi at Bethlehem.

For your reading —

Begin strongly with Isaiah's call for attention in verse 1, and maintain your slightly raised voice through verse 4.

At verse 5 comes the self-evaluation which establishes the prophet's worth. This verse serves as a long comma, during which your voice does not fall.

With verse 6 Isaiah must repeat the introduction, "he says." The words of the Lord now take center stage, so that your delivery of the last two verses, the central thrust of the passage, will be at a slower pace and with increased intensity.

1 Corinthians 1:1-9

General sense —

In these joyous post-Christmas days, all are one in adoration of the Christ who is made flesh and dwells among us — "both their Lord and ours," says the Apostle. Jesus' coming has already enriched us (verse 5), as we wait for the total revelation of the Lord (verse 7).

Today's reading is the first of seven from this letter to Corinth, taking us through the Epiphany season.

For your reading —

In verse 3, after you have delivered Paul's opening salutation, drop your voice after "grace" and after "peace." The verse climaxes the opening of the entire letter.

Verses 4 through 9 ring with joyful echoes of the recent feast of the Incarnation, as the Apostle praises the coming of the Lord five times by name, for a total of nine times during today's passage. Read these lines with a smile in your voice, making frequent eye contact with your hearers.

John 1:29-41

General sense —

As Paul so intensely did in our previous reading today, John here makes the Christ the focal point of attention for the crowds, crying out, in prophecy of Jesus' sacrifice, "Behold, the Lamb of God!" As he supports that statement with his own inspired witness, two of his own disciples begin following Jesus instead.

For your reading —

When you read, "Behold, the Lamb of God!" whether in verse 29 or verse 36, be careful to let those words stand out, as they must have arrested the attention of those who first heard them. They were enough to attract Andrew and Peter.

The conversational exchanges are short, which means that you must read them carefully, to bring out their importance.

The passage today is a fine challenge for your storytelling skills. In this Epiphany season we are all called to become disciples of Jesus.

THIRD SUNDAY AFTER EPIPHANY

Suggested theme for today's readings —

The revelation that the Lord centers our lives includes with it our responsibility to keep his commandments.

Amos 3:1-8

General sense —

This passage is the keynote of Amos' prophecy. Preparing the nation for the invasion of the Assyrian army, he reminds them that their election by God means a responsibility to heed his laws. He defends his authority to speak: things happen for a reason, he insists in verses 3 through 6, just as the call of the Lord is his reason for speaking out.

For your reading —

You are delivering today a call for attention, the introduction to an examination of conscience for a nation going astray.

Read these lines strongly, with conviction. You will find the rhetorical questions to be not a part of our modern way of speaking. Nevertheless, give them the insistence the prophet intended.

The interruption in verse 7 was added later, most scholars agree, in praise of prophecy. But verse 8 concludes the reading with a reminder that we feel compelled to pass on what the Lord makes clear to us.

1 Corinthians 1:10-17

General sense —

We continue our readings from this letter, as Paul appeals for unity and charity, claiming his particular vocation to be the preaching of the Gospel.

For your reading —

Paul's appeal is to us as well. As we celebrate the season of the Epiphany, we are also to be one in Jesus Christ.

The passage has no particular climax. Verse 17, the final verse, should be read a bit more slowly, since it is Paul's clearest statement of how he thinks of himself, even as Amos did in our first reading.

Matthew 4:12-23

General sense —

Jesus' first open proclamation of the Gospel takes place after the imprisonment of John. Perhaps Jesus knew that John would be seen no more, or felt that the Baptist had introduced him sufficiently well. At any rate, he travels to a place which centuries before had felt the wrath of the Lord, to fulfill Isaiah's prophecy by making the people there the first to hear of the Lord's salvation.

For your reading —
Jesus' opening of his public ministry is a Gospel milestone; as such, it merits emphasis as you read verse 17.

Change the mood to the narrative at verse 18. From here to the end in verse 23, you are the storyteller.

FOURTH SUNDAY AFTER EPIPHANY
Suggested theme for today's readings —
Holiness is totally available to everyone, thanks to the mercy of God in Jesus Christ.

Micah 6:1-8

General sense —
Most regard today's passage as the classic text for prophetic religion. The charge by God, both prosecutor and judge in this world-sized courtroom, is forgetfulness of all the Lord has done for his people. And the divine sentence is not burnt offerings, sacrifices, or even "the fruit of my body for the sin of my soul," but simply the change in one's ways, which is the only true sign of fidelity.

For your reading —
Verses 3 through 5, with many more additions, used to be read some years ago as part of our Good Friday services.

This is a difficult passage to deliver, because of its accusing tone and because it is the Lord almighty who first speaks. Be mindful of the dignity as you read these lines.

In verses 6 and 7, after a pause, the prophet — or, more accurately, Israel, the defendant — asks what the sentence might be.

Pause again after verse 7, and read verse 8, the amazingly lenient verdict, calmly and quietly, yet with some intensity, that your hearers may remember in their hearts how deeply it resonates the voice of truth.

1 Corinthians 1:26-31

General sense —
This remarkable passage exemplifies the irony of the Gospel — that God never seems to choose according to our ways. "Even things that are not," the nonentities — the Gentiles — are chosen to hear the Word, so that the pretensions of those who account themselves as something might be brought down. We are to boast of nothing but the Lord.

For your reading —
Read these lines carefully, so that no one misses the point of this shocking paradox. There are only a few verses, so that your pace need not be hurried. It is important that everyone understands what is said here.

Verse 30 is the climax of the reading; it brings the paradox home to its single point, and should be read in a stronger tone of voice.

Matthew 5:1-12

General sense —
We begin today a series of five readings from Matthew's account of the Sermon on the Mount. This is the proclamation of the Kingdom of God, the Good News. Matthew introduces it solemnly, in verses 1 and 2.

The beatitudes enumerate not commandments, as Moses brought down from Mount Sinai, but they gently draw forth the quality and activity of the virtuous person.

Paul, in our second reading today, singled out the lowly as God's beloved, echoing the tone of the Sermon here, the charter of the New Covenant.

For your reading —
There is no new, or unusual, or striking way to deliver these immortal lines. They must be read slowly, one at a time, so that the words will speak for themselves, resonating in the hearts of all of us who long for the coming of the Kingdom, in the world and in ourselves.

FIFTH SUNDAY AFTER EPIPHANY
Suggested theme for today's readings —
As Christians we are witnesses to God's care for all people.

Habakkuk 3:2-6, 17-19

General sense —
The Lord comes in power to avenge his people, as he did centuries before, in the day of the mighty Exodus under Moses. The prophet, in verse 2, remembers history, and prays for the return of divine justice. Whatever loss comes, the Lord is trusted and rejoiced in.

For your reading —
As you deliver this heartfelt prayer of trust, based on the prophet's vision, your appreciation for the "sound of words" in the first section, verses 3 through 6, will be your best ally. Make these wonderful sights and sounds come alive by the raising of your voice.

The second segment, verses 17 and 19 — the act of faith — concludes the reading. Be aware that the entire verse 17 is only a dependent clause. The principal point comes in verses 18 and 19: the joy of the divine Epiphany, or manifestation, which we celebrate this season. Conclude with a strong emphasis on the prophet's declaration of trust.

1 Corinthians 2:1-11

General sense —

Paul had attempted, at Athens, to speak to the Gospel as a philosopher, in Acts 17:16-34. But he was poorly understood and coolly received.

Now, he will reveal "a secret and hidden wisdom of God," not for the wise but for those of faith, through God's Spirit. Gone is the philosophical approach: "I decided to know nothing among you except Jesus Christ and him crucified."

For your reading —

Paul sets down here a rather personal witness. It is not easy for an educated person to forego his learned ways and speak so openly of "weakness and much fear and trembling."

Typical of the Apostle, the ideas come tumbling forth; your reading must slow them down somewhat, so that your hearers may appreciate the growing spirituality of this man.

Verse 2 is the key to his mindset, and ought to be delivered strongly, from this point through verse 5.

Verse 6 returns to the topic of his letter; but be careful to render the remaining verses in a clear, unhurried tone. They are our basis for understanding the mystery of the Epiphany.

Matthew 5:13-20

General sense —

With these homely metaphors of salt and light, readily grasped by the peasants to whom he speaks, Jesus continues his revelation of the Kingdom of Heaven.

Verse 17 begins Matthew's effort to state Jesus' position toward the Law. The Savior speaks boldly to a very tender point. The Law was, in a tradition four thousand years old, the safe and secure guide of conduct, assuring all of good relations with God. Jesus does not accept this value, because he knows that letter-perfect observance can generate hypocrisy (verse 20).

For your reading —

Verses 13 through 16 reflect the tone of a proclamation, as Jesus raises his voice so that everyone on the hillside may hear.

At verse 17, after a pause, Jesus changes to a more explanatory mode of speaking. Your voice ought to do the same.

Remember, nevertheless, that the tone remains insistent. Jesus is deliberately contradicting tradition here.

SIXTH SUNDAY AFTER EPIPHANY

Suggested theme for today's readings —
The gentleness of God's leading us lies in his recognition of and respect for our free will.

Ecclesiasticus 15:11-20

General sense —

This book, called either Ecclesiasticus or Sirach, is a part of the Greek Old Testament which was not taken into the Hebrew canon at the time of the establishment of that canon by Jewish scholars in A.D. 90. Along with thirteen other books, it is one of the Apocrypha, or hidden writings.

The passage we read today is an affirmation of our free will, which is masterfully coupled with the teaching that God is the source of all human activity. Our comments are on the text of the Jerusalem Bible.

For your reading —

Direct, clear and to the point, these lines should be read with confident assurance, in a calm yet firm tone.

Verses 18 through 20, summarizing the reading, ought to be separated from the first six verses, 11 through 17, by a pause. Then, your reading pace slows a bit, as you tell of the true position of God with respect to our freedom.

1 Corinthians 3:1-9

General sense —

The Church at Corinth, split by factions, here learns of Paul's realization that they are still rather young in the ways of the Spirit, as well as his compassionate understanding of that situation. The ancient words of wisdom in our first reading find an echo in verses 3 and 4. We are always free to choose.

For your reading —

The earnest appeal of the Apostle strikes a very personal note; its directness of approach should put an edge in your voice as you share in his anxiety to set things in perspective.

The final verse, 9, brings the passage to its climax, and should be delivered in an authoritative way, to settle the issue with finality.

Matthew 5:21-24, 27-30, 33-37

General sense —

Jesus' Sermon on the Mount takes three commonplaces in the life of weak and sinful people, and turns them around to the way it is in the Kingdom of Heaven. We are to ask forgiveness; we are to avoid occasions of sin; we are not to fall into the emptiness of futile oath-taking.

For your reading —

If you pause after each of the verses which separate the three segments of this reading, namely, verses 24, 30 and 37, you will make their individuality clear to your hearers.

Otherwise, no special emphasis marks these three counsels of the Master. Read them calmly and in a normal tone of voice.

SEVENTH SUNDAY AFTER EPIPHANY

Suggested theme for today's readings —
Our Christian lives are by their nature opposed to the ways
of the world.

Leviticus 19:1-2, 9-18

General sense —
We read today admonitions on charity and consideration for
others, framed by the primitive outlook of the ancients, long before the Jews became a nation. The Exile was centuries in the
future; the only law of the time was the Ten Commandments.

What makes this primitive theology relevant to us today is
its introduction in verses 1 and 2. Holiness is to motivate every
area of life behavior, whether it be leaving something for the
poor, or dealing justly with other people.

For your reading —
Read these lines as if you were speaking with the lips of
Moses. Although there are no points of special emphasis, your
voice will not be raised in vain. The grace of the Lord will move
us at some point to be more kind, and more generous with our
worldly goods.

1 Corinthians 3:10-11, 16-23

General sense —
Further motivation for the homely precepts in our first reading now comes from a more sophisticated theology: we are temples of the Spirit, and we are chosen to belong to Christ despite
our foolish weaknesses.

For your reading —
Pause after verse 11, as the Apostle turns, in verse 12, from
a general principle to direct address.

Verses 16 and 17 are spoken in a reverent tone, expressing
a profoundly affecting truth for all of us.

Again Paul changes the subject, in verse 18, as he speaks of
the wisdom of foolishness. These three verses, 18 through 20,
bear a personal application, to be delivered rather strongly. Paul
is disturbing the self-sufficient here.

The summation begins in verse 22b, with "all are yours,"
and continues to the end of verse 23. Back into your voice should
come the tone of reverence, as you slow your pace and reduce
your tone, to drive home the fundamental principle of the whole
passage: we are God's.

Matthew 5:38-48

General sense —
The Sermon on the Mount must have stunned its hearers.
One after another, Jesus revokes the old ways. The old law of

retaliation is replaced by "do not resist." Then, to take it out of the abstract, Jesus enumerates four concrete examples: physical violence is to be suffered (verse 39); legal contention is to be yielded to, and more (40); so is forced labor (41); and beggars and loan-seekers are to be honored (42).

Finally, most remarkable (and most difficult) of all, we are to love even the unlikeable, and on top of that, not as an extra work but as what is expected of us.

For your reading —

There is no mistaking the severe tone of this reading. Our familiarity with these precepts today can be an obstacle to delivering them with the pointedness they had when Jesus first uttered them.

Try to place yourself in Jesus' frame of mind as he boldly confronts these comfortable people. This is a stern reading, devoid of the Savior's usual compassion.

EIGHTH SUNDAY AFTER EPIPHANY

Suggested theme for today's readings —
In our fidelity to the ideals of Jesus is the source of our happiness.

Isaiah 49:8-18

General sense —

The author of these lines, writing nearly two hundred years after Isaiah, proclaims the marvelous reversal of the fortunes of Israel, and sees the redeeming compassion of the Lord overcome even the humiliation of being forgotten.

For your reading —

For your hearers to grasp the mood of this oracle, or saying, they must depend on the enthusiasm for this "Second Spring" which is reflected in your raised, upbeat voice.

In this difficult reading, the writer is on an exceptional "high," as he contemplates what good things lie ahead.

Pause after verse 13, as you begin the objection in verse 14. Then pause again after 14, to let this most touching expression of divine love make its fullest impact, in verses 15 and 16.

Verses 17 and 18 conclude on the same joyful note, as the Lord swears fidelity by his very life.

1 Corinthians 4:1-5, 8-13

General sense —

Paul, though a servant of the Gospel, will brook no invasion of his conscience by human judgment. He applies the same principle, that God alone is our judge. With biting irony he contrasts the sufferings of an apostle with the smugness of those who think themselves better than others.

With this passage we conclude our eight readings from this letter.

For your reading —
Read the first five verses with the self-assured confidence of one who has been stung by opinions he does not care about, and who now stands apart from them.

With your voice raised, verse 8 begins Paul's attack on the people's self-satisfied nonchalance. Keep up a fairly rapid pace through to the end in verse 13, as Paul tries to make them realize what a lowly and demanding vocation he has chosen.

Matthew 6:24-34

General sense —
Jesus, as did Paul many years later, takes aim at our selfish preoccupations with creature comforts. With the divine genius which is his birthright, he can speak simultaneously on three levels: the fields of lilies, destined for the oven, the ancient glories of a long-ago king, and the care of his Father for all creatures.

For your reading —
This entire passage should be delivered with some urgency. Jesus is speaking to all the ages; we need to be told these things as much as his audience did.

Keep your voice at a steady pitch until the mood eases in verses 31 through 34, so that you may conclude as Jesus did, with words of consolation.

To avoid sexism, you may wish to make some word substitutions. Suggested are "you" for "he" in verse 24; "your" for "his" in verse 27; "you" for "man" in verse 30.

LAST SUNDAY AFTER EPIPHANY
Suggested theme for today's readings —
Living according to Jesus' teachings will transfigure our lives and values.

Exodus 24:12, 15-18

General sense —
Moses has received the Ten Commandments and many other laws for the newborn nation. Now he is called to ascend the mountain again, so that we may hear more of this ancient Epiphany as the season closes.

This manifestation of the absolute "otherness" of God, and his practise of teaching his people through an intermediary, such as Moses, are perennial Old Testament themes.

The numbers seven and forty are sacred designations in Old Testament history, not necessarily indicative of any specific time period.

For your reading —

In the few moments you have in which to deliver these lines, your story-telling skills will be your strength. This is a tale of obscurity and mystery, bearing little relevance to our modern-day routines.

Invest it, through your use of the sense of wonder we all possess, with the awe the people must have felt when they first experienced it.

Philippians 3:7-14

General sense —

The great Apostle has thoroughly assimilated the Lord Christ into his life. Now, in his maturity, twenty years after his conversion, Jesus has become his center, far surpassing any other worldly advantage.

As he reflects on how different his outlook is, he lays down the same challenge for all: righteousness not through any observance of law but through faith. It is a fitting attitude in which to end the Epiphany season and look toward Lent.

For your reading —

Very few are ever granted the grace of regarding an entire career, with all its struggles and achievements, as nothing — even rubbish — compared to the possession of Jesus Christ.

Your delivery of this passage should reflect something of the atmosphere of awe Moses must have experienced on Mount Sinai. No one, at least in the pages of the Bible, has ever spoken like this.

Accent the victory in verse 8, and the sudden realization in verse 12 that Paul may be bragging a bit.

The last two verses conclude the passage with Paul's looking beyond his hearers, beyond his present state, and ahead to whatever is in store for him. It is a note of triumphant hope.

Matthew 17:1-9

General sense —

The Transfiguration completes today's readings with yet another manifestation of the glory of the Lord.

Yet Matthew's account of the incident ends with a revealing glow of humanity, as Jesus touches his disciples and bids them not to be afraid, but to keep the episode to themselves.

For your reading —

Pause before verse 2, then speak in a tone of reverence and awe as the hidden glory of Jesus suddenly appears.

Quicken your pace as you begin verse 4, to reflect the excitement of Peter, and resume your natural pace for the appearance of the bright cloud.

Verses 7 and 8 are read in a gentle tone, as the Master returns to himself.

ASH WEDNESDAY

Suggested theme for today's readings —
Our life is a showcase for our values. Lent is the time to take stock of them.

Joel 2:1-2, 12-19

General sense —
A great locust plague has come over the land. Joel's account of it swarms through the first two chapters of his book.

But events always evoke the presence of the Lord. The cloud of locusts is his hand, his judgment, overshadowing an unfaithful nation with the darkness of remorse.

In the end, nevertheless, his mercy wins over all, as we, his people, gather to fast and do penance, to begin the holy season of Lent.

For your reading —
Your hearers are very well disposed today for this two-part reading. The spirit of Lenten penance moves us all. As you announce verses 1 and 2, let your voice ring out with the tone of the six weeks to come: weeks of fasting, of prayer and penance, and sorrow for our sinfulness.

Suddenly, at verse 12, the mood changes completely. Our prayers reach the ear of a God "gracious and merciful, slow to anger and abounding in steadfast love." Your voice softens, becomes gently insistent with the real message of Lent: "rend your hearts and not your garments."

Finish with the strong reassurance that we will be spared, and that our devotion will never allow anyone to wonder where our God is.

2 Corinthians 5:20b – 6:10

General sense —
How could anyone better urge us on to a happy Lent than in these words? "We beseech you, on behalf of Christ, be reconciled to God." So Paul opens today's passage as we enter on this holy season. These next few weeks will be a source of grace: "We entreat you not to accept the grace of God in vain." And as in all strivings of the spirit, "now is the acceptable time."

The writer leaves no doubt as to what he has been through for the Gospel, as he masterfully turns each loss into a profit.

For your reading —
Open somewhat slowly, yet with firmness; these lines sum up the purpose of Lent. Accent the "we" in verse 21.

After the quote from Isaiah in verse 2, make its application as strongly as you can: "*Now* is the time; *now* is the day."

The remainder of the reading deserves repeated emphasis on each of Paul's sufferings, in verse 5, and his virtues in verse 6. It would be over-reacting and annoying if you were to "punch" each one of them, but they do rate some importance. Verse 6 should be read in a more gentle tone than verse 5, as Paul seems to contend that the virtues overcome the troubles.

From verse 8b on, mark the contrasts clearly by the tones of your voice, as you conclude on a strong and positive note.

Matthew 6:1-6, 16-21

General sense —

The Sermon on the Mount is halfway through, as Jesus here corrects the self-seeking of the Pharisees; and he does it on their own grounds; almsgiving, prayer and fasting. We are to be generous, prayerful and abstemious, he says, but not for the admiration of others. True righteousness seeks to conceal itself.

People of Jesus' time hardly ever saw hard money. What they did have they tended to hoard by burial rather than spend it. The same was true of costly garments being saved for special occasions. Verses 19 through 21 refer to those customs. Jesus was very much in tune with the people.

For your reading —

The contrasts Jesus makes between the old and literal following of the Law and the grasp of its true spirit are sharply drawn. Verses 2b, 5b, and 16b accent that updating, and "truly I say to you" should reflect the difference he wants to emphasize in each case.

Verse 21 sums it all up: what we think has lasting value takes most of our time and energy. Make sure your hearers are left with this final word strongly accented.

FIRST SUNDAY IN LENT

Suggested theme for today's readings —
As Lent begins, it is well for us to study the mechanics of sin.

Genesis 2:4b-9, 15-17, 25 — 3:7

General sense —

The beauty of God's creation, his setting of man's first moral boundaries, and man's almost immediate violation of those boundaries, begin our Lenten reflections this year. In seven brief verses is forged an amazing link between today's sophisticated lifestyles and the primitive ways of our ancient forbears (3:1-7).

For your reading —

This is storytelling at its best. There is no way to dramatize the events here more powerfully than the words of Scripture do. We still follow the same process of sinning that the first people did.

Let the words, then, speak for themselves; observe the conversational changes in tone as you speak, and your story will remind us all, as Lent begins, to be more aware of our sinfulness.

Romans 5:12-19

General sense —
Adam and Jesus Christ both affected humanity profoundly, but in different ways. Adam, the father of unredeemed man, was the symbol of the sin and death which controlled him. Christ, the new Adam and the head of the new humanity, through the superabundance of his grace, did our race incomparably more good than Adam had done it harm.

The sinfulness incurred, or revealed, in our first reading today, has been healed, "so that grace might reign, through Jesus Christ our Lord."

For your reading —
The significance of this passage has been debated for centuries. Your work as a lector is of course not relevant to that dispute. But to make it crystal clear, the reading must be delivered with frequent pauses, born of a preparation thorough enough for you to grasp what is being said.

Paul wants us to understand how Jesus Christ's grace negated the dreadful episode in our first reading, restoring man from "death" — spiritual death — back to God's friendship.

Verses 18 and 19 are the climax of the comparison, to be delivered even more carefully, as Paul repeats the thesis stated in verse 12. A slowing of your pace will drive the argument home as you conclude.

The adding of verses 20 and 21 would form an even more effective conclusion. Those are the triumphant words Paul chose to praise the intervention of Christ in history, for our righteousness.

Matthew 4:1-11

General sense —
As the study of human sinfulness continues in today's readings, Jesus is seen to be tempted. But the temptations all involve the use of miraculous power, not the satisfaction of common longings we all suffer. What is being tempted is Jesus' Messianic mission — the work of the Church. The Savior's victory rests in meeting the spiritual dangers which always threaten the Church: the abuse of power, whether to satisfy ordinary needs (verse 3); to provide a great sign compelling us to believe, rather than work toward faith (verse 6); or to wield political power, making Jesus a secular Messiah (verse 9).

For your reading —
The dialogue which forms this passage and gives it life, so markedly similar to the temptation dialogue in our first reading, is yours to deliver, yours to give to it the significance it deserves.

Tell your story with the conversational modulations (always in moderation, never overacted!) which will make its import clear to your hearers.

The contrast between the stern rebuke of Jesus in verse 10, climaxing his refusals to yield, and the abruptly quiet end in verse 11, should be well marked by two different tones of voice.

SECOND SUNDAY IN LENT
Suggested theme for today's readings —
The purpose of our Lenten penances is our conversion of heart by a deepening of our faith.
Genesis 12:1-8

General sense —
With the appearance of Abram, later to be Abraham, the story of our origins takes a completely new turn. Mankind had been turning from God since the dawn of his creation. Now, with this man's response in faith, begins the return to God which still goes on today.

For your reading —
Read the first three verses as if you were trying to get someone's attention, which was their purpose in the first place.

The divine claim to all the earth appears in verse 7a; Abram's official designation as a priest of his nation is told in 7b, and also in verse 8, where worship is first performed.

You are reading a story, basically, and that is the tone in which this passage will make the most sense to your hearers.

Romans 4:1-5, 13-17

General sense —
Paul here reflects on Abraham's faith, which we heard about in our first reading today. Even back in those days, says the Apostle, faith was the principle of justification, as it is (he insists) for us today.

For your reading —
Typical of Paul, the urgency of his argument impels him to tumble forth one idea after another. This makes for a reading which does not lend itself to a leisurely pace.

Read, therefore (not without thorough rehearsal), rapidly enough so that what stays with your audience is not the barrage of words but the constant insistence on faith, as against the inability of the Law alone to justify.

Retard your pace somewhat at verse 17, in order to show the

wonderful results of faith — for example, the calling into existence of what did not exist: the miraculous birth of Isaac to a barren old woman.

John 3:1-17

General sense —
Nicodemus came by night, looking for signs that this man was the Messiah. But he was looking for the old signs — the wonderful works of the Old Testament holy men.

Jesus proposes a new sign: a change of heart, within. And Nicodemus' hesitancy to understand draws from Jesus a magnificently lucid statement of his mission on earth.

For your reading —
What better opening for a story? "Now there was a man. . ."

The remarkable conversation in these lines makes this an important — and vividly human — reading.

Allow a pause after verse 3, while Nicodemus absorbs the standard the Savior proposes.

From verses 4 through 8, Jesus speaks at a more insistent pace, after which you should pause again; Nicodemus is still struggling to understand.

Jesus becomes a shade impatient at verse 10. Let your hearers know that, through your voice.

Pause again after verse 15. Jesus turns to thoughts of his loving Father, whose will it is to heal and to save. Conclude your reading on this gentle note of assurance, voicing more slowly the truths announced by the Lord.

THIRD SUNDAY IN LENT

Suggested theme for today's readings —
In shaping our conversion of life, God always takes the initiative by his grace.

Exodus 17:1-7

General sense —
Griping about our lot has been a human failing since the dawn of time. Moses hears it here, and answers in kind. But the Lord is merciful and generous, providing water from a rock to satisfy the people's thirst.

These nomads were not a nation of Israelites yet. From the ancient word for dusty shoes, they were called "the dusty ones," or "abiru," from which has evolved our word for them, Hebrews.

For your reading —
As you tell your story, raise your voice to convey the murmurs of the people and Moses' exasperation with them.

Verse 5, the generous answer of the Lord, who does not complain but simply gives, is delivered in a calmer tone, as is the rest of the narrative.

At verse 7b, the incident ends with the author's explanation of the names Massah, a testing, and Meribah, a quarrel. There is no need to stress the final quotation, since it is a part of that explanation.

Romans 5:1-11

General sense —

As in the incident of the water-giving rock in our first reading, God loves us unquestioningly, even in our weaknesses, because, "while we were yet sinners, Christ died for us."

For your reading —

This passage sets down a firm and faith-filled declaration of our new status with God, despite our human condition. Read its lines with the earnest conviction Paul intends for it.

Verse 6 begins a re-statement of the theme, with an easily understood example. Verses 7 and 8 make a strongly expressed contrast. Your pace in verse 8 should be slower, to add to the intensity of the argument's conclusion.

Verses 9 through 11 end the reading on a gentle tone, as the author describes the process of the reconciliation Jesus has earned for us.

John 4:5-26, 39-42

General sense —

Jesus greets an alien woman and heals her thirst for truth as she heals his thirst for water.

Thus John adds another narrative in his development of the theme of life. Once again Jesus Christ is the fulfillment of what the Law could only promise (verses 12-14), despite our sinfulness, personified in the Samaritan woman.

For your reading —

This story demands all the voice modulations in the dialogue which carries it along.

Take advantage of the length of this episode to draw your hearers into the significance of Jesus' mission as the bearer of life. Both he and the woman compare the old ways with the new.

There is a climax in verse 26 as Jesus reveals himself. Read it slowly and with some intensity, to heighten the drama; then deliver the last four verses in the narrative tone as you conclude with Jesus' identity again.

FOURTH SUNDAY IN LENT

Suggested theme for today's readings —

Through our Lenten penances, we move from the darkness of our old ways to the light of Jesus' way.

1 Samuel 16:1-13

General sense —

Samuel, the last of the Judges in Israel, had set up the ill-fated Saul as the first King.

Now, with the anointing of David to replace the rejected Saul, begins the rise of a new dynasty, in this man who was "ruddy, and had beautiful eyes, and was handsome (verse 12)."

For your reading —

The search for a new king begins suspensefully, with the fear of the present king's anger.

Your hearers' understanding of this episode, so full of the courtesy and tact of the old Israelite ways, depends on your familiarity, through preparation, with these ways. The voice of the Lord is accepted as a member of the discussion with perfect ease, as usual.

There are no points of special emphasis; in keeping with the theme of today's readings, you are telling the story of a call into the light of God's grace.

Ephesians 5:8-14

General sense —

The Apostle here describes the contrasts between pagan life and the new Christian way. He uses the analogy of light and darkness, instantly familiar to all, to illustrate his point with maximum effectiveness.

For your reading —

Verses 1 through 7 could be read here, but to begin with verse 8 accentuates more sharply the positive results of conversion. Reading the first seven verses privately, as part of your preparation will, however, give you a more complete picture of Paul's train of thought.

The reading itself is brief, to be delivered at a moderate pace. There are no obvious pauses indicated. As usual, your clarity of speech, based on your knowledge of the passage, will be the best vehicle for the understanding of those who hear you.

John 9:1-13, 28-38

General sense —

The ancient holy men were the bearers of the oral traditions which endured through the ages, through the medium of story-telling.

As Lent passes the halfway mark, we are witness today to another story. The subject is light, in the cure of the blind man, and darkness, in the failure of the Pharisees to understand it.

For your reading —

You need little help here; the story tells itself. Once again Jesus climaxes it, as he did with the Samaritan woman last week, by revealing his identity and eliciting an act of faith from one who has felt his healing power.

Thorough preparation is the key, so that your hearers may catch every nuance of this miracle. Since the reading is fairly long, move at an even but not leisurely pace, retarding your speed at the last verse, 38, for the act of worship.

FIFTH SUNDAY IN LENT
Suggested theme for today's readings —
Our restoration to life is the reason God became man and died for us.

Ezekiel 37:1-14

General sense —

Few ancient writers seize the imagination as does Ezekiel. His breathtaking imagery and gift for metaphor illuminate his basic focus: a future in the hands of God.

For your reading —

Even a trip to the land of the dead — perhaps he saw piles of unburied bones on an old battlefield — sets afire the soul of this mystic. Your task here is to draw your hearers into this imaginative vision. They will need to hear you deliver all fourteen verses to understand this episode clearly.

Imagine the silence, as the prophet wanders through this spectacle, stricken mute with wonder, in verses 1 through 3. Let your voice be hushed, intense, filled with awe.

From verses 4 through 6, the story gathers momentum, as the Lord utters the life-giving words of prophecy.

Verses 7 through 10 demand your greatest effort, as the vision surges into action. Raising your voice involves great self-discipline here, lest you be caught up in over-dramatizing. Practise it well beforehand. Read verse 10 slowly, phrase by phrase, as the miracle happens.

When the meaning of the vision is finally revealed — the restoration of the defeated nation by its God — speak more quietly, but with intensity, to the end. We need to hear, in the shadow of our Lenten penances, of our eventual healing.

Romans 6:16-23

General sense —

Restoration to life, as in our first reading, forms the theme of these lines from Paul's exhortation on the effects of Christian Baptism. Sin is death; it leads to death. "The wages of sin is death, but the free gift of God is eternal life in Christ Jesus our Lord."

For your reading —

As we carry out our Lenten penances, our habits of sin and

slavery to self should decrease in strength.

We need these words of encouragement; we need to know, as you deliver these lines, that we are at least on our way to a closer following of Jesus Christ.

The tone, then, is an upbeat, happy one. As Lent comes down to its last two weeks, read with the assurance that your hearers know now, from experience, the futility of slavery and the joy of freedom.

The final verse, the oft-quoted 23, climaxes the reasoning, and should be read more emphatically, as you conclude.

John 11:17-44

General sense —

Ezekiel saw resurrection in a vision or dream. Paul described it theologically. Now, in our third reading, through Jesus we witness a personal resurrection. The words of the Savior literally and physically fulfill his teaching, as well as demonstrate the power of God to bring not only the body but the soul back to life.

For your reading —

This story speaks so well for itself that it should be a fine exercise of your narrative skills.

There are two places worthy of particular emphasis. The first occurs in verse 25. Jesus affirms Martha's faith, but reminds her that he is its source. It is most important, to bring out what the Master wants to say, that you lean strongly on the word "I."

The second place of emphasis is at verse 43, the climax of the episode. As Jesus raises his voice, your voice ought also to reflect the intensity of this moment. A pause before verse 44 will help your hearers to visualize the miracle before you conclude quickly, as does John.

PALM SUNDAY

Suggested theme for today's readings —
As we witness Jesus' death, we give thanks for the grace he has earned for us this Lent.

Isaiah 45:21-25

General sense —

From the cross-shadowed eminence of Holy Week, this is a call to salvation, with only one requirement: "turn to me." To the homesick exiles far off in Babylon, the sacred writer thrusts forward the palm of truth: regardless of your situation, forgetful of your many sins and infidelities, "all the offspring of Israel shall triumph and glory." The moment of salvation, we read in verse 21, was prepared from the beginning.

For your reading —

The courtroom style of this passage sounds like the pleading of God's defense attorney, which indeed a prophet is.

You must discipline yourself here to keep your voice raised, with an edge of insistency and confidence that despite our forgetting it so often, this message is the truth.

The climax is verse 22, the key to the passage. It should be your most intense and earnest statement.

Verse 25's mass amnesty of all sinners will help you end strongly and confidently.

Philippians 2:5-11

General sense —

In this classic passage, an ancient liturgical hymn is modified a bit by the writer and inserted here, to strengthen a point of exhortation. But in these few sentences is contained all of the mystery we celebrate this Holy Week.

Jesus' divine pre-existence, his Incarnation, his death, his being raised up for the adoration of the universe, and his new title, the Lord — every jewel in his crown radiates forth in this magnificent summation of his identity: from eternity, through earthly life and death, back to eternity, he is indeed the Lord.

For your reading —

Verse 6 means that Jesus made "no big deal" about reflecting the glory of God. He never treated it as a privilege to be exploited, nor did he stand on his dignity.

This passage, then, has no special climactic verse; it is, in its entirety, the highlight of this chapter.

Read it in the same tone throughout, mindful, by the solemnity of your voice, of its awesome dignity. You are reciting a biography unlike any other. Moments after you leave the lectern, we will hear the Passion, so that the mood is the somber tone of Palm Sunday.

Raise your voice slightly to make the last verse the most important of all. It sums up Jesus' glory completely.

Matthew 26:36-75, 27:1-54

General sense —

The Passion narrative — this year we read Matthew's account — was the first Gospel recital to be included in the liturgy. The earliest proclamation of Jesus centered on his death and resurrection, the great saving act of the Father and the climax of salvation history.

Matthew's version of the Passion, longer than the other Evangelists', is still in close agreement with them, a feature rarely seen in other Gospel narratives.

For your reading —

In most places nowadays the Passion story is read by several people who re-enact the roles of its characters.

Those of you who share in this privilege also share in the discipline of presenting each role in as lifelike a fashion as possible. Voices must be changed and modulated to suit each moment.

The supreme tribute to your individual and collective skills will be when some of the congregation put down their texts to listen to you.

EASTER SUNDAY — PRINCIPAL SERVICE

Suggested theme for today's readings —
Christ's resurrection is the seal of God on the authenticity of our faith.

Acts 10:34-43

General sense —
Today we read the last sermon of Peter in Acts. It is brief enough, but not relevant to the story of Cornelius' conversion which precedes it.

The writer of Acts develops the same outline in other speeches of both Peter and Paul. By this device he wants to show what Christian preaching is and ought to be. Thus he is less concerned with recording history than he is with a literary-theological task.

For your reading —
This is a good summary of our Christian faith, very suitably chosen for the triumphant close of Jesus' life which we celebrate today.

Therefore you are to read it like a speech. Verse 35 is the ear-catching opening sentence, to be declaimed in a strong and clear tone.

Verse 41 is another ear-catcher, certainly for the people of that time. Imagine being chosen to eat and drink with someone risen from the dead! Make your voice an instrument of wonder here.

Conclude verse 43 with the most important and lasting gift of Jesus' life and the reason for our Easter joy: the forgiveness of our sins. It makes a fine and strong ending.

Colossians 3:1-4

General sense —
Paul has been criticizing the material religious practices that are in opposition to the risen presence of Christ. But Christ's victory over the Old Law removes the fear of being punished for its non-observance. This is the victory we celebrate at Easter. There is only one law left: the law of love.

For your reading —
You have a few seconds here to join in today's general rejoicing at the Resurrection, by repeating the promise that we will,

after a life hidden in Christ, rise with him in glory.

Make the most of your time at the lectern by announcing these lines in a strong and clear voice, full of the conviction born of your faith.

John 20:1-10

General sense —

For all their devoted loyalty, the disciples were mere spectators at the mysteries of Jesus' final days on earth. The reason, John says today, is simple: "as yet, they did not know the Scripture." The enlightenment of the Spirit at Pentecost was yet to be theirs.

For your reading —

The first rays of the Risen Light of the World fall on, of all people the most unlikely, Magdalen.

Your presentation of this incident will receive its dramatic force from the gradual increase in the action.

Verses 2 through 7 should be read with some urgency, as Mary passes on the shocking news to the two disciples, who run to the tomb, followed shortly by Peter.

At verse 8, when John sees and believes, your voice softens and slows. John can speak here only for himself, even though with hindsight many years later, he can write that the Spirit was yet to come.

Verse 10 concludes quickly. The rest of the story of Easter could be added here, with the appearance of the risen Lord, to verse 18.

SECOND SUNDAY OF EASTER
Suggested theme for today's readings —
Jesus' resurrection is the keystone of our faith.
Acts 2:14a, 22-32

General sense —

Today, and for the next four Sundays, we share some of Luke's history of the early Church. The present passage is the first sermon of Peter, wherein he places the burden of Jesus' death on his fellow Jews (an onus lifted officially by the Universal Church in recent years), then demonstrates the Scriptural authenticity of the Resurrection.

For your reading —

This is a speech, proclaiming the Good News. Read it in a raised tone of voice, with two strong points: verse 22a, to attract the hearers' attention; and verse 24, when the fact of the Resurrection overcomes the cruelty of Good Friday.

Pause after verse 28, as Peter ends his quote and begins

speaking in verse 29, directly to the people.

Conclude with emphasis on the final verse, 32, repeating the central truth of Peter's discourse: Christ is risen.

1 Peter 1:3-9

General sense —

Peter has told us, in our first reading for today, of the primacy of the Resurrection in grounding our faith. Now, writing to the Christians of Asia Minor, he gives thanks for Jesus' renewal of our life, and relates it to our devotional life.

For your reading —

Exclaim the first verse, 3, as you begin, in the same way Peter does.

The remainder of the passage teaches, in a close, personal manner, the results of the wonderful event of the Resurrection. Although no particular verse seems to warrant emphasis, your reading of these lines is a basic instruction in the foundation of our faith.

John 20:19-31

General sense —

John's attention remains fixed on Easter Sunday — "the first day of the week," so that in his Gospel perspective, as well as in the judgment of most scholars, the animation by the Spirit takes place on the day of resurrection.

What is basic here is the close connection of Jesus' rising with the coming of the Spirit, which our teaching and liturgies have always reflected.

The episode of the doubting Thomas is added today to the Gospel we will read on Pentecost. It is used by John to corroborate the authenticity of Jesus' resurrection through the most explicit act of faith (that of Thomas) in all the Gospel stories.

For your reading —

You are telling a story. Dramatize Jesus' words in verse 19 by a pause before you say them, as also when he repeats his blessing in verse 21.

It would be well too to pause before Thomas' act of faith in verse 28, to set it apart and accent its importance.

Otherwise, tell your story simply and quietly, with the sense of wonder which must have stricken the people in the upper room.

THIRD SUNDAY OF EASTER

Suggested theme for today's readings —

The order of salvation as a result of the preaching of the Word.

Acts 2:14a, 36-47

General sense —

In this second of five selections from Peter's first sermon in Acts, the reaction to his remarks in the verses we read last week is predictable. He has stung the national pride as well as individual consciences. Immediately, however, the speaker proposes the next stop in man's cycle of redemption: repentance and incorporation into Christ by Baptism, for the forgiveness of sin.

Verses 41 through 47 condense the events of a period of time into a few lines, as a summary which creates the impression of a continuous history.

For your reading —

Be the storyteller here, as you trace for your hearers the outpouring of grace resulting from Peter's strong words. Recount its wonders with frequent pauses (e.g., after verses 37, 39, 40, and 42).

1 Peter 1:17-23

General sense —

Again we are urged by the Apostle Peter to put off the old ways and conduct ourselves as children of a loving Father.

Each of us, moved by grace, passes through the "order of salvation" many times during our lives, every time we repent of our sins and turn over a new leaf.

For your reading —

To vary the tone of this calmly reasoned passage, pause before verse 22, as Peter applies the Resurrection to our obligation of mutual charity as a corollary of our hearing of the Word.

Raise your voice slightly at verse 24, to make the quotation from Isaiah stand out from the text.

Conclude pointedly as the Old Testament praise of the Word is exemplified in today's preaching.

Luke 24:13-35

General sense —

In this beautiful and oft-quoted incident, the order of salvation begins with the appearance of Jesus, in the breaking of the bread, to two unknown disciples (representing all of us). Their recognition of him stirs their hearts and urges them to pass their experience on to others, as preachers do.

For your reading —

The best way to the heart and meaning of this story will, as always, be your own thorough preparation. Meditation on it will show you how to pace it, how to vary the tone from the disciples' original discouragement to Jesus' somewhat edgy impatience in verses 25 and 26, then to his calm exposition of the Scriptures.

Pause now, after verse 27, to indicate a passage of time. Then, be aware of more variations: their appeal for Jesus to stay; the climax of verses 30 and 31; and the joyful conclusion of the story, as they tell what they have heard.

FOURTH SUNDAY OF EASTER
Suggested theme for today's readings —
To serve God is to have life to the fullest.
Acts 6:1-9 – 7:2a, 51-60

General sense —

The Hebrews and the Greek-speaking Hellenists, both groups being Jewish converts to Christianity, provide the first indication of dissension in the Church at Jerusalem. The Hellenist Stephen, one of seven deacons chosen in a restructuring move, first delivers a stinging rebuke to Jerusalem's leaders, then gives his life as the Church's first martyr.

For your reading —

These are exciting times to read about. The differences in the community and the election of Stephen occupy the first segment, which lends itself well to your storytelling skills.

In verse 51 your voice sharpens, as Stephen rails against the rejection of the Spirit, his principal accusation and the climax of his speech.

Pause after verse 53 as the speech ends. Now your voice is lower, as you describe the crowd's reaction in verse 54.

Verses 55 through 60 are not easy to deliver. The climax of the episode demands that you transmit the rage and resentment, the ecstasy of Stephen, and his last words, as faithfully as you can. The intensity of such scenes is best captured by a slight lowering or raising of the voice and a slowing of your pace. There is never a reason to shout.

Be sure to pause before the last sentence, to heighten the drama of Stephen's death.

1 Peter 2:19-25

General sense —

Rather than try to get a national and cultural institution like slavery abolished — that idea would not have occurred to him — Peter aimed at Christianizing it. He sees it as part of our duty to suffer unjust wrongs, after the example of Christ. The reading continues today's theme of true life through faithful service.

For your reading —

The omission of verse 18, which gives the passage its point, bespeaks of today's more democratic society.

Your reading here, still holding up the example of Christ, is nevertheless valid for its urging us to put up with injustice.

Verses 24 and 25 will be more effective if you deliver them at a slower pace, as the climax of this brief exhortation.

John 10:1-10

General sense —

The sheep of the village, kept in one corral at night, would answer only the voice of their master at the morning call to pasture. Jesus draws the analogy to signify the Pharisees as unlawful intruders into his sheepfold. In verse 6 they prove his point by missing it. They are not the sheep who hear the voice of the shepherd. They do not share his life of service.

For your reading —

The expression, "truly, truly," in verses 1 and 7, is most effectively rendered by stopping after the first "truly," then reading the second "truly" as part of Jesus' address: "truly I say to you."

Our Savior uses this expression to refer to something already said but now expanded or put in a new light. Your reading, therefore, continues his explanation of the previous episode of the blind man in chapter 9. Adopt in your rendering his teacher-like tone of insistence, both in verses 1 through 6, then again in verses 7 through 9, as he underscores his meaning again. Let your hearers catch the force of this repetition in your voice.

The final verse is an echo of John's portrait of Jesus in chapter 1, verse 4 of this Gospel. Pause before you read it, and give it the slower-paced emphasis Jesus intended for it, as a summary of his mission.

FIFTH SUNDAY OF EASTER

Suggested theme for today's readings —
Our dignity as God's people is that Jesus adopted our image and likeness.

Acts 17:1-15

General sense —

Paul made three missionary journeys. This episode occurs during his second, to northern Asia Minor. Thessalonica was one of the district capitals of Macedonia, called today Saloniki in northern Greece. The incidents described follow the usual pattern: Paul finds a synagogue and preaches Jesus; some of the congregation stirs opposition to him; he leaves for the next town.

Synagogues were always the first stop in a new town, because Paul still believed that the priority of salvation was the privilege of Israel.

For your reading —

This is a good storytelling exercise, particularly in verses 5, 6, and 7, where the jealousy of the Jews boils over into action.

Drop your voice after "King" in verse 7, to mark the replacement of Caesar by Jesus.

Pause after verse 9, as the first incident closes. The remainder of the passage repeats the cycle: some converts, some opposition, then flight. Conclude as the storyteller, as before.

1 Peter 2:1-10

General sense —

Peter bids the new Christian converts to live up to their call as a chosen race, even as Paul did in the synagogues of Asia Minor. We constantly need this reminder of our dignity and worth in God's eyes.

For your reading —

Render this passage in the tones we usually associate with a speech or a letter of encouragement. Be sure of yourself, confident, and as positive as your study and preparation will inspire you to be.

Drop your voice after "come" in verse 4, as also after "stone," in the same verse.

Pause after verse 8, to prepare your hearers for the tribute which climaxes this passage. Each phrase is important; each one deserves your most heartfelt emphasis, so that we may let these sublime, faith-given qualities sink into our hearts and be part of us.

John 14:1-14

General sense —

For the third time today we are reminded of our dignity as God's people. This time we see our Father in Jesus, as we do, through faith, the work that he does. Our Savior promises us total accessibility to the Father for our needs, as long as we ask in his name.

For your reading —

Read the consoling thoughts of verses 1 through 4 calmly, then raise your voice slightly as Thomas asks his question.

In verse 6, your stressing of the word "I" is vital to its meaning. Thomas has already mentioned "the way" in the preceding verse, so that that becomes secondary to Jesus' identification of himself. *He* is the way.

Philip's next question and Jesus' insistence on himself as our vision of the Father will require modulations of your voice to suit this exchange.

Drop your voice after the first "truly" in verse 12, then join the second "truly" to "I say to you," as one phrase.

Verse 14 concludes strongly with Jesus' universal promise to us all: we are objects of God's deepest care.

SIXTH SUNDAY OF EASTER
Suggested theme for today's readings —
God's loving care for us requires our intimate attachment to the goals of his mission.

Acts 17:22-31

General sense —

Paul stands as a Christian missionary before pagan Gentiles. His discourse mentions Jesus only indirectly, at the end, in verse 31. These people know nothing of Christ or of his mission, so that Paul must speak of a God who "does not live in shrines," but "gives to all life and breath." As usual, some mock him, but others are interested: their God is still the unknown.

For your reading —

The Apostle begins with a proclamation of a popular religious idea: there must be a god somewhere. In verse 24 he makes clear how your rendering of these lines should sound: you proclaim, as he did. Simply raise your voice slightly, imagining yourself a sidewalk preacher trying to attract a crowd.

Thorough preparation of this passage will make its natural segments more clear, as well as suggesting the pauses you ought to make:

1. verses 22-23 introduction
2. verses 24-25 the reality of God
3. verses 26-27 the nearness of God's care for us
4. verses 28-29 our response to him
5. verses 30-31 God's plan for us

1 Peter 3:8-18

General sense —

When we remember that Peter was speaking to a shipwrecked people, anathematized as pariahs in their own society, we can better understand passages like this one today.

Goodness in the face of persecution, "that those who revile your good behavior in Christ may be put to shame," is his principal admonition to fidelity and loyalty.

For your reading —

The power of these lines lies in their relevancy to today. All of us are called to live in harmony; everyone suffers some misunderstanding and/or abuse from time to time.

Your reading, then, will be in a somewhat urgent, insistent tone. Separate the quotation from Psalm 34 by a pause after verse 12. Return to Peter's words with renewed vigor, as he proves his point by the Old Testament reference.

A final pause after verse 17 will set forth the climactic idea in verse 18 as you conclude. God's care for us is best exemplified in Jesus Christ.

John 15:1-8

General sense —

How intimately our goodness, such as it is, is bound up with the concern of the Lord for us, stands out today. Parallel with that good vinedresser's devotion to us is his demand that we bear fruit in proportion to our union with him, as a requisite for discipleship.

For your reading —

Jesus speaks simply and directly, without introduction, possibly, after the end of the previous chapter, as the little company moves out toward the Garden of Olives.

Since the entire passage consists of Jesus' words, read it at a measured pace, pausing before verses 4 and 8 to indicate slight changes in tone. In verse 4 Jesus bids us abide in him. In verse 8 the central thrust of the passage is expressed: the purpose of this intimacy of concern is that we bear fruit.

ASCENSION DAY

Suggested theme for today's readings —
Jesus' last command is that we be witnesses of him.

Acts 1:1-11

General sense —

There is so much information crammed into these eleven verses that it may be difficult to absorb its basic sense, except to say that it chronicles the first days of the new missionary Church.

Luke's idea was to present a quick summary of his Gospel, then get on with the task at hand: how the word of the Lord spread from the Mother Church, Jerusalem, outward from its Jewish matrix "to the ends of the earth," all of this under the guidance of the Holy Spirit.

For your reading —

After the initial run-through of what has transpired, pause after verse 5, really to take a breath and to make a transition to the words of the Lord.

The burning question of the day is now settled in verses 7 and 8. The Second Coming of Christ will not be soon at all, as many had thought. The Word must first be witnessed to the ends of the earth.

Speak the Lord's words here with strength and authority.

Suddenly, at verse 9, we are into "live action." Slow down here — this is the departure of the Lord we celebrate in today's feast. Read these last three verses as if everything that went before was their prelude.

The key phrase is the promise in verse 11 — "he will come in the same way" — that is, in glory. This is your strongest and most direct statement. Conclude your reading on this high and joyful note.

Ephesians 1:15-23

General sense —

Had Paul been present at the Ascension, these lines might have been an appropriate conversation among the disciples on the way back into Jerusalem.

It is a happy passage, fitting for this great feast, because it not only summarizes the purpose of Jesus' mission and its total accomplishment, but also relates his victory to the present, for our hope and consolation.

For your reading —

This is an authentic acknowledgment of the joy in our hearts. Read it in an upbeat fashion, as if it were the first time we'd heard it.

Every sentence teems with the bursting blooms of our new life in Christ. There are so many meaningful phrases just as relevant and practical today as they were then.

Let us, your hearers, treasure each of these great joys. Make every one stand out by your frequent pauses, after this phrase or that sentence.

Finally, the grace of Christ reaches the ends of the earth in the last verse, 23, so that you conclude with almost a shout. It is good news indeed.

Luke 24:49-53

General sense —

Now that today's two previous readings have reflected on the Ascension and its effects throughout the world, this brief account seems anti-climactic.

But one more element is present here. "They returned to Jerusalem with great joy." Joy is one of Luke's favorite themes. He has understood that the Spirit of Pentecost grants us a stronger, more personal union with Jesus, within the community of the Church.

If you read for yourself all of Chapter 24, you would agree with most Scripture scholars that the Ascension happened on Easter day. We keep it as a separate feast because it is too important to be absorbed in the Easter celebration.

For your reading —

Though the shortest of the day, your assignment is the only account written like that of an eyewitness. How inspiring for your audience to hear the final wish of Jesus on this earth! Linger over the beautiful words of his last blessing in verse 49. Look up and wait until you have everyone's attention before you begin your reading.

Go as slowly as you can: you have but four more verses, barely thirty seconds, to impress your hearers with Jesus' official passing on of his Father's promise and the joy it created in the hearts of those who saw and heard it.

SEVENTH SUNDAY OF EASTER

Suggested theme for today's readings —
Any departure of Jesus from our lives saddens us. But he does it to reinforce his presence right here, within us.

Acts 1:8-14

General sense —
Jesus' return to his Father could have happened some time after his resurrection, at least physically. Rising up in the air, however, is figurative language at best, imagining that heaven is "up there somewhere." But as Jesus himself reminds us in John 20:17, the ascension, theologically, was an integral part of his resurrection. Most scholars agree that the Resurrection and the Ascension were not separated in time. They may well have both taken place on Easter day.

Somehow, Jesus concluded his appearances among us. Somehow, we must not stand here idly. We have a world to change.

For your reading —
These are mysterious lines. Whether the Ascension was an event or a reflection of an early church tradition is beyond our ken. Your reading of the first four verses, 8 through 11, will therefore be as a storyteller, in a tone of wonder. Pause a bit after each verse, to heighten the dramatic effect of this vision.

Verses 12 through 14 evoke very effectively the departure of a group from an event and their sequestering themselves to reflect on it. Quicken your pace for these verses. We have placed the group in their waiting room for the earthquake of Pentecost next week.

1 Peter 4:12-19

General sense —
The departure of Jesus is a "fiery ordeal" for anyone who has experienced his seeming absence. Peter here encourages, consoles and strengthens the Gentile Christians of Asia Minor in the mid-sixties, A.D., just before his own ordeal of martyrdom at Rome.

For your reading —
Be as urgent as the writer of these lines in your transmitting of his care for his readers' welfare. This is a strong passage, one we need to keep in mind in our own troubles.

No particular place of emphasis appears to stand out, so that your reading will continue with the strength of your own faith-filled conviction to the end.

John 17:1-11

General sense —

Just before his earthly departure, Jesus, in this sublime meditation, sums up the significance of his life. Now that "the hour has come," he extends his blessings, exemplified by the accomplishments he recalls, over the Church he is to bring forth in his glorification.

For your reading —

This is a meditation and a prayer, a most unusual revelation of the inner soul and desires of this man we call Son of God.

Let yourself drink deeply of his love for us as you prepare to deliver these lines. There is more of him — and of us — in them than we could ever comprehend.

Read them slowly, with frequent pauses whenever your sense of them notices a change in his address. Examples of this would be before verse 5, before verse 9 and before verse 11.

The final thought of the passage, verse 11b, is one of the climaxes of this chapter. Raise your eyes to your hearers, and pray with Jesus for their unity, with all the earnestness at your command.

PENTECOST SUNDAY

Suggested theme for today's readings —
The Holy Spirit has made the Lord our most intimate friend.

Acts 2:1-11

General sense —

Pentecost needs no setting. It begins a whole new world, a monumental change in the course of history. It provides its own setting: the universal appeal of the Spirit of God to everyone, regardless of who and where we are.

For your reading —

The scene is established quickly, in one brief sentence. As you read verses 2, 3 and 4, do whatever you can to dramatize this moment. Raise your voice; speak with the intensity and wonder you would use in telling a story to young people. Let your every work convey the excitement of this wondrous happening.

At verse 5 the intensity slows somewhat, because here you begin to build toward a second climax: the extension of the Spirit out to the people. Assisting this buildup will be your putting a period, or at least a semicolon, after each national designation. Like this: Parthians. And Medes. And Elamites. And so on through all of them. We're not suggesting that you slow down, just that you drop your voice to let each nationality stand forth in importance. Remember that you are relating what was at that time an incredible incident.

It is impossible to overemphasize the last phrase in verse 11, as you conclude. Give this grand climax the strength it deserves, as we hear you tell of the mighty works of our God.

1 Cor. 12:4-13

General sense —

St. Paul lists here the endless varieties of gifts given to us by the Spirit of Jesus, as we celebrate today the source of all our gifts, even the same blessed Spirit.

Each manifestation of the Spirit is ours "for the common good," even today as it was then.

For your reading —

Except in the opening verse, 4, the best rule here is not to emphasize the word "Spirit." It happens in nearly every verse. What needs to be made clear to our hearers is the enunciation of so many gifts. The words to be remembered are best delivered by the dropping of the voice we have suggested on other occasions, as, "wisdom. knowledge. faith. healing. miracles. prophecy." Each word is of equal stature. All of us have one or another of these gifts.

This is a very heartening passage, designed to make us hearers of the Word aware that the Spirit is manifested in our own personal gifts just as much as it was on that Pentecost day so long ago.

John 20:19-23

General sense —

With these beautiful words Jesus passes on his own power to act as our mediator before God. He begins by granting us that which is necessary for all conversions of hearts: his own peace.

For your reading —

After the word: "Jews," in verse 19, wait a beat. Accentuate the comma. Then announce the presence of the Master — even dropping your voice after "Jesus."

Drop your voice, too, to dramatize Jesus' greeting, as he says, "Peace be with you." Then, up again with your voice, to tell us that the disciples "were glad." Then do it again: *"Peace* be with you."

Read verse 22, as Jesus gives his Spirit, breathing on them, very gently and solemnly. Lean toward the microphone as you do this, so that no one misses a syllable. Then conclude in tones of affection with the charter of forgiveness.

TRINITY SUNDAY

Suggested theme for today's readings —

The invocation of the Trinity on our lives provides us with three basic necessities: a loving Father, a Brother who suffered like us, and a Spirit to warm our hearts.

Genesis 1:1 – 2:3

General sense —

This majestic burst of divine expression, man's reflection on how the universe might have come to be, begins the Bible story as it ends our Easter cycle of redemption. It signifies God's absolute power to create again and again in us, wherever we are, in whatever circumstance.

For your reading —

One way to capture the rhythm of these action-packed lines is to be aware that the eyes and ears of all your audience are fixed on you, ready to hear of the spectacle which justifies our existence.

Read it as the storyteller that you are, captivating us with your sense of drama, reinforced by pauses after each phase of creation.

Pause before verse 26. This is the magnificent insight which brought us to life. It is the climax of the account.

Pause again after verse 31, to let our imagination wander through this entire pageant. Then read the three verses of chapter 2 in a somewhat lower tone. Conclude, unhurried, as the Lord reflects on his handiwork.

2 Corinthians 13:11-14

General sense —

In the creation, God delivered us into a world in perfect harmony. Our second reading instructs us on how to keep that harmony alive, by living as closely as we can to the love and peace in which our seed came to bloom. Finally, Paul invokes the presence of God's three manifestations, Father, Son and Holy Spirit, on our struggles.

So rich and instructive is this brief blessing that in many places the last verse is used, both as greeting and as farewell, every time we celebrate Eucharist together.

For your reading —

This explicit wish for everything necessary for our salvation should be rendered with as much eye contact with your hearers as possible. The words are simple, familiar and direct, and with a modest effort on your part could be memorized.

Brief though your time at the lectern may be, your reading will be effective to the degree that you can personalize it.

Matthew 28:16-20

General sense —

Matthew concludes his Gospel, a catechism for Jewish converts, with some interesting images. The Old Testament image of the mountain evokes the sacredness of Mount Sinai, where Moses gave the law, even as Jesus' phrase, "all that I have commanded you," draws on the memory of the Great Lawgiver himself, in the person of the new Moses. The mention of some doubt in verse 17 is an undercurrect running through all the resurrection stories. And in verse 19, the apostolic commission reflects well the Church's self-image in those early days.

Finally, the visible manifestation of the Trinity assures us of his living presence with us for always.

For your reading —

From verse 18, the commanding and consoling words of our Savior invoke the Trinity on our entire life and our mission as witnesses to him. Read them with raised voice, to set them apart from the narrative in verses 16 and 17. Be aware, too, that with this Sunday we end the resurrection cycle of the year, as we prepare for next week's revelation of the Spirit and the instructional Pentecost cycle which takes us through to Advent.

NOTE – For Propers 1, 2 and 3 after Pentecost, please refer to the readings for the 6th, 7th, and 8th Sundays after Epiphany, respectively. The readings overlap because of the variations each year in the date of Easter.

PROPER 4

Suggested theme for today's readings —
The test of the true Christian is not only good works but the faith which underlies them.

Deuteronomy 11:18-21, 26-28

General sense —

This reading introduces the time after Pentecost. The cycle of the life of Jesus is over for another year. Now we are to be nourished by what he taught.

Behind all divine teaching lies the notion of covenant, based on the primacy of the Word (verse 18), the fundamental choice of blessing and curse (verse 26), and the nature of the encounter with the Lord: the need to decide "today (verse 28)."

For your reading —

Today you are the wise teacher, setting out the Word of the Lord and its conditions. Your tone of voice is kind but firm, gentle yet insistent. Read at a measured pace, treating every sentence as of equal importance.

Pause before verse 26 as the writer begins his statement of sanctions. These last three verses strike the keynote of our entire summer and fall readings from Matthew. Read them slowly and strongly as you conclude.

Romans 3:21-25a, 28

General sense —

These important lines formulate the essence of Paul's teaching: our salvation comes by our faith in the Christ-event, through which God has manifested his divine uprightness and fidelity, "apart from the Law (verse 21)."

For your reading —

Today you are explaining a point in Christian theology. It is rather brief: you will be at the lectern only a moment or two. Be careful to go slowly enough, pausing after each sentence, to make its significance as clear as you can.

Read the last sentence, verse 28, with more intensity; it sums up what went before. You may want to replace the word "man" with "person," or with "we are."

Matthew 7:21-27

General sense —

Today we open the Gospel of Matthew. It will be our companion and guide for all the Sundays after Pentecost this year.

Matthew's is the Jewish Christian Gospel, in which Jesus, lowly, suffering, a friend of the poor, comes as the foretold Messiah of the Old Testament, unrecognized by the very ones who should have known him.

Providentially, it is their unbelieving hostility which begets the fulfillment of the Church, the new Israel, in the Gentile world.

For your reading —

Verse 21 opens this reading strongly, as Jesus separates the empty protesters from the doers.

Verses 22 and 23 are dialogic exchanges. Show in your voice the whining tone of the protester and the stern response of the Lord.

In the last four verses Jesus returns to the teaching mode. Let your reading reflect the graphic illustrations he provides, so familiar to his hearers.

Pause before verse 26, as the Savior applies the simile to his hearers' reception of his Word. Conclude with firmness and conviction.

PROPER 5

Suggested theme for today's readings —
Our faith is what makes everything else happen in our relationship with God, self and neighbor.

Hosea 5:15 – 6:6

General sense —
This plea for repentance and conversion is a familiar theme with Hosea. He continually reminds his people that God has always been Israel's savior, despite the shallowness of its love for him (verse 4a).

For your reading —
Glide through (or over) the word "saying" in verse 15. The important words are what is said. Drop your voice after "seek me."
Verse 4, the Lord's frustrated complaint, and the three verses of his response, are to be read in a stronger voice, particularly verse 6, in which he tells us how important to him is our continuation in love, rather than our performance of exotic penances and sacrifices.

Romans 4:13-18

General sense —
Paul, from whose letter to Rome we will read for the next few months, balances the practicalities of the Gospel of Matthew with his own accent on faith.
Today the Apostle pits the experience of Abraham against the Mosaic Law itself. Abraham was blessed, even before he was circumcised, because of his faith.

For your reading —
The constant stress here is on the absolute primacy of faith. As you read, look for this key concept and lean on it when it occurs. It is the accent which unifies Paul's whole train of thought.
Otherwise, there is no particular place of emphasis. Your careful preparation will reveal to you that this is a short discourse on the necessity of faith as the ground of all good things.

Matthew 9:9-13

General sense —
Matthew responds to the call of Jesus promptly, as unlikely a subject as he seems to be. Better still, he invites Jesus to meet his friends, "tax collectors and sinners." Jesus not only comes but is instantly at home with these people, even designating them as objects of his special care.

For your reading —
Matthew does nothing but play his role of extortionist — until he receives, and accepts, the gift of faith.

Pause after verse 9, to reinforce this remarkable moment, and let it penetrate your hearers' minds and hearts.

Verses 12 and 13 contain Jesus' sharp response to his needlers. Read them with an edge to your voice which exposes their snobbishness and teaches us all a lesson about judging people.

PROPER 6

Suggested theme for today's readings —
We are accepted and loved by God exactly as we are, faults and all.

Exodus 19:2-8a

General sense —
This classic text reveals two attributes of God we sometimes have trouble believing in: 1. his election of us, in the person of the Israelites, as his own dearest possession — the word "possession" in Hebrew is "segullah," or "sweetheart (verse 5);" 2. his choice to leave this sublime destiny to our own free option, in the same verse (*"if* you will obey my voice").

The eagle flies below her fledglings, so that should they fall in learning to fly, she will catch them on her outspread wings. This is the beauty and power of the figure in verse 4.

For your reading —
The magnitude of this promise is almost too great for us to grasp. Generations of preachers and spiritual writers have so schooled us in self-abasement before God's majesty that we quail at being as free and as noble as he constantly invites us to be.

Read these words of the Lord with dignity and deep conviction. Pause at their conclusion, after verse 6. The principal stress after that will come when you mark the people's enthusiastic response in verse 8.

Romans 5:6-11

General sense —
Paul reminds us of our election, as did the Lord so many centuries before, through Moses. He adds more than the Old Testament writer did: the reality of our sinfulness does not stand in God's way, on account of Jesus Christ, in whom we are forever reconciled.

For your reading —
Verse 8 is the forceful one here. It begins the explanation of the fruits of Jesus' sacrifice. Proceed carefully, making certain that Paul's reasoning is clearly expressed to your hearers.

The last half of verse 11 is the story of our access to heaven.

It deserves particular emphasis as you conclude.

Matthew 9:35 – 10:8, 9-15

General sense —

The disciples' marching orders reiterate today's theme of our undeserved salvation. The Good News is to be passed on without cost, and its final acceptance or rejection is left to its hearers. There is no need to debate or dispute; the response to non-acceptance is simply to depart.

For your reading —

Read the first two verses a little faster, to illuminate the hustle and bustle of a missionary trip. Suddenly, in verses 37 and 38, your tone is lower, reflecting the observation of Jesus about the crowds.

The remainder of the passage is narrated as a story. Jesus goes into great detail to help these men who have never done this before, so that the entire instruction is read in the tone of one who is patiently teaching a lesson, or rehearsing a program.

Lay particular stress on the final verse, in which Jesus leaves the unbelievers to the judgment of God.

PROPER 7

Suggested theme for today's readings —
No matter how mysterious are God's ways with us, Jesus Christ has acquitted us all, driving out our fears by faith.

Jeremiah 20:7-13

General sense —

Reflections on the meaning of some of the prophet's experiences include today's passage, the feelings of despair undergirded by absolute trust in the Lord. The two emotions tumble out almost in the same breath, typical of our psychological and spiritual crises.

The word "deceived" and the paraphrase, "Thou are stronger than I," translated literally, "you seized me," are both in verse 7. They are the same words used elsewhere in the Old Testament for a man's act of seducing a virgin. We mention this to lend more power to Jeremiah's denunciation of the Lord. The prophet accuses God of more than just deceiving him.

For your reading —

Jeremiah used to be the sage of the royal court; now, in his old age, they laugh at him because the Lord seems not to pronounce judgment on Israel's enemies.

Your reading, then, ought to reflect his anger and despair, as well as his sudden disclaimer in verse 11 that he still trusts, no matter what.

The change in tone at verse 11 moves from a shout of angry despair to cries of unflagging trust and faith in ultimate victory. Jeremiah speaks to God more than he addresses the people any more.

Romans 5:15b-19

General sense —

Paul presses on in his description of the reconciled Christian. Here he prefigures Adam as the head of the "old" humanity, to be replaced in a far superior way by Christ, the new head. The centrality of Jesus in history lies in his eradication of all the evil wrought by Adam's descendants, assuring our reconciliation.

For your reading —

As clearly as Paul struggles to express it, the significance of this profoundly meaningful comparison will escape a mind not prepared for it by contextual study. If your time permits, it would increase your own understanding of these thoughts if your preparation included reading for yourself the entire letter up to this point, tracing Paul's reasoning.

The best way to pass on these ideas to your hearers will be the tried and true method of moving along carefully, pausing after each verse or idea, whichever helps your understanding the most. Your grasp of this passage will determine how successfully you assist others in appreciating it.

Matthew 10:24-33

General sense —

Jesus reassures us, in accordance with today's theme of our own worthiness, of our Father's care for us, even to the hairs on our head. In return, he demands that we acknowledge him, by our lives, in a confession without fear.

For your reading —

Read the words of Jesus with a pointed urgency. They concern, as usual, all of us; we must hear them as a part of the Master's missionary discourse at the departure of his disciples, continuing from the beginning of this chapter.

Move along at a measured pace, especially from verse 29 on. It is here that his address becomes personal and comforting.

Finish at verses 32 and 33 with the Savior's clear demand for what is involved as a result of our commitment to him.

PROPER 8

Suggested theme for today's readings —

The Lord is intensely jealous of us; no longer slaves of sin, we are to love him only.

Isaiah 2:10-17

General sense —
Isaiah's favorite theme, the humiliation of human pride before the irresistible power of God, is here invoked against a double-pronged evil of his day: the wealth and influence of King Uzziah's reign, and its prosperous alliances with the foreign powers with whom Israel traded. The direct object of the prophet's wrath is the pride, superstition and unbridled luxury rampant at Israel's higher levels.

For your reading —
Beneath and between these thundering lines lie their relevance to our modern temptations to pride. Read them with raised voice and stern bearing. What you seek here is the cumulative effect of this affirmation of divine power on our often selfish and avaricious devotion to material things.

As you summarize the passage in the final verse, 17, slow your pace, so that you will remind your hearers, as you conclude, that the Lord is the Lord.

Romans 6:3-11

General sense —
Paul's description of our Christian life moves on. Through Christ, our very "self" is being transformed. By Baptism into his death, we are not taken around death; we do not ignore death; we do not cover it over. The journey to resurrection leads straight *through* death. "We are buried with him." Today's passage attempts to explain the effects of that incorporation into the death of Jesus.

For your reading —
The same insistence which has marked our Pauline readings for the last four Sundays remains here. Like the others, this passage defends a developing theology of sin and grace in terms totally new to those who read it first.

If you can invest your delivery of these lines with the urgent tone of a defense attorney trying to explain our motivation, you will strike the mood in which they were written.

As is so often the case, the final verse concretizes the argument into an easy-to-remember aphorism. Read it more slowly, after a pause, because your hearers may want to remember it too.

Matthew 10:34-42

General sense —
The jealousy of the Lord for us can be divisive. We are asked to imagine here how disruptive the proclamation of the Gospel came to be in the early Jewish community, of which Matthew's lines are a reflection. Even family relations would be affected, in

a striking bit of irony, by, of all people, the Messenger of Peace.

Perhaps more than any other in the Gospels, this passage represents Jesus' outspoken resolve to reverse the values of our secular world.

For your reading —

Begin strongly. Jesus flatly contradicts what might be supposed of him: that he will cover our human weaknesses with a veil of sweetness and light.

As you read on, be aware that in this passage Jesus destroys eight of our misconceptions about what his coming, and our discipleship, will mean. Pause after nearly every verse, as your sense of their significance, obtained by your preparation, seems to indicate.

PROPER 9

Suggested theme for today's readings —
It is our friendship with Jesus which makes the heavy burden of our continual wars with ourselves easier to bear.

Zechariah 9:9-12

General sense —

We read today of a vision of future triumph, by an unknown author who lived during the last two centuries before the Christian era. He describes, in terms both obscure and rather mystical, a Messianic panorama of the days to come, when the world will be at peace.

For your reading —

Begin your reading in a slightly raised voice, announcing the coming of the Messiah-King. At once the tone is softened in verse 9b, as you detail his humble bearing.

The remainder of this brief announcement completes the prophecy in the warlike terms typical of the ancient visionaries.

Romans 7:21 – 8:6

General sense —

Paul surely speaks for all of us. The war goes on within, but the Spirit of Jesus is our strength and hope, as long as we walk "according to the Spirit."

For your reading —

As you quickly identify, through your life experience, with Paul's predicament, your reading will take on the life and the urgency it requires, rendering the first five verses in a tone of anxious bafflement.

Now Paul shows us how well he has dealt with himself in this eternal conflict we all share. Verses 1 through 6 transmit his triumph over despair. Read them in a lower tone, with self- assurance and peace. Lean on verse 6, which reveals the Apostle's great discovery about himself.

Matthew 11:25-30

General sense —
Jesus prays in thanksgiving for the success of the disciples' mission, as well as for the understanding they have received, even though they are novices in their work. In his Father's design, this wisdom — his message of salvation — has been hidden from those people ordinarily assumed to be "wise and prudent."

The oft-quoted beauty of the last three verses invites us to accept the yoke of submission to the reign of a Lord of love.

For your reading —
Since the words of Jesus occupy this entire passage, you will do well to deliver them as he might have done. Forego the narrative mode in which you so often tell stories. Use, rather, tones of fervent gratitude for the first two verses, then of information, almost as an aside, for verse 27, as if the Savior had noticed a questioning glance in the group.

Finally, as you deliver the last three verses, you, giving voice to the Master, are tenderness itself. Pronounce these consoling words gently, quietly, yet with great earnestness, as you conclude.

PROPER 10

Suggested theme for today's readings —
Our hearing of the Word of the Lord sows the seed of life in us, so that we can walk in the Spirit.

Isaiah 55:1-5, 10-13

General sense —
The writer of this second half of Isaiah, dated long after the Prophet's death, is the herald of future Messianic glory, which all humanity is about to witness. In this passage, perhaps written from Babylon as the Jews were preparing to go home after their exile, he invites his countrymen to a banquet of divine joy, as the Word of the Lord at last bears its fruit.

For your reading —
Do you, as a capable Lector or Lay Reader, need to be advised about a meaningful mode of delivering these beautiful lines? Their joy and exultation fairly shouts out the message of the Lord for us.

Remember, as always, that there is no need, in rendering this proclamation, to be shrill. The voice is raised, of course, but the secret here is the intensity of conviction which, through your preparation, should seize you and make of you a modern-day prophet of the joy of the Lord in us, his people.

Romans 8:9-17

General sense —

Because of the gift of the Spirit, writes Paul, the Christian is a real child of God, born anew of God, and calling him "my Father."

For your reading —

As the Apostle contrasts the life of our natural inclinations with the life we accept from God, this passage becomes rather difficult to deliver.

The best way to have this closely-wrought reasoning make sense to your hearers will be to take it one idea at a time, pausing after each sentence, even if only for a heartbeat, for the first three verses.

At verse 12 Paul begins drawing his conclusions. This portion of the passage will flow more smoothly, with its climax coming at verses 15 and 16. Drop your voice after the first "heirs," in verse 17, to accentuate our new status as children of God.

Matthew 13:1-9, 18-23

General sense —

The parable was commonly used by the holy men of Jesus' time to make a point, or to expound a teaching. Though fictitious, it leads the listener to concede a point not readily perceived as applying to oneself, since the scope of the answer is broader than first imagined.

The parable offers a theme to reflect on, and to draw from it as much meaning as one wishes.

God's reign will happen, says this parable, despite any obstacle. It is as inevitable as the growth of the harvest.

For your reading —

Read these lines in the narrative mode, being careful to dwell on the details, so that your hearers may easily grasp them for their reflection.

Stop for a moment after verse 9, as the parable ends. Then begin Jesus' explanation, once again attending to the parallels he draws for us.

There is no particular place of emphasis. Let the words speak for themselves. You cannot improve on the logic of our Savior.

PROPER 11

Suggested theme for today's readings —
Our troubles are neither interruptions, delays or distractions in our lives. They are part of the fabric of life and salvation.

Wisdom 12:13, 16-19

General sense —

We read today from a book not present in the Hebrew canon.

The passage is part of a homily about how the punishment of the Egyptians became the blessing of God for the Israelites. God's might is indeed the source of his mercy; by his leniency with us we learn to be gentle with others.

For your reading —

What these lines amount to is a hymn of praise and appreciation for the goodness of the Lord in our regard.

Read them in a rather prayerful mode, for they will touch the hearts of all your hearers, as we acknowledge that similar thoughts have crossed our minds, too, which by these lines we humbly admit.

Verse 19 is the down-to-earth closing of the passage. Lean on it a bit, as you conclude, for our reflection.

Romans 8:18-25

General sense —

Paul gets straight to the point. Far from making a Pollyanna-like comparison to cheer us on our way, he uses verse 18's contrast to testify to our Christian destiny of glory in three ways: the material universe, in its chaotic state, cursed by Adam's sin, groans with expectation; humanity itself (verse 23) also awaits redemption; and, as we will read next week, the Spirit shores up our hope that despite our weaknesses, with Christ we will win out in the end.

For your reading —

The opening, verse, 18, is the strong one; with it the writer immediately seizes our attention. Lean on it as you begin your reading.

No further places of emphasis are evident. The predominant tone throughout reinforces Paul's optimism, and optimism should be your mode as well.

Matthew 13:24-30, 36-43

General sense —

Re-echoing our theme for this week, Jesus demonstrates that his Kingdom will grow irresistibly, despite difficulties. Explaining the parable, he postpones the solution of the problem of evil till the end of the world, when in God's justice all will be evened out.

Verse 43b was a common story ending in Jesus' time, inviting the hearers to take the story's meaning to themselves.

For your reading —

In the first seven verses, the parable tells itself. Read it with your storytelling skills; then pause after verse 30 to let your hearers reflect on it for a moment.

Once again you are a storyteller, as the Master explains what the parable means. The last verses, from 39b to the end, must have startled Jesus' first hearers, who would expect a more mundane interpretation. Let your voice intensify here, as the Savior surprises us with the breadth of his vision and future insight.

PROPER 12

Suggested theme for today's readings —
God's unceasing love for us is the principle of the Kingdom's growth in us.

1 Kings 3:5-12

General sense —
Solomon's dream has an age-old precedent in Bible stories. Revelation by dream was a standard means of discerning God's wishes.

The ancients commonly equated wisdom with success in life in any chosen field of endeavor. Solomon's prayer for that gift above all others is the writer's way of showing how readily his prayer reached God's ears.

For your reading —
This is a story, and should be read as such. The detailed elaborations are a part of the author's praise of a good man. Read the passage with a sense of wonder at the closeness of the Lord to our desires, and his joy in granting our prayers.

Romans 8:26-34

General sense —
Continuing his testimony to our glorious destiny, the Apostle confirms that the Spirit even prays for us when there are no words. God's purpose and plan so pervade our lives that they are behind whatever happens to us. We are predestined not as individuals, but, by the Lord's design, his plan is aimed at our final destiny as a family of Christian believers.

For your reading —
Speak these lines with strength and conviction. They express fundamental Christian beliefs, and your hearers need them for reflection and reassurance.

In verse 31 the author bursts into a hymn of joy, couched in the rhetorical questions of one who has no doubt of the answer. This only increases the intensity of your voice.

The passage ends with a question, as it breaks off, to be continued in next week's reading. Whether you drop your voice after verse 34, or read it as a question, will be a matter of your judgment, based on your preparation.

Matthew 13:31-33, 44-49a

General sense —

The parables of the Savior continue, for our instruction. Today we hear of the mustard seed, the leaven, the treasure, the pearl, and the great net in the sea — all evidence of the growth of God's Kingdom.

In each parable Jesus teaches us four things: the inevitability of the Kingdom, despite its insignificant start; the infinite value of each one's discovery of that Kingdom as an individual; the universality of God's ultimate reign; and the fulfillment of the Kingdom on the last day, as its false members are expelled.

For your reading —

Today you tell five separate stories. With a pause after each one, you will give each its proper importance, as well as providing reflection time for your hearers, each of whom might respond to a different story.

Pause especially after verse 48, as Jesus applies all the parables to our final destiny.

PROPER 13

Suggested theme for today's readings —
The Christian's response to God's nourishing love is unfailing loyalty.

Nehemiah 9:16-20

General sense —

God's unwithdrawn love for us remains, despite our obstinacy. In this excerpt today from what may have been a public liturgical prayer, the author praises the divine mercy and generosity.

For your reading —

Since we have here what sounds like an invocation, your voice will take on that tone. It is a slightly raised voice, though full of humble petition. The passage is brief, so there is no need to hurry. Though the circumstances bespeak the ancient culture, the feelings are familiar to us today. Your voice will be our public confession of the mercy of the Lord in our behalf.

Romans 8:35-39

General sense —

The theme of the love of God for us made manifest in Jesus has echoed through our last several Pauline readings. Today, with no little emotion, a burst of rhetorical questions, and a smashing of all barriers to the divine love in our lives, the author concludes his exposition of the Christian's destiny.

For your reading —

It will be difficult not to be caught up in the driving force of these lines. They are aimed directly at the emotions.

Never be afraid to raise your voice to convey the utter conviction of Paul's mind and heart. He wants us to be convinced of these truths as well.

Verses 38 and 39 should conclude the passage at a slower speed, yet with still deeper intensity. These are words from the heart — the kind that can evoke a sudden burst of applause, or a shout of "Amen!"

Matthew 14:13-21

General sense —

Jesus, according to Matthew, has just heard of the killing of John the Baptist. His attempts to find some solitude are in vain. But his compassion urges him to nourish those who have followed him.

Matthew omits the usual note of wonder after the miracle, so that his purpose seems rather, in this instructional Gospel, to prefigure the Eucharist, the banquet of life, also freely given.

For your reading —

This episode passes so quickly that one of your storytelling skills will be to slow it down. Pause at the changes of scene, after verses 13 and 14. And assume an even and measured pace throughout, so that your hearers will be able to absorb all that is going on.

The final verse needs no particular stress. The size of the crowd sounds like about ten thousand, which is unlikely and very exaggerated by years of oral tradition.

PROPER 14

Suggested theme for today's readings —

God's omnipotence delivers us from all peril, but mostly from our faithless selves.

Jonah 2:1-9

General sense —

The Lord here demonstrates his power over all creatures and events by using them as his instruments. Rather than imagine the prophet praying from the belly of the fish, it seems more realistic and appropriate to treat the entire episode as a symbol of Israel's deliverance from the Exile in Babylon. In this sense we can sing, with Jonah, our own daily prayer that we be delivered from all evil.

For your reading —

A passage full of emotions like this one will challenge your ability to come out of yourself and take the place of this Israelite Everyman.

Make your reading an expression of your own gratitude for deliverance from darkness and ignorance, and convey that to your hearers with deepest sincerity and conviction.

Romans 9:1-5

General sense —

Paul turns now to a specific problem in the new Christian economy of salvation: the relationship of Judaism to the Christ-event. He has spent the last chapter expounding the Christian experience in terms of our reconciliation with God through Jesus Christ.

Now he speaks with "great sorrow and unceasing anguish" of his "kinsmen by race," who have let their inheritance pass to the Gentiles.

For your reading —

The passage selected for today represents only the merest introduction to Paul's treatment of the Jewish question, which occupies the next three chapters.

Nevertheless, the situation weighs on his heart. As you read, your tone ought to show the great urgency which moves him to reach out toward his fellow Jews.

The climax, or at least the most intense part, of the reading, is at verse 3. Otherwise, no particular emphasis is necessary.

Matthew 14:22-23

General sense —

Some think this incident might have happened after Jesus' resurrection, so singular is it. Most agree, however, that the little boat far out on the water represents symbolically the Church, from which Jesus is never far, despite the storms and darkness through which it sails.

For your reading —

We love stories; we will always give our best attention to a good storyteller. It is not that we receive any new information; we need, rather, to recapture experiences we have already had, to reaffirm the view of the world, contained in the story, that we hold.

Your narration of this incident has all the qualities of a wonderful tale: the lonely figure at night; the fury of the storm at sea; the fear of the boaters; the ghostly apparition; and the final reassurance, after Peter's momentary danger, that everything is all right.

In your preparation, practise the voice modulations which suit the action, and you will reassure your hearers that the Lord is always near to help us, as the Gospel intends to proclaim.

PROPER 15

Suggested theme for today's readings —
The ever-present mercy of the Lord is our steady rock of
hope.

Isaiah 56:1(2-5) 6-7

General sense —
Is the entire world invited into the community of believers,
to worship in the "house of prayer" with "the children of promise"? Evidently so, as these lines seem to foreshadow the revelation of the Gospel to the Gentiles. The Exile is over; salvation is
near; we must "hold fast to the Covenant."

For your reading —
References to the proximity of salvation and the Lord's deliverance, which abound in the Old Testament, carry a deeper
immediacy when taken to refer to our own personal destiny.
Hence your reading today will strike a note of relevancy, as
the Word invites all to live righteously while we await the Lord.
If you think of this brief passage in such fashion, your voice
will bring to its delivery the encouragement we all need.

Romans 11:13-15, 29-32

General sense —
The burden of Paul's thesis on the Jewish question, in chapters 9 through 11 of this epistle, is that the disbelief of the "dis-
obedient and obstinate people" is actually a part of the plan of
God. The Gospel was intended all along for the entire world.
The "Apostle to the Gentiles" now states that the disbelief is
only temporary, not final — "until the full number of the Gentiles
come in" — and that God's mercy is ultimately available to all.

For your reading —
Be as firm and direct as you can here. The author is explaining a delicate point as he suggests a ray of hope in Israel's rather
dark past.
Verse 15 is a key verse to be stressed, as it represents the
core of the argument: the Jews are grasped by the Lord despite
themselves.
Keep up your assertive tone of voice to the end, laying special
emphasis on verse 32 as you conclude. Verse 32 is the story of
our lives.

Matthew 15:21-28

General sense —
Jesus rarely encountered the Gentiles; he was sent principally to the children of Abraham (verse 24). Here, however, is a
chance for Jesus to teach: he does not refuse faith wherever he
happens to find it.

His exchange with the woman exemplifies the duel of wits, the matching of riddle with riddle, typical of Palestinian conversation.

The woman's turning of Jesus' witty insult around into a commitment in verse 27 is a master stroke which stops the Savior in his tracks and provides the climax of this episode: the mercy of the Lord is present the instant we need it and ask for it.

For your reading —
As in all your storytelling, you remind us, as we hoped you would: God's mercy always responds.

In your preparation, go over this rapid-fire dialogue until you have penetrated its nuances, as mentioned above in the General Sense paragraphs.

Pause a beat before verse 28 as Jesus is stricken with momentarily speechless admiration, then becomes deadly serious. Then conclude with authority.

PROPER 16

Suggested theme for today's readings —
Remaining faithful to God's love, despite discouragements, is a sign of our Christian vocation.

Isaiah 51:1-6

General sense —
We deliver today a poetic call to salvation. In this three-level tribute of appreciation, the poet masterfully gathers the creation of man, the history of Israel, and her divinely ordained destiny. And in a brief six verses he combines them all in this moment of salvation, trying to shake to attention a nation grown languid with despair.

To receive the maximum impact of this stirring evocation of Israel's glorious past, it would be well, as part of your preparation, to read the entire chapter.

For your reading —
It should go with out saying that your voice will rise as you read these noble encouragements. Deliver them strongly, vigorously, at a good pace. Pause after verse 2, verse 3 and verse 5. Each pause represents a new idea, or a change in address.

Romans 11:33-36

General sense —
The merciful wisdom of God has stopped Paul's train of thought in this conclusion to his analysis of the Jewish question. God has arranged, it seems, for the mutual assistance of both Jews and Gentiles in attaining salvation. Israel's role in this plan would never have been suspected otherwise. Paul can rationalize no further. He stops, awestruck by the mystery, and bursts into song.

For your reading —
This is not an easy reading. Frequently during the year we are called upon to transmit deeply-felt emotions. The idea here is to be completely unafraid to let your wonder at the mysteries in your own life inform your preparation. You will find, according to your diligence, that Paul's words will carry a conviction you may not have suspected.

Read at a slower pace than usual. Pause after each sentence. Your hearers deserve the time to reflect on their own mysteries too.

Matthew 16:13-20

General sense —
Jesus picks a place glorious in the past to promise Peter his future. Caesarea Philippi, far to the north, was an entirely Gentile community, and the site of many ancient shrines. Here, among the ashes of the old ways, the Master lays down the fundamentals of a new way: the primacy of faith rather than of the Law (verse 16); its origin not in human reasoning but by the revelation of God (verse 17); and the dependence of the faith community on divine rule (verse 19). It marks a pivotal episode in our history.

For your reading —
Despite its theological focus, this is basically the story of one of Jesus' encounters with his disciples where he had something of lasting impact to discuss with them.

So it is a story. And your delivery will be in the measured pace of the dialogue mode. Be sure to observe all the necessary voice modulations your preparation will suggest to you, which includes the dramatization of verses 17 through 19, the key to the episode.

Verse 20 is then spoken in a more reflective tone. Jesus knew that the disciples' faith was strong enough for such an injunction.

PROPER 17

Suggested theme for today's readings —
God's fidelity to his promises never fails. He is our helper in our struggles against evil.

Jeremiah 15:15-21

General sense —
The theme of the sins of the people and the vengeance of the Lord permeates chapters 14 through 17 of Jeremiah. The law of retaliation, a common procedure in ancient criminal cases, far from showing a vindictive mentality, was really an attempt to apply the principle of equity to all, as opposed to the chaos of uncontrolled vendettas. Jesus was to abrogate that practise, replacing it with charity. Jeremiah's appeal to retaliation in verse

15 must be understood in the framework of his culture.

For your reading —
Besides being a storyteller, you are sometimes called upon to act out a passage. Today's reading contains a vivid account of Jeremiah's inner crisis, his anger with the Lord, and God's final renewal of his mission. Challenge yourself to read it as if it were your own story. Then conclude at verse 21 with the Lord's promise, in almost the same words as the prophet's original call years before.

Romans 12:1-8

General sense —
These are general counsels, not necessarily concerned with the Church at Rome. Paul outlines them as the cost of our discipleship: our lives are to be a sacrifice to God; our struggles with evil are necessary for the good of the community. And, as with Jeremiah, God is always faithful.

For your reading —
Read these admonitions in the tone of a gentle and wise teacher, appealing for a better understanding of the mercies of God and the proper use of his gifts.

No special emphasis marks any verse: we have here an exhortation to a better life. Your tone ought to be the same throughout, perhaps bringing out the positive virtues cited in verses 7 and 8.

Matthew 16:21-27

General sense —
The instruction at the old pagan shrines of Caesarea Philippi is now impressed upon the minds of the disciples. They are glad to hear of the Messiah. Now Jesus reveals the other half of the picture: the Messiah must suffer and die — an idea entirely foreign to the Jewish tradition.

His rebuke of Peter stings all the more for the humiliation of hearing it in the presence of the others.

For your reading —
The sharp exchanges between Jesus and Peter in verses 22 and 23 should be marked in your voice by a sternness on both sides, and a slight quickening of your pace, just as we would express the same feelings in a heated conversation today.

The final verses, 24 through 28, possibly prompted by Peter's warning, are delivered in a calmer tone, as Jesus sets down the price of entering his Kingdom.

PROPER 18

Suggested theme for today's readings —
Our mutual charity is a reflection of God's wish for our salvation as a people.

Ezekiel 33:7-11

General sense —
Under the figure of the watchmen who stand on the hills of Palestine and warn of a hostile army's advance, Ezekiel defines the role of the prophet. He saves his own life by being alert to danger for others. Today's moral shadings were not a part of ancient reasoning. Everything is black and white. We are either wicked or virtuous.

For your reading —
The relevance of this idea is that we are all watchmen for each other in charity, joined in a common trust that God wills our salvation and our deliverance.

These are the words of the Lord, so that your reading will adopt the style of a proclamation.

Pause before verse 10, at the climax of the reading, as the Lord reveals that he wills not the death of the sinner, but that the sinner turn from his ways and live. Verse 11 should be strongly accented as you conclude.

Romans 12:9-21

General sense —
These maxims about mutual charity update the Old Testament counsels about our being watchmen. Christian charity extends even to one's enemies. And it is always to be exercised without sham or hypocrisy, as a sacrifice offered to God.

The attribute of God called "wrath" or "vengeance" is left to the last day. It is not to be a part of our lives.

For your reading —
These appealing counsels will always stand as staples of our everyday conduct. Straightforward and simply worded, you will find them easy to deliver. Maintain a smooth, even tone throughout.

As happens so often, the reading has been selected so that its last verse sums up the entire passage. If you have paused frequently, letting each maxim be clearly enunciated, you will leave your hearers with much to reflect on.

Matthew 18:15-20

General sense —
One of the ways in which we care for one another is to seek out those who have wandered. The art of correction is an exquisitely delicate one today, when we are more aware of our spiritual

heritage. In the early underground Church, the unity of the brethren was absolutely vital to its existence.

We should remember that these procedures borrowed considerably from Old Testament ones, somewhat discordant with the Gospel proclaiming Jesus' love for sinners. Their tone suggests that they were a product of the primitive Jewish Christian community.

For your reading —
Although these lines relate in little more than a general fashion to our world today, they are to be read, as in all instances of this kind, with a keen sense of how important they were to those who first saw them. Make your delivery as animated as you can, especially the final verses, 19 and 20. They are still true today, as we are so often engaged in common prayer.

PROPER 19

Suggested theme for today's readings —
We are forgiven, as Jesus teaches us in the Our Father, only as we forgive.

Ecclesiasticus 27:30 – 28:7

General sense —
Since this book is not a part of the Hebrew Canon, and does not appear in the Revised Standard Version of the Bible, we will use here the Jerusalem Bible's text.

Ecclesiasticus, the church book as it is called, contains a synthesis of revealed religion and experiential wisdom. An apology for Judaism, it seeks to demonstrate that true wisdom resides in Israel.

Today's passage counsels against anger and resentment.

For your reading —
Read these wise admonitions calmly, like a teacher instructing a class. They contain nothing we have not heard a thousand times, not only from our teachers but in our hearts of hearts.

The climax and principal emphasis in the passage come at the last three verses — the three "remembers." In these lines is the motivation for the killing of our anger and resentment.

Romans 14:5-12

General sense —
What really counts, as Paul concludes his discussion of the Christian life for us, are the values which inform human conduct, not the details of holy days or rules of eating.

He is dealing with age-old problems: the careful versus the carefree, the progressive versus the conservative. All will stand before the Lord in judgment.

For your reading —

As in all our presentations from the lectern, we are dealing with the Word of the Lord. This means that even in what seems to be a rather matter-of-fact reading like today's, the grace of the Word will touch someone who hears your voice.

Accordingly, move along carefully, as if this were the most important reading you will ever do. For example, in verses 7 through 12, the author passes over all our petty human differences to evoke our equality before Christ. Be sure you speak these words clearly and with some intensity. Pause after verse 9 as Paul asks a question, and again after verse 11, as he capsulizes this principal point in a few words we all need to hear.

Matthew 18:21-35

General sense —

Most of us recite the Our Father every day of our lives. Here, Jesus enlarges on the fifth petition of that prayer in an unusually stern and uncompromising parable. Forgiveness of our trespasses will only happen to the degree that we forgive those who have trespassed against us.

For your reading —

The first two verses today form a prelude to the main story. It is Peter's question which moves the Master to exemplify his answer.

Once again you are a storyteller. Let the story be your guide; there will be no difficulty in your hearers' understanding what it means. The action moves along at a good pace, with hardly a wasted word.

The principal pause is after verse 34. The story is over; Jesus has captured his audience. Now, after your brief stop, he punches home the application in a way that is clear and unmistakeable. That is the effect you ought to create too.

PROPER 20

Suggested theme for today's readings —
The goodness and mercy of the Lord toward us transcends every human circumstance.

Jonah 3:10 – 4:11

General sense —

For the Israelites, the sea was the kingdom of death. The Book of Jonah is about God's mercy in delivering us — all of us — from death.

But Jonah, who has been shown God's mercy, is resentful that the Lord extends it to others. The prophet is Everyman, who would limit divine freedom by presuming to decide how much of it should be handed out, and in which direction.

For your reading —

As the Lord challenges Jonah to examine the motive for his anger, your storytelling skill will reflect the edge in Jonah's voice, through verse 5, where the prophet goes off by himself to sulk.

In verse 6, as God shows his mercy again by shielding Jonah from the sun, soften your voice. Beginning with verse 7, the pace picks up again.

As the author makes his point in the final verses, be free to close as suddenly as the writer does, by an arresting literary device.

Philippians 1:21-27

General sense —

Enduring Roman imprisonment, possibly facing death, because he is known to be a witness for Christ, Paul reflects here on the alternatives of living and dying. But he feels, in verse 25, that he may survive the experience.

For your reading —

Although these feelings, grounded in faith by a man of steadfast courage, are beyond the experience of most of us, read these lines imagining that you are leaving a final testimony to the people you have cared for.

Give the passage, through the tone of your voice, the strength of Paul's conviction, ready for whatever might befall him. Conclude, with him, with a fervent wish that they remain true to "the faith of the Gospel."

Matthew 20:1-16

General sense —

Jesus gives us today a parable about salvation for the Jews and the Gentiles. Even though the Gentiles arrive late in the day, they are "paid" no less than the others, while taking nothing away from the earlycomers. Whoever is admitted to the Kingdom is allowed the fullest participation; arrival time has no relevance to standing. Otherwise the Kingdom would not belong to God (verse 15).

For your reading —

Parables are stories. As you read, you reassure us of the justice of the Lord.

Be sure to observe, through your careful preparation, the shadings of the dialogue which forms the substance of the story.

The ending strikes a note of finality; in the Gospel, Jesus' mysterious remark, sounding like a putdown of the Jews, concludes the encounter.

PROPER 21
Suggested theme for today's readings —
Action is the true test of obedience. Our individual responsibility means nothing unless we carry it out in practise.

Ezekiel 18:1-4, 25-32

General sense —
Today's passage deals with individual responsibility and its implications. It concludes with another affirmation of the unwithdrawn love of the Lord for us, whatever our past sins may have been.

For your reading —
There is an edge to these lines; the prophet is defending the Lord's right to his creatures, as well as his justice in rewarding and punishing our actions.

Read the entire passage in that defensive mode. The prophet appeals throughout his book to the holiness of God and his vindication among the Gentiles.

There are strong accusations in verses 30 and 31, followed by God's promise of life. Read the last verse gently as you conclude.

Philippians 2:1-13

General sense —
Paul here recasts the notion of individual responsibility in a whole new mode. Where the prophet declaimed against sin, the Apostle affectionately encourages and counsels toward virtuous Christian ways.

The hymn to Christ which makes this passage so memorable (verses 6-11) might have originated in Jewish-Christian liturgy. It is still used every year during Holy Week. We, like Christ, should not be overly proud of being chosen by God to bear the name of Christian.

For your reading —
The reading begins gently, although it will be effective to lean on the phrase "complete my joy" in verse 2, to establish the tone Paul intends for the first four verses.

From verse 5 through verse 11, read the hymn to Christ at a somewhat slower speed, being careful, through your preparation, to make the logic of these sublime and oft-quoted words very clear.

Verses 12 and 13 should be preceded by a pause, to return to the gentle mode which marked the opening four verses.

Matthew 21:28-32

General sense —
Jesus contrasts empty promises with action, and even his

enemies admit that action is the true test of obedience. The Master flares up at them, because although they know enough to give him the right answer, they have never practised the obedience which arises from faith.

For your reading —

You have but a moment or two to deliver this sharp-edged lesson on true obedience. Get right into it as Jesus does, making clear the contrast he draws.

At verse 32b, intensify your voice as Jesus shows his annoyance at the hypocrisy of his hearers. Continue in this mode of impatience until the conclusion. The ending, though rather abrupt, will serve as a good starting point for your hearers' reflection.

PROPER 22

Suggested theme for today's readings —
Fidelity to our faith will mean disappointment, and many temptations; but God's fidelity will never fail.

Isaiah 5:1-7

General sense —

We could call today's passage a first-person parable, cast in the form of a song, a ballad that might be rendered at a village festival. It begins pleasantly enough, but the truth emerges in the end: it is a parable about Israel's infidelity.

For your reading —

The opening joy of this song should be evident in your tone of voice — happy and upbeat — until the last phrase of verse 2: "but it yielded wild grapes." That disappointment, inedible fruit, lets your voice fall as you conclude this introduction.

Verses 3 and 4 speak the disappointment of the vintner, and are delivered rather plaintively.

In verse 5 we see that he knew all along what he was going to do. Be firm, and, impersonating the owner, have your mind made up, from this verse to the end. Pause before verse 7, to isolate the revelation of the parable's meaning, then read verse 7 in a stern tone of voice.

Philippians 3:14-21

General sense —

Paul, lashing out at those who would undermine the faith of the Christians, tries to encourage the Church at Philippi to strive even harder, ending with a picture of their eternal reward.

For your reading —

Aside from verses 18 and 19, where the author refers to the subject of this chapter, this is an upbeat appeal for the very best that is in us. Deliver it in a tone of encouragement, treating verses 18 and 19 as a momentary interruption, then hastening back to "our commonwealth" and concluding on a note of earnest joy.

Matthew 21:33-43

General sense —

All three readings today seem to deal with the notion of fidelity in the face of subversion by the forces of evil. Matthew here echoes the vineyard theme of Isaiah in our first reading.

Note how the Evangelist intensifies the action by placing it in dialogue form, so that the Jews themselves pronounce the words of condemnation.

For your reading —

Be the storyteller here. Jesus makes the same point as he did in his parable last Sunday: that the Jewish nation will not be the sole heirs of the Kingdom, because they have not appreciated its value. So your responsibility is to narrate without embellishment, letting the story speak for itself.

Jesus asks a direct question in verse 42, which will require a slight raising of your voice in this verse and in the last one.

PROPER 23

Suggested theme for today's readings —
Whatever the trials of this life, God's fidelity provides a joyful destiny for us.

Isaiah 25:1-9

General sense —

Chapter 25 is the second of four entire chapters devoted to a vision resembling in scope the Apocalypse of John. The prophet looks behind the events of his time to forsee the everlasting banquet of the Lord.

In today's passage he celebrates God's victory as something that has already taken place.

For your reading —

Ideally, this passage is read with raised voice throughout. It expresses in language relevant to its time and culture, the same hope of future salvation we all cherish today.

Verse 6 contrasts present poverty with future riches. It begins the second half of the proclamation, the happier, more positive side, and should be preceded by a pause after verse 5.

Verse 9's expectations will resound more familiarly in the hearts of your hearers. Make it, by your increased intensity, a true climax for our reflection.

Philippians 4:4-13

General sense —
These happy lines, read last year on the Third Sunday of Advent, deserve another hearing today. Paul's care for his beloved Philippians shines through, as he bids them all farewell.

For your reading —
Although "rejoice" leads off the sentiments here, the original word seems to have been "farewell." Nevertheless, the smile in your voice should be evident here from beginning to end.

The Apostle's fondness for these people casts his words in a mode of peace, their best assurance of a joyful future, echoing Isaiah's vision in our first reading.

Matthew 22:1-14

General sense —
Jesus makes several points in this parable of the wedding feast: the universality of the guest list; the indifference, then the violence, of those who receive the invitation, and their swift and fatal punishment; and the necessity of the wedding garment of grace for attendance. As do his other parables, the banquet exemplifies the Last Day and the final judgment.

For your reading —
Tell your story as Jesus does — calmly, letting the quickly recognizable lessons it contains sink in with your hearers.

It will be well to read verses 6 and 7 in a more intense way, to signify the bad treatment of the king's son and his father's retribution.

The reference to the last days in verse 13 also deserves particular emphasis.

PROPER 24

Suggested theme for today's readings —
Our Christian joy is founded on the sovereignty of the Lord over all creation.

Isaiah 45:1-7

General sense —
So overjoyed were the Israelites with their deliverance from their Babylonian exile that they called Cyrus, King of Persia, their Messiah. The prophet excitedly looks forward to the moment when this benevolent despot will worship the true God himself. But the King had only asked that their freedom include worshiping their gods and praying for him.

Today's passage proclaims the divine decree announcing Cyrus' royal enthronement.

For your reading —
For us, the relevancy here, as in so many of the Old Testa-

ment texts we read, lies not in the deeds recounted but in the sovereignty of the Lord, his dominion over all creation, and his calling us by name.

As you enunciate this theme, be the proclaimer of this great dominion. Read with uplifted voice of the center of the prophet's vision, the action of the Lord.

The impression you wish to leave for your hearers' reflection will be the overpowering presence of the Lord in our lives.

1 Thessalonians 1:1-10

General sense —

The value of Paul's two letters to the Church at Thessalonica in northern Greece lies in their treatment of the Second Coming of the Lord. This expectation should motivate the people to courage and patience in tribulation.

We begin today a series of four readings from the first of these letters, in which Paul outlines his personal relationship with the Church there, and gives his views on the Second Coming.

For your reading —

You read today the words of a man who speaks to a well-beloved Church. His appreciation of their goodness and steadfastness gives this reading a glow which good preparation will lend to your voice.

Imagine the people he addresses gathered about you with shining faces, reveling in the unqualified praise contained in the letter you have delivered. There are no particular places of emphasis; just a load of good news and smiles.

Matthew 22:15-22

General sense —

Jesus makes no political statement here, no judgment as to right or wrong. He simply recognizes the right and power of the government to levy taxes. What belongs to Caesar and what belongs to God he leaves to the personal decision of each individual conscience.

For your reading —

Drop your voice after "Herodians" in verse 16, so that you will not accent the word "saying." What is said is more important.

Verses 16 and 17 drip with unctuous flattery, as the Pharisees try to trip Jesus into taking a stand. If there is something of a smile in your voice you will catch the mood here.

Jesus answers sternly and resentfully in verse 18, as he sees through their trick.

The remainder of the episode is told calmly; Jesus has already solved the problem. As you conclude, they simply have no answer.

PROPER 25

Suggested theme for today's readings —
Love of our neighbor for the sake of Jesus is the greatest commandment of all.

Exodus 22:21-27

General sense —

The theme of care for strangers echoes through the Old Testament. No one was to forget that the Israelites themselves had been aliens in Egypt many years before. And the chief advocate of that cause, as appears in our reading today, is the Lord himself.

For your reading —

Your delivery of this excerpt from the ancient code of law called the Book of the Covenant should be in a mode of announcement, with no special emphasis. Its point that we act compassionately with strangers, who represent the Lord in our midst, resounds in our lives today as it did when it was written.

1 Thessalonians 2:1-8

General sense —

The Apostle here differentiates himself and his companions in mission from the many charlatans and false preachers of his day. Despite his anxiety over the disciples' rough treatment at Philippi (described in Acts 16:19-40), the Gospel gave him courage to preach here. Evidently his motives were believed, for the people here "had become very dear to us."

For your reading —

Read these rather personal lines with deep sincerity and conviction. Imagine yourself as Paul, having overcome the natural fear of a repetition of his treatment at Philippi.

Verses 7 and 8 express the author's total giving of himself to people who understand what he is trying to do.

Matthew 22:34-46

General sense —

Jesus dealt with five important controversies in the last days of his public ministry. His authority was questioned; he was asked about tribute to Caesar. Again, his preaching of resurrection from the dead was resisted because resurrection did not appear in the Law.

In today's reading Jesus settles the last two controversies: that of the Greatest Commandment, and the question of his being a son of David.

For your reading —

As a storyteller here, you are challenged to reproduce faithfully the flattering inquiry in verse 36, and the straightforward answer beginning in verse 37.

Now comes Jesus' turn to ask questions. Pause after verse 40, to indicate a second episode. In verse 42b the answer of the Pharisees sounds very assured, yet because of false theological assumptions on their part, they are unable to respond to Jesus' final questions.

A pause after verse 45 will give your hearers a moment to imagine the silence of the outwitted Pharisees. Then conclude with the inevitable result of their embarrassment.

PROPER 26
Suggested theme for today's readings —
Practising what we profess gives our faith and our witness the authenticity which leads others to Christ.
Micah 3:5-12

General sense —

Micah was the last of the four great prophets of the eighth century before Christ. With Isaiah, Amos and Hosea, he proclaimed the wrath of the Lord against the social evils of his day, never forgetting that God is also Mercy.

In the passage assigned for today, he castigates the unscrupulous preachers "who lead my people astray," and who give religion a bad name.

For your reading —

This scathing diatribe against the venality of both religious and secular leaders, probably delivered before a gathering of Israelite men of influence (verse 9), makes for difficult reading. The emotion of anger ill befits the lector at our modern devotions.

But as transmitters of the Word, we do owe our hearers a faithful rendition of the Scriptures. Keep your voice at the level of intensity which you feel best brings out that anger.

Verses 8, 9 and 10 are especially strong. Your conclusion will lower your pitch somewhat, as you reveal the dire consequences of the leaders' conduct.

1 Thessalonians 2:9-13, 17-20

General sense —

The Church at Thessalonica, there remains no doubt, is Paul's pride and joy. He insists how hard he has worked for them, how zealously he strives for their Christian perfection, and how much he has missed them since being on the road. He is proud of them.

For your reading —

From verses 9 through 13 the writer urges the people to remember the genuineness both of his interest in them and of the Gospel of Christ. Lend to these verses your own conviction of the truth of the Gospel.

At verse 17, in the second segment of the passage, Paul becomes much more personal. Absence from these friends draws out a deeper level of feeling. The principal change in your voice here will be an increase in enthusiasm, signified by greater voice modulations. Paul really wants the people to know how much he cares for them.

Matthew 23:1-12

General sense —

Jesus' entry into Jerusalem, to face the events of his Passion, Death and Resurrection, lies directly ahead. Chapters 19 through the end of Matthew's Gospel cover a period of only eight days — the last of the Savior's earthly life.

In today's passage, Jesus attacks neither the right of the Scribes to teach nor the teaching itself. What he is critical of is the discrepancy between their teaching and the way they live.

For your reading —

Imagine the shocking impact these words must have had on the crowds, as you study them during your preparation. Then deliver them with an edge in your voice which will mirror Jesus' mounting impatience with the institutional religion of his day.

Verses 8 through 12 sound like a digression, but Jesus here addresses his own disciples as much as he does the crowd. His mood seems to soften for a moment. Conclude your reading on this somewhat gentler note.

PROPER 27

Suggested theme for today's readings —
Keeping the lamp of honesty lit will make us ready for Christ's coming.

Amos 5:18-24

General sense —

Steeped in the old Mosaic tradition, Amos speaks as the conscience of social justice, the decrier of Israel's sins against the ancient Covenant.

In this passage, typical of the tough-minded approach of this hardened old shepherd, the prophet catsigates religious practises which do not spring from sincere and contrite hearts.

For your reading —

Careful attention to some key words will illuminate the harshness of these judgments, such as "have" in verse 18, and "bear" in verse 19.

Pause after verse 20, because the writer gets to his principal point in verse 21, with a direct attack on organized religion's excessive formalism.

Verses 21 through 24 are difficult to read because you must tread a path between imitating the outrage of the prophet, which would render your presentation rather shrill, and on the other hand delivering only his words, thereby robbing the passage of its life. If you slow your pace a bit, and read with a deeper intensity, you will reproduce the author's feelings without hinting to your hearers that it is they with whom you are angry.

1 Thessalonians 4:13-18

General sense —
We read today one of the classic texts for our belief in the afterlife. Using a favorite attention-getting device, Paul "would not have us ignorant" of the fate of our departed brothers and sisters.

His description of the Second Coming, grounded in true Christian hope, reassures the people that their friends who have gone before them will also share in Christ's glory.

Verses 16 and 17 describe the end of the world in terms of the "up in the air" cosmology of his day.

For your reading —
Even though the Apostle's cosmology is dated, his picture comforts our sense of wonder about the Last Day. Read it, climaxing with the act of faith in verse 15, in a gentle consoling mode. Those were important words for those people to hear.

The tone of comfort is especially strong and clear as you conclude at verse 18. Pause before you read that verse, to let the message sink in.

Matthew 25:1-13

General sense —
This homely yet sad wedding parable preaches not vigilance but foresight. With no set time, apparently, for the bridegroom to appear, vigilance would be too exhausting. Human nature demands sleep, and all ten maidens do sleep. The point of the parable lies in our need for foresight. We have no knowledge of Christ's coming, but that knowledge is not necessary if we are ready, as five of the maidens were.

For your reading —
Verses 12 and 13 carry the application of this parable. After you have related the experience of the ten maidens in your very best storytelling style, pause after verse 12 for a beat, raise your head, and speak verse 13 directly to your hearers, as you conclude.

PROPER 28

Suggested theme for today's readings —
All Christian life takes its meaning from our awareness of the coming of the Lord and our accountability to him.

Zephaniah 1:7, 12-18

General sense —

These lines teem with the clamor and dust of battle, as this prophet of the seventh century B.C. likens the coming of "the great day of the Lord" to the approach of an irresistible army, because of the sins of an unfaithful nation.

For your reading —

Zephaniah's tough-minded nationalism and his anger at Israel's infidelity make this a reading to be prepared carefully. Read the dreadful curses strongly, of course, but not in a shrill way. Remember that our modern theology and devotional attitudes regard the Lord in much more gentle terms, as our loving Father.

The hoped-for effect of this passage is simply to remind us, albeit in terms from another age, that the great day of the Lord looms for each of us as well.

1 Thessalonians 5:1-10

General sense —

Casting the dire predictions of Zephaniah in the new mode of Christianity ("God has not destined us for wrath"), Paul has words of encouragement for his beloved Church at Thessalonica.

We speak of the coming of the Lord because Advent is only two weeks away.

For your reading —

Once again we deliver the message of the Apostle in the mode he uses throughout his epistle: kindly encouragement.

Even so, season this friendliness with a note of insistence. Paul wants no one to be in doubt, as we read last Sunday, about the desire of the Lord to welcome us as we leave this life.

Conclude with a smile in your voice as you read the final verse.

Matthew 25:14, 15, 19-29

General sense —

For the third time today, our readings, as we approach Advent, turn on the coming of the Lord. In this parable the accent is not so much on the uncertainty of that coming, as with the parable of the ten maidens last week, but on the fact that we are accountable for our gifts and talents. What is more, as in verse 29, our powers grow with use and wither with disuse.

For your reading —

Parables are stories, as we know, and as you read this detailed, rather personal reminder of our individual responsibility, proceed at an even pace, pausing frequently to allow your hearers time for reflection.

Verses 26 through 29 drive home the stern lesson Jesus intends to teach. Put an edge in your voice as you speak directly to the hearts of your hearers.

PROPER 29

Suggested theme for today's readings —
We will be judged on how we have treated others.

Ezekiel 34:11-17

General sense —
All the bitter invectives of the prophets now fade away, and as we end another year, the voice of the Lord proclaims that he will be the shepherd of his people. Not only will he feed them, he will actively search them out — even the lost, the strayed and the crippled.

For your reading —
Proclaim this consoling announcement as you begin today. Each verse fills in another detail of the picture. Make them count, as you pause after almost every verse. Be careful, however, not to let these pauses make your presentation choppy. For example, verses 11 and 12 can be treated as one, as can 14 and 15.

The final pause would fit after verse 15, as the Lord now turns to those who will need more help, in verse 16.

He concludes with a word to those who have been faithful and are held more responsible than others.

1 Corinthians 15:20-28

General sense —
Paul here offers one of his frequent descriptions of the last day. He depicts it as the crowning event of salvation history and the victory of man over sin, Satan and death. Perfectly suited to this last day of the Church year, it manifests God our Father as the final end of all creation and our ultimate destiny.

For your reading —
This is a teaching passage, to be read as carefully and clearly as one would draw a picture.

Pauses are not indicated here. The picture is to be sketched without interruption, the last stroke in verse 28 as important as the first.

Matthew 25:31-46

General sense —
A homely analogy of animal care, the transfer of sheep and goats to other pastures, marks this sublime lesson of Jesus on the primacy of active care for others. He describes, at the Last Judgment, the one quality by which our lives have meaning, and the sign of our movement toward God: charity.

For your reading —

Of all the stories you have told from the Bible during the past year, this panorama grips the imagination as no other. Jesus draws us intimately and individually into the core of his moral teaching: he is present in all his people; to honor others is to honor him, and save our souls.

Lean on this application, as Jesus brings it down to earth in verses 40 and 45. These are the verses where you will slow your pace and make eye contact with your hearers. They form a fitting and motivating climax to all the lessons we have heard this year.

Year B

FIRST SUNDAY IN ADVENT

Suggested theme for today's readings —
Watchfulness in prayer enriches our knowledge of the ways of the Lord.

Isaiah 64:1-9a

General sense —

Today's lines, as we begin a new Church year, are painted in somber shades of desolation and despair. The Temple is no more; Jerusalem lies in ruins. The ravaging Babylonians have deported the people to a faraway, inhospitable land. As we admit in verses 5 through 7, the Lord has not heaped sorrow on us, but simply abandoned us to our guilt.

For your reading —

The prophet calls out to God in prayer. Lend your voice to this Advent plea for his coming, from the first words through the end of verse 2.

The remembrance of old sorrows softens your voice in verse 3, and the accumulation of guilt-filled despondency builds up through verse 7.

At verse 8, after a pause, comes the beginning of consolation. You are praying again. This last verse and a half, to the end of the reading, speaks fervently and humbly, admitting that we are nothing without our Father.

You may not even want to drop your voice after the final word, "forever." It can be more appealingly prayerful to leave it up in the air.

1 Corinthians 1:1-9

General sense —

Paul opens his letter to the Church at Corinth with this typically Pauline salutation, identifying himself and giving thanks for the faith of the people, as he reminds them of the everlasting fidelity of God.

For your reading —

Drop your voice after both "grace" and "peace" in verse 3. There should be a comma after "peace." Read as if there were one.

Pause after verse 3, which concludes the opening, so that you can mark the transition to Paul's direct address to the people's faith.

Drop your voice after "gift" in verse 7. It marks the end of a thought.

The remainder of the accents in the reading will become apparent to you from the text itself.

Mark 13:33-37

General sense —

This is the classic urging to Christian vigilance. It is true for all times and ages.

Verse 35 contains the four divisions of the night hours used by the Romans. The final verse, 37, lifts the entire thought beyond the immediate situation (the coming ruination of Jerusalem) to apply it to all people for all time.

For your reading —

This is not a difficult reading, in that it is delivered in one somber tone of voice throughout. Lean on the word "watch," which occurs four times. By doing that, you will be able to communicate to your hearers the Advent spirit in which this passage has been chosen.

SECOND SUNDAY IN ADVENT

Suggested theme for today's readings —
The Advents of our lives are always times of comfort and healing.

Isaiah 40:1-11

General sense —

The last twenty-seven chapters of Isaiah differ greatly from the first thirty-nine. The latter chapters were written as a Book of Consolation for the exiled Israelites. Isaiah himself had been dead and gone for nearly two hundred years, so that these chapters are called Second Isaiah.

The Book of Consolation begins with today's reading, promising that the Lord of comfort will surely come to the rescue and end Israel's healing sorrow.

For your reading —

Begin gently — how could you otherwise read these first two verses? A mother's murmurings to her child would sound the same.

Verse 3 begins the expectations of Advent with the traditional lines quoted years later by John the Baptist. If the voice "cries," your own voice should rise to reflect that cry.

This elevated tone of hope and encouragement should be maintained all the way through the end of verse 10. Is this difficult to do? Yes, it is. This is not an easy reading. But its tone demands that you make the effort to proclaim this Good News.

The gentle tone of verses 1 and 2 is then resumed, as the reading comes full circle in verse 11. End quietly, to reflect the atmosphere of this beautiful season.

2 Peter 3:8-15a, 18

General sense —

The author of this letter expresses the fundamental Christian — and Jewish — teaching of the coming Day of the Lord in the popular imagery of the times.

This is the only place in the Bible describing a final day of fire consuming the universe. Overall, it is a testimony to the sovereignty of God and the power of his will to end the world as efficiently as he created it.

For your reading —

These are dire words, but the exhortation to good lives is designed to mitigate the fear they naturally would generate. Therefore, the first three verses, 8, 9 and 10, are not really the point of the passage, so that you need not read them in too solemn a tone.

The point is the good lives we ought to lead in order to fulfill God's loving design in verse 9. Verse 11, then, is to be read only after a pause, with the word "you" leaned on, to catch the people's attention.

In verse 13, drop your voice in a "mental period" after each use of the word "new;" this marks the contrast between before and after the fire.

Mark 1:1-8

General sense —

Mark begins his Gospel with John the Baptist as a prologue to the coming of the Messiah. He quotes two Old Testament prophets (one unnamed here) to certify that if Jesus, who had not yet appeared, is not the true Messiah, then John's ministry has no place in the Gospel.

For your reading —

Pause for a beat after verse 1, as those words are simply a title.

Raise your voice for the official proclamation in verses 2b and 3. After that, the narrative tone is used.

Verse 8 sets the tone of the Incarnation: baptizing with the Holy Spirit will now inaugurate the visitation of the Lord himself to purify all our deeds and forgive us our sins. This verse should end your reading with a strongly-marked contrast between the old dispensation and the new.

THIRD SUNDAY IN ADVENT

Suggested theme for today's readings —

The joy of Advent symbolizes our perpetual waiting for the Lord.

Isaiah 65:17-25

General sense —
The Book of Consolation ends with a panorama of joy: an entire new creation, as the universe shares in man's redemption. The word "create" occurs three times in rapid succession; the achievement is clearly God's. The Lord and his people unite in common joy, even as we today look forward to the advent of our Savior at Christmas.

For your reading —
As long as you keep your voice elevated and joyfully enthusiastic, this reading should, by its text, be truly an Advent encouragement.

Pausing frequently will be a great help in maintaining that tone. Pausing gives you a chance to catch your breath and plunge on. Let your hearers sense the joy the prophet must have felt.

1 Thessalonians 5:16-28

General sense —
If we are expecting something (or someone) great, we rejoice. To our Advent waiting, Paul adds this cheerful greeting, as he signs off his letter to the church community at Thessaly. To follow the Lord Christ means more than the obligation of charity toward our neighbor. It is a way of life oriented to God in joy and thanksgiving.

For your reading —
These short, punchy maxims are typical of the Pauline address. Be careful not to read them too quickly; each has its own importance. As we end a letter or a phone conversation, we linger over our goodbyes in much the same fashion, adding this thought and that as they occur to us.

Do the same here, as if these pithy amenities are just popping into your mind.

John 1: 6-8, 19-28

General sense —
This is the Evangelist's testimony to the authenticity of John the Baptist as the Messianic forerunner. As John's identity and role are examined in some detail, he avows that the Messiah is among the people but not yet revealed, and that he, John, is merely sent to announce that event.

For your reading —
As deeply as its significance and symbolism lie, this is an unvarnished introduction to the events to come. Read it in the concise, straightforward manner in which it is told.

In verse 19 there ought to be a colon after "who are you?" Drop your voice here; this verse serves only to present John's testimony.

Pause after verse 23, as John's witness is interrupted by the author's footnote in verse 24. Then resume your narrative tone until you close, with what we would call today the "dateline."

FOURTH SUNDAY IN ADVENT

Suggested theme for today's readings —
The one who comes, and makes our best moments, is always the Lord.

2 Samuel 7:4, 8-16

General sense —

Israel understood its religious history as a succession of saviors sent to deliver the people from their troubles. Moses; the Judges after him; men like Nehemiah and Ezra, and now David, all were looked on as sent by God. To the people, the King-savior governs with justice, helps the poor and needy, and always defeats his enemies.

Nathan, in today's passage, delivers an oracle (an Old Testament sign that God is speaking officially) promising that the house of David, meaning his dynasty, will last forever.

For your reading —

Read these lines in the tone of a world-class announcement. The passage happens to be the basis for the whole idea of a royal Messiah in the Israelite hopes and dreams. It is a milestone in their history.

Verse 11a concludes the first half of the personal covenant with David himself. Pause after "enemies," and begin again with a new idea: the house, or dynasty, which is the covenant with his offspring and successors.

Continue, however, in the same "big news" tone throughout your reading.

Romans 16:25-27

General sense —

Paul concludes his missionary's reflections on the salvation now offered to all people through Jesus, and looks forward to his coming visit to Rome. His farewell (whether written by him or added later has never been fully determined) forges a crucially important link with the Old Testament revelations, establishing the sovereignty of God over all the ages, both ancient and latter-day.

For your reading —

This short passage will challenge your ability to deliver an important idea in a few words.

The thing to accomplish here is to read all the way to the end of verse 26, without dropping your voice once. Verses 25 and 26 are only a development of "to him." The thought is not completed until verse 27, so that your voice should not drop until after "forever more." Then, as the author adds, "through Jesus Christ," as a conclusion, you add the "Amen" strongly, to conclude the reading on a positive note of thanksgiving.

Luke 1:26-38

General sense —

The account of the Annunciation is a meditation on absolute faith, unquestioning obedience, and the acceptance of a difficult (public, unmarried pregnancy, in those days) and mysterious role.

The Evangelist offers here not just "a day in the life of" Mary, but a Gospel of salvation. Jesus' Jewish background, his descent from David, the call of the shepherds to signify universality, and the promise of everlasting rule, all work together to overwhelm the details of what happened with the communication of the mystery of redemption.

For your reading —

Drop your voice after "David" in verse 27. Do *not* drop your voice after "said" in verse 28. The important words here are the angel's greeting.

There is a "mental period," a voice-drop, after "son" in verse 31.

Pause before verse 34, when, as Mary speaks, the tone changes a bit.

Drop your voice after "spirit" in verse 35, and especially after "also" in verse 36.

Pause a beat before the last verse, 38, concludes the episode. Mary's consent is the key to the whole mystery. Say her words humbly and quietly, then those about the departure of the angel in the same manner.

CHRISTMAS

NOTE – Readings for all three Christmas services, as well as the first and second Sunday after Christmas, are identical in cycles A, B and C. See cycle A for general sense and reading hints.

THE EPIPHANY

NOTE – The readings for the feast of the Epiphany are identical for cycles A, B and C. See cycle A for general sense and reading hints.

FIRST SUNDAY AFTER EPIPHANY

NOTE – First and second readings are the same for all three cycles. See cycle A.

Mark 1:7-11

General sense —

The baptism of the Lord Jesus is celebrated at this time of year, as he begins his public ministry. Mark's is the only Gospel to mention it. Apparently, in verse 10, Jesus was the only one to see the Spirit descending on him. In this way Mark keeps Jesus' true identity a secret known only to the reader. It is not time yet for the revelation of the Kingdom to his contemporaries.

For your reading —

Be sure to drop your voice after "preached," in verse 7. The word "saying" is to be glided over almost as if it were not there.

The rest of this brief reading presents no special problems. As usual with short passages, you must take time and be sure that no one misses the significance of this public appearance of our Savior.

SECOND SUNDAY AFTER EPIPHANY
Suggested theme for today's readings —
The "day" of our conversion to the Lord is hidden from us.
1 Samuel 3:1-10

General sense —

We read today of the call of Samuel — or at least of some of it. The message of the Lord to the young temple helper is announced in the verses which follow today's passage, so that we may hear only of the importance of lending a careful and obedient ear to the unmistakable voice of the Lord.

Samuel grew up to be the last of the ruling Judges, a prophet, a kingmaker (Saul and David), and a key figure in the transition of Israel from the Judges' rule to a monarchy.

For your reading —

This reading will test your ability to modulate your voice rapidly, as the conversation flows between Samuel, Eli and the Lord.

Raise your voice as the Lord calls out each time. Try your best to make this remarkable conversation as lively and real as you can, especially the last verse, when the call finally gets through.

1 Corinthians 6:11b-20

General sense —

This letter is Paul's response to news about disorders in the Church at Corinth. Among these, in today's reading, is his advice to those who were invoking Christian liberty to justify serious violations of morality. Paul's remark in Romans (14:14) that "nothing is unclean in itself" had been raised to a byword for all of life, instead of just in dietary matters, as he had intended it.

For your reading —

Slow your voice in verse 12. That is the key to the entire passage.

Verse 15 is to be read strongly; as Paul raises his voice, be sure to raise yours.

Verse 17 comes back to Paul's spiritual reason for avoiding immorality, as he softens his warning words with a positive approach to his message.

The last three verses are intended by the Apostle to clinch his basic idea: that our bodies are made for the Lord, temples of the Spirit and members of Christ. Read them more slowly, as earnestly as they were written.

John 1:43-51

General sense —

The phrase "the next day," which opens this passage, is John's fourth mention in this chapter of a sequence of days. He began his Gospel with a reference to the creation of the world, which took place in "days." Now he gradually unveils the reality of Jesus in daylike stages, culminating in "manifesting his glory" at the marriage feast at Cana, which immediately follows today's reading.

For good reason are the early chapters of John called "The Book of Signs."

For your reading —

Verse 46 touches a bit on the sarcastic, which your voice should reflect as you read it. It is especially important here because it is followed right away in verse 48 by Nathaniel's conversion.

It would be well to pause a beat in verse 49. As the truth suddenly dawns on Nathaniel, he hesitates and then blurts out, "Rabbi, you are the Son of God!"

Jesus' promise that Nathaniel hasn't seen anything as yet is the same promise he makes to each of us in our moments of conversion. Read his words clearly and strongly as you finish.

THIRD SUNDAY AFTER EPIPHANY
Suggested theme for today's readings —
Our conversion must come only from within ourselves.
Jeremiah 3:21 – 4:2

General sense —

Jeremiah here pleads with his people for their conversion, and ends today's passage with a promise of the fruits of conversion, in terms of the dedication of all our internal values to God.

For your reading —

If you could manage a rather pleading tone of voice for this reading, you would picture graphically for your hearers the anguish Jeremiah felt at seeing every day how far his people had backslid from the virtuous life they began with.

The basic appeal of this passage is to our own sense of personal sin.

1 Corinthians 7:17-23

General sense —

Paul's fondness for the status quo is not at all the stodgy passiveness that appears on the surface of this reading. Rather, he, like other Christians of his day, was convinced that Christ would return to end the world and establish his Kingdom any day. There was no time to spend searching out new lifestyles.

For your reading —

Your presentation of these lines today may suffer a bit from the virus of irrelevance. But there are some verses good for our times.

In verse 19 Paul realizes that what counts is keeping God's commandments. In verse 25 he reminds us at what a price we were bought.

These two verses, when leaned on and accented, will bring home to your hearers two practical thoughts for today.

Mark 1:14-20

General sense —

In this first of seven consecutive readings from Mark, Jesus begins the recruitment of his disciples. He has done some preaching, but now is the time to speak with authority. His imperative call begins to change lives, disrupt families, and fulfill the ancient promises. "The time is fulfilled," he announces.

For your reading —

Speak verse 15 strongly; it is the first word of Jesus in this Gospel, his invitation for all of us to be fishers, as were his disciples.

The remainder of this passage is in simple narrative form, and presents no special problems in delivery.

FOURTH SUNDAY AFTER EPIPHANY

Suggested theme for today's readings —
In our Christian witness, we are responsible for our actions.

Deuteronomy 18:15-20

General sense —

One of the most theological of the Old Testament books, Deuteronomy could be called a sermon on the Law. It pictures the ideal, charismatic, liturgical community. It is quoted and referred to more than any other book by the New Testament writers, to illuminate the person and mission of Jesus as the ideal prophet, prefigured today in verse 18.

Today's passage deals with the prophet as a vital link with God. The days of a "nature" religion, where the gods were controlled and manipulated, have passed. The new Jewish theocracy is to live by obedience to God's saving word. The prophet speaks only what the Lord commands.

For your reading —

As we continue the Christmas season in the Sundays after Epiphany, we rejoice in the appearance of Jesus, the divine prophet.

Your reading today is therefore rather like a proclamation, as you announce in strong tones the fulfillment of the prophecy contained in verse 18.

At verse 20, as the contrast comes, lower your voice. Make the words a real threat, an ominous warning that we ought to be careful how we advise people; for we are to be prophets too.

1 Corinthians 8:1b-13

General sense —

Today, advice comes from Paul on foods, as he responds to a very good and practical question from Corinth: can we eat meat that has been sacrificed to idols? The markets were full of it; the butchers bought the leftovers from the temple priests, since the whole animal was not needed for the sacrifice.

Of course, an idol has no real existence, argues Paul. But there are, he says, two kinds of people who must eat with their pagan friends and/or families: those with weak consciences and those with an enlightened conscience about Christian liberty. Rather than criticize the weak ones, or scandalize anyone, Paul says he would rather not bother eating meat at all.

For your reading —

This is down-to-earth practical advice, to be delivered in the calm, reasoned manner in which it is phrased.

The principal stress should be on the very last verse, 13, because, after all the discussion, it represents Paul's final conclusion, very practical even for us today: if what you do is going to bother somebody, and you are in a role of responsibility, don't do it.

Mark 1:21-28

General sense —

We continue the early ministry of Jesus according to Mark. His rapid sketch of a day's work at Capernaum teems with detail, as the Evangelist gradually unfolds the mystery of this Man. His power over evil, the hatred he evokes in the evil spirits, his stern rebuke and dismissal of them, and the astonishment of the crowd, all mark him as a dramatic and affecting new presence. He is recognized by the demons — and by us — in verse 24, yet remains an enigma to the people, even as "his fame spreads everywhere."

For your reading —
This is a rather dramatic reading. Modulate your voice to bring that drama to your hearers. The demon cries out: Jesus speaks sharply as he exorcises him; and the crowd exclaims its wonder in verse 27.

All these changes are to be reflected in your voice. Without them the reading will lose the immediacy it must have to re-create the original scene.

FIFTH SUNDAY AFTER EPIPHANY

Suggested theme for today's readings —
Hospitality is the one virtue in which we are most certain to meet the Lord.

2 Kings 4:18-37

General sense —
The only way to grasp what is going on here is to read the text from verse 8 onward, where the incident begins. It is a typical holy-man story, common to the time and culture, but it has a message for us in its touching tribute to the virtue of hospitality.

The holy man, Elisha, had been given life in the upstairs room provided for him. Now, in return, he himself becomes the agent of life on that same bed.

For your reading —
It might be well, even at the lectern, to read this story from verse 8, so your hearers can know the whole story from the beginning.

Tell it smoothly and without much change in your voice. Your greatest discipline will be to let the words and the actions here speak for themselves.

1 Corinthians 9:16-23

General sense —
In our reading last Sunday, Paul said he would rather give up eating meat than scandalize anyone. In today's passage he explains why he has given up some of his own rights. "It is all for the sake of the Gospel," he says in verse 23, that he strives to identify with the needs and weaknesses of others.

For your reading —
Lean on the final phrase in verse 16: "woe to me," because it supports all of Paul's other reasonings here.

One of his apostolic rights given up is that he does not charge anyone for his preaching. Another right is his freedom. Verse 19 is a strong one, summing up the reason he cares less about his rights.

Finish strongly in verse 23, as the final reason embraces all that went before it.

Mark 1:29-39

General sense —

Today Jesus, in an unusual eyewitness detail, enters into a home for a cure, then holds court that evening for the crowds who flock to him — "the whole city," it seems.

As this scene challenges our imagination, we notice the Savior's withholding of his identity in verse 34. The mystery is not to be revealed as yet. But the turbulent action charges on, reinforced by pre-dawn prayer, in verse 35.

For your reading —

Read this passage with a touch of excitement, trying to communicate the rapidly moving action and the changes of scenery. Jesus is in the first flush of his early, uncritical popularity, or what we would call today the "honeymoon." He has not yet challenged anyone or made any trouble. We ought to feel, through your voice and the tone of your delivery, the rush of affairs in these episodes.

SIXTH SUNDAY AFTER EPIPHANY (OR PROPER 1 AFTER PENTECOST)

Suggested theme for today's readings —
We are witnesses to our faith in everything we do.

2 Kings 5:1-15

General sense —

This is another of the holy-man stories which surrounded men like Elisha. His fame is such that he can admonish even his king. Of course, the king of Syria had given the king of Israel the wrong message to begin with, says the author. Naaman was sent to Elisha, not to the king of Israel. But the way the story is told enhances the prophet's glory, as it was intended to.

Rather than simply follow instructions, Naaman thought he was important enough to be made a big fuss over. That was not to be. But his conversion was.

For your reading —

This is such a smoothly-told tale that it should lend itself quite logically to our hearers' understanding.

Your own experience with our human conversation should take you through the variations in tone and emphasis without trouble.

As the climax to the story comes in verses 14 and 15, your voice should slow down and become a bit lower. You are evoking the powerful presence of the Lord, after telling of all the confusion and self-seeking of people.

Since the last few words in verse 15 refer to what follows after this reading, please omit them by concluding your reading with "Israel."

1 Corinthians 9:24-27

General sense —

We continue our readings from Paul's letter with an observation on sports, in which the writer compares us to athletes competing in the race for eternal life — not against one another but against ourselves.

For your reading —

As in all short readings, go slowly. You will be off the lectern and gone from view before anyone hears you, if you race through these brief lines.

Pause before verse 26. As Paul makes the comparison with the connective, "well," make eye contact with the people before you go on.

But be sure to keep your leisurely pace. You have only a few moments up there. Make the most of them.

Mark 1:40-45

General sense —

As the fast-moving first chapter of Mark unfolds, Jesus still demands secrecy: it is not time for him to reveal the Kingdom as yet. But the leper, humanly enough, fails to contain his joy and spreads the word anyway.

Jesus has already begun to nettle his future enemies: he saves a person excluded from Israel by the Law of Moses.

For your reading —

As in all brief passages, make the most of your reading, You have but a few moments.

Dramatize Jesus' cure by stressing the first three verses, 40, 41 and 42. They are the heart of the story. You must read them slowly, because everything else depends upon how convincing you have made the actual cure.

Stop for a beat after verse 44, as the encounter with the leper concludes. Then, in the last verse, 45, you are listing the consequences Jesus had to put up with: his loss of privacy and freedom of movement. They, even as today, are the price of celebrity.

SEVENTH SUNDAY AFTER EPIPHANY (OR PROPER 2 AFTER PENTECOST)

Suggested theme for today's readings —
The heart of the Gospel is God's prodigal forgiveness.

Isaiah 43:18-25

General sense —

Lest his people glory in past deliverances, God insists today that his forgiveness is an entirely new thing, like a new road in the wilderness.

But the theme of these remarkable lines lies in verses 22 through 24. In courtroom style, God, the prosecutor, remembers the ingratitude of his people: "You have not . . . not . . . not . . ." In the Jerusalem Bible's text, these negatives occur eight times.

But the bottom line in both texts makes the same amazing promise: "Yet I will blot out your sins; I will not remember them."

For your reading —
This is a proclamation of the most important divine communication we can ever experience: God's forgiveness. It is to be read in that way, as an announcement of something new.

After verse 21 the first half of the reading is over. The Lord has recalled his favors. Pause now, to prepare for a change in tone, as he reminds the people, in as stern a tone as you can manage, of their ingratitude, through verse 24.

The final verse is the fatherly concession, in virtually the same words we use with our own children: "All this, yet I still have to forgive you because I am your Father and you are my child." This verse is to be read more slowly. It sums up, almost with a sigh, how prodigal is his love for us. Make it as humanly real as you can.

2 Corinthians 1:18-22

General sense —
Paul has no reason to be ashamed of his conduct with the people at Corinth. His sincerity is absolute, a gift of the Spirit, neither inconsistent or deceiving. Jesus was and is absolute truth. There could be nothing in him but Yes to the faithful carrying out of God's promises.

For your reading —
Read these lines with the urgent conviction of one who must prove his sincerity and the authenticity of his gospel.

End as strongly and positively as you began.

Mark 2:1-12

General sense —
An unusual setting for a miracle occurs. Not only does Jesus disclose himself as a divine forgiver of sin, but the revelation comes in front of hostile people. The key to the story, and its fundamental announcement, is the connection between faith and forgiveness, an abundant Gospel theme.

Verse 10 is a teaching comment by the writer, not a saying of Jesus.

Notice, in verse 12, that they all fail to see in the cure a sign of Jesus' power to forgive. All they see is the physical miracle.

This little episode shows us, finally, the unfailing courtesy of our Savior, interrupted while he was talking in an already hot and crowded enclosure. He looks up and sees, not the commotion caused by the interruption, not even the paralytic, but their faith.

For your reading —

In verse 8, be careful not to accent the word "hearts." The key word in this sentence is neither "hearts" nor "question," but "why." Jesus already knew they were questioning; where else but in their hearts?

In verse 10, lift your eyes to your hearers to deliver the teaching comment.

EIGHTH SUNDAY AFTER EPIPHANY (OR PROPER 3 AFTER PENTECOST)

Suggested theme for today's readings —
The Lord has changed the world with the coming of Jesus.

Hosea 2:14-23

General sense —

The Book of Hosea reflects the rapid and violent changes in Israel during the eighth century before Christ, just before the final disappearance of the nation from the political scene.

Hosea sees through the bad kings, the overdone national pride, and the endless political infighting and corruption. He sees them as but symbols of the basic disorder: Israel has forsaken the Lord.

The prophet frames his indictment of Israel in the metaphor of an unfaithful wife.

For your reading —

Reading this richly allegorical language is a challenge to your ability to create a picture of the prophet's anguish at the evil in his world.

The printed punctuation in this passage will be your best guide. Following it faithfully will help you transmit well the sense of the passage.

Two references will help: first, the Valley of Anchor led into the fertile land of central Palestine. It is a "door of hope" because Israel's future restoration will follow the historic trail of the Exodus, and thus connect with the grand scheme of salvation history.

The second reference, in the final verse, 23, is to verses 6, 7 and 8 of Hosea's first chapter, wherein the children are so named and the reasons are given for those names.

2 Corinthians 3:17 – 4:2

General sense —

Now that our Savior is here, as we reflect in these closing days of the Christmas season, we resolve not to lose heart and to be courageous in our determination to do better. In the Spirit of Jesus we are gradually transformed into his image.

For your reading —

The first two verses are the most important ones. Speak them carefully, not missing a syllable, because the rest of the passage depends on them. The Lord is indeed the Spirit.

Pause a beat before verse 1 of chapter 4, to change the tone from the explanation of this teaching to its application. Lean on the general premise which concludes this verse: "we do not lose heart."

Mark 2:18-22

General sense —

Jesus' point in this passage — the sixth of the seven we are reading from Mark in these Sundays after Epiphany — is twofold: the superiority of his Messianic authority over the old law of Moses, in verse 19; and the two comparisons he makes in verses 21 and 22, stressing the incompatibility of the old Law, under which John the Baptist had come along, and the new law of his Kingdom.

For your reading —

Jesus seems to refer to himself rather openly here, in verse 19. Lean on this wording, so your hearers will be sure to grasp it, as well as the ominous prediction in verse 20.

Pause before verse 21, as Jesus returns to his original premise, that the old Law is gone. Everything is new, not merely patched up. Stress, almost like an announcement, the newness of the Christian era, symbolized by the figure of wine.

LAST SUNDAY AFTER EPIPHANY

Suggested theme for today's readings —
God speaks to us in any way he can get our attention: by a flash of insight, or a "still, small voice."

1 Kings 19:9-18

General sense —

If verses 13 and 14 seem like a duplication of verses 9 and 10, the reason is that the editor probably added the two former verses — a common happening in the ancient manuscripts — since the action continues only after verse 13.

The point of the passage can be found in the "still, small voice" of God's working within us to achieve his plan.

For your reading —
Be careful here of the variations in conversational tones. Most of the passage is the dialogue between the prophet Elijah and the Lord, told to enhance the reputation of the holy man, as was the custom in those days.

Speak the words of the Lord gently, and those of Elijah in a slightly complaining way. He is upset; he even thinks he is the only one left on earth to speak for God.

Elisha is mentioned by the Lord in verse 17, indicating the transition from the Elijah cycle (of stories) to that of Elisha.

2 Peter 1:16-19

General sense —
Jesus, as we recite in the Nicene Creed, "will come again in glory." In Peter's day some had objected to this belief. The writer's object here is to show, by an apostolic eyewitness account, not so much that the Transfiguration happened, but that the way they had seen Jesus in that shining moment was the way he will appear at his Second Coming: with majesty, honor and glory from the Father, clothed in Messianic and divine sonship. It is a beautiful recollection, perhaps more spiritually expressed here than in Mark's ninth chapter.

For your reading —
The tone is insistent, argumentative. The author says, in effect, "We didn't make this up. I am near my death, and I don't lie to anybody. I saw him as he will appear. Yes, I know we thought he would return any day, and it hasn't happened yet. But it will."

There are no particular punctuation difficulties here. The main thrust you are to communicate to your hearers is that of Peter's insistence on the truth of his testimony.

Mark 9:2-9

General sense —
On this last Sunday before Lent, we end our sevenfold reading from Mark's Gospel with the account of the Transfiguration referred to in Peter's letter, also read today.

God's Kingdom has truly arrived, says Mark. He offers three proofs: the Transfiguration, the coming of Elijah, and the conquering of the devil in an exorcism, performed in public with many witnesses.

Here is the first proof: this is the way Jesus looks as the son of God; this is the truth of this mysterious Man.

For your reading —
This is a dramatic episode. Jesus will not appear in this way again until after he has risen.

Heighten the drama by reading verses 2, 3 and 4 with suspense and excitement.

Peter is overcome and incoherent in verse 5. Exclaim with him as he witnesses something no one has ever seen.

Intone with some gravity the voice of God in verse 7, as he approves his beloved son.

Verse 8 is shrouded in mystery, as the vision suddenly passes. End your reading quietly, as the Apostles, either symbolically or physically, "come down," as we say today, and are warned, so typically of Mark, to maintain secrecy about this remarkable experience.

ASH WEDNESDAY

For Ash Wednesday, all readings are identical for cycles A, B and C. See cycle A for general sense and reading hints.

FIRST SUNDAY IN LENT

Suggested theme for today's readings —

God's loving mercy arches over our entire existence like a rainbow.

Genesis 9:8-17

General sense —

The authors of this first record of man's reflections on his existence draw from them a profound religious insight: the end of the Flood, the sacred covenant with Noah, and the bow across the sky are the Lord God's merciful permission for history to continue.

In times more ancient than even these, the mighty arch across the heavens was thought to be "the bow of the gods," used to shoot arrows of punishment at man. Now its many-hued beauty is a sign of peace that speaks to us even today of the quiet end of a storm.

For your reading —

We need God's promises to steady our resolve, as our Lenten penances take form. Read these consoling and grace-filled lines in a joyous, upbeat fashion, making the promise of the Word our own.

Pause after verse 12; then, as if you were to invite everyone to glance skyward with you, slow your speed as the Lord sets the beautiful rainbow over us. It is the climax of the passage, as God promises to think of us every time we see a rainbow.

Pause again before verse 17, so that you may separate what has been said from the final summary of the covenant. Read that last verse strongly as you conclude.

1 Peter 3:18-22

General sense —

This reminder of Jesus' Passion and Death at the outset of Lent serves to put the Lenten ideal of his suffering as the example to encourage our season of penitence.

The Flood was the subject of today's first reading. Here, Peter uses the memory of it to recall God's saving power in the waters of Baptism, a power realized now through the crucifixion and resurrection of Jesus Christ.

The eight persons referred to are Noah, his wife, their three sons and three daughters-in-law.

For your reading —

Maintain a smooth and even tone here in this brief exhortation to our Lenten fervor.

There are no particular climaxes in this passage. Your task will be to use your few moments at the lectern to make Peter's connection with God's past mercies and his present grace clear and understandable.

Mark 1:9-13

General sense —

Lent, we might induce from this reading, can be a new Baptism, a new beginning, for us. But with our new life also come temptations, we find.

The brief reference to Jesus' encounter with Satan reflects his redemptive power to conquer our personal devils. That he succeeded is shown throughout the Gospels by his exorcisms, of which five are recorded explicitly.

For your reading —

The purpose of your reading these few lines at the beginning of Lent may simply be to evoke for us the commanding entrance of Jesus Christ into our history. Within just a few verses, he accomplishes, in the Jewish mind of the day, the two most basic qualifications for a Messiah: he has the approval of the God of Abraham, Isaac and Jacob; and he overthrows in one stroke the empire of Satan.

You have five verses — probably twenty seconds or so. Can you pack into these few words the magnificence of this appearance, pausing after verse 11 to move from one event to the other?

Your understanding of the importance of these two events will make them as meaningful to your hearers as they are to you.

SECOND SUNDAY IN LENT

Suggested theme for today's readings —
God's redeeming love blesses our sacrifices for others.

Genesis 22:1-14

General sense —

By his conception in his mother's advancing age, Abraham's

son Isaac was a product of faith, in the previous chapter 21 of Genesis. How ironic that this reward of obedience now becomes its test! The Lord demands of Abraham the only reason he had for his faith: Isaac, in whom the divine promise of a great nation was to be fulfilled.

The absolute clarity of God's expectations — "take your son, your only son, Isaac, whom you love" — and Abraham's unquestioning acceptance of them, are what pierce our selfish hearts and thus make this story so moving.

For your reading —
These early reflections on man's state strive to understand his condition, long before there was any theology. In this is their utter fascination for us, which seems to suggest that you pass these lines on to us as the learning experience they are intended to be.

Let wonder and suspense color your voice. Here is man directly facing his Maker, doing God's bidding in darkness, plunging ahead in obedience to a clear call. Modulate your tones for these awe-inspiring exchanges, both between the Lord and Abraham, and between father and son. Imagine yourself being asked to offer your own child for an unrevealed reason. Hospital waiting rooms teem with such parents today.

Make this a memorable event. It is our own story.

Romans 8:31-39

General sense —
It is our privilege today to share one of Paul's most emotional — and beautiful — insights, In this triumphantly joyous hymn to the presence of Christ among us, he can see no obstacle to our Savior's awesome redemptive power in us.

The Apostle could be alluding to the sacrifice of Jacob, which was our first reading today, in verse 32.

But his insistent cry rings forth across the ages: the love of God for us in Christ is the unshakable foundation of our Christian hope.

For your reading —
This is a difficult reading, fast-moving and full of the emotions of a person caught up in a moment of deepest fervor.

Exclaim every line. Try your best to reproduce the courtroom-style, rapid-fire questions in verses 31 through 35. Paul considers them rhetorical questions only, as if he were urging an audience to shout the answers back to him.

Verses 37 through 39 are read in a lower voice and in a more intense fashion; the author is answering his own questions. All the zeal he can muster crackles through this climactic act of faith from one who has been through it all, and who urges us on, this Lent, to even greater things.

Mark 8:31-38

General sense —

Jesus hints of his coming Passion today. Peter will not accept it and is warmly scolded. More than that, Jesus insists, first, that his sacrifice will be the model for our own, that no worldly goods could be exchanged for the loss of eternal life; and secondly, that acceptance of his words means acceptance of him.

For your reading —

In verse 33, be sure to reproduce Jesus' sternness to Peter in your voice.

After that, Jesus regains his composure and speaks in a friendly way about what his mission means. Sadly, the Apostles still have no idea of what he is talking about, as later events will prove.

But we know; and we read today this Lenten reminder of how important our spiritual lives are, as Jesus identifies himself with the Good News.

THIRD SUNDAY IN LENT

Suggested theme for today's readings —

God wants us to understand how radically new his plan is for us.

Exodus 20:1-17

General sense —

This episode is part of God's design to form Abraham as his prophet. The sub-plot here is an encounter between two good men. Women were fair game, especially single ones, so Abraham had tried to protect himself, in verse 11. As it turns out in verse 12, she was his half-sister. But Abimelech, after some confusion and a little advice from the Lord in a dream, not only understands the mistake but restores the lady's honor as well as her husband's, in verse 16. For this delicacy and tact he is rewarded by the Lord, in verse 17.

For your reading —

As a lector or lay reader, you are first of all a storyteller. Here is a good story of how God protects those he has chosen for his work, and how he arranges events to suit his plan.

There are no particular accents here. Your understanding of what the story means, which is the unfolding of God's plan, will carry you through it. Read it as if you had been a witness to it, knowing that Sarah, in the very next chapter, will bear Isaac. He was to become the father of Jacob, whose twelve sons were the founders of the twelve tribes of Israel.

Romans 7:13-25

General sense —

Are there any lines in the Bible closer to our human situation than these? The age-old conflict still rages in every one of us. And in the chapter from which we read today, Paul has difficulty explaining something which deeply shocked his Jewish and scholarly sensibilities: the Law — the holy Law of God — was the enemy of human righteousness, just as much as sin. The Law and sin were on the same side, at least potentially.

For your reading —

Since the reasoning in these lines is so tight, you must be especially careful to move along slowly and clearly. You will need maximum attention from your hearers.

Pause after verse 13. As Paul begins his chain of thought in verse 14, mark the contrast in that verse between "spiritual" and "carnal."

Verses 15 through 20 are a supreme test of your ability to handle a "stream of consciousness" sequence of not-very-well-organized thoughts, as Paul struggles for some answers. A pause after each verse, to let the thought sink in, will help you to go more slowly and carefully.

At verse 21 pause again. Paul's thinking begins to come more clearly, and your delivery will now assume a bit more confidence and authority.

Verse 24 is a cry from the heart. Lean on it strongly. But your preparation has told you that it is merely a rhetorical question, setting up the final shout of victory in verse 25. And in 25b, you end calmly, as the reality makes itself known.

John 2:13-22

General sense —

The significance of this incident lies not so much in Jesus' anger at the money-changers. Since no Roman money was accepted in the temple, they performed a necessary function.

Rather, Jesus is impatient with the organized religion of his day, and uses the cleansing to promise that a new house of his Father, validated by his death and resurrection, would replace the temple forever.

For your reading —

Let your voice rise as you reach verse 15, where the action begins. Let it take on the tone of sternness which motivated Jesus, through verse 16 as well.

In verse 19, lean on Jesus' smoldering impatience, as he speaks words which no one will understand, as verse 22 reminds us, until after he was risen.

FOURTH SUNDAY IN LENT

Suggested theme for today's readings —
Whoever his agent might be, there is no end to God's merciful love for us.

2 Chronicles 36:14-23

General sense —

This is one of many references to the Babylonian Exile — its beginning in verse 20, and its end, predicted to be "seventy" years, in verse 23. "Seventy" is an old Semitic term for "many." As it turned out, the actual period of the Exile was about forty-eight years.

Cyrus, who just happened to come along to be the Israelites' deliverer, was looked upon as a great savior and messenger of God, as would any stranger who extends a hand in dire need.

As usual, all Israel's troubles spring from her infidelity, and those who conquer her are God's punishing angels.

For your reading —

These references to God as the immediate cause of all troubles and blessings are Old Testament commonplaces, and should be read as the truth, in a grave and prophetic tone.

Your voice brightens at verse 22, after a pause, as Cyrus enters the picture. Whether the Lord stirred up his spirit or not, he was the enemy of Babylon and finally its conqueror, allowing the Israelites to go back home.

So the Hebrew Bible ends, here at Second Chronicles, the last book in the official Canon, on a note of optimism and enduring faith.

Ephesians 2:4-10

General sense —

As the season of Lent passes its midpoint, we need today a reminder that we are already saved by the God who is rich in mercy, simply because he loves us, even though we have lost his grace by our sinfulness. Jesus Christ has bought us back and "raised us up with him."

For your reading —

This is an important word of encouragement, in case we are tired and disheartened by our Lenten penances.

Read these hope-filled lines in a happy, upbeat fashion, leaning on "the great love" in verse 5, and "kindness toward us" in verse 7.

Repeat the thesis with Paul as you insist, in verse 8, that God's gift to us is the faith which saves us.

Pause before verse 10, and conclude with a strong and clear summary of our true destiny.

John 6:4-15

General sense —

John usually cites a feast day to locate and make theologically significant the ministry of Jesus.

Today he begins the "Chapter of the Eucharist" with a miracle of courtesy and compassion, in response to our hunger for our daily bread.

The Old Testament Passover feast celebrated the deliverance of the nation from its wanderings in the desert centuries before. Here, it is incorporated into the mystery of our own deliverance in the new Passover, as the people surmise, in their own primitive way, without understanding it, in verses 14 and 15.

For your reading —

The episode we read today is a straightforward narrative, and should be read as such, with its conversational modulations faithfully reproduced in your voice. Let your skill as a storyteller come forth here.

The one climax, true to John's purpose, occurs in verse 14, and should be delivered with a rising tone of voice to accent the people's reaction.

Verse 15 is a quiet one as you conclude. Jesus wants no part of kingship. His point has already been made.

FIFTH SUNDAY IN LENT

Suggested theme for today's readings —

We respond to the Kingdom within us through our kindnesses to one another.

Jeremiah 31:31-34

General sense —

The heart as God's place of written revelation is a creation of Jeremiah, so that these lines convey a monumental revolution in legalistic Israelite thinking. Since God will henceforth guide us directly, intermediaries such as Moses, or prophets, or priests of the temple are less necessary.

This is of course no new doctrine but the realization of our gift of acknowledging God's presence to every circumstance of life. To the Israelite mind, this "new covenant" (the only time this phrase occurs in the Old Testament) is a new means of assuring fidelity through interiorization of each person's commitment, and a statement of the primacy of our interior values.

For your reading —

Verse 31 is an announcement, so begin strongly. Verse 32 compares it to the old ways, and is of a bit less importance.

Verses 33 and 34 are the meat of this extraordinary prophecy. Read them more slowly: they represent the discovery of what

Jesus would later express in his own way: "The Kingdom of God is within you."

Make sure that no one misses any of these important words. Since your reading is so short, there is no hurry. We need this reassurance, as Lent winds down.

Hebrews 5:5-10

General sense —

We too, as did Jesus, offer up prayers and supplications with loud cries and tears, as we perform our Lenten penances. And like our Savior, through these humiliations we learn obedience to the Spirit who guides us along the way. Finally, in the kindnesses we do one another, we become sources of salvation. Our calling as Christians is a noble, priestly one indeed.

For your reading —

This reading presents no difficulty of expression, but simply explains the intercessory nature of Jesus' relationship to us whom he redeemed.

You have but a few seconds at the lectern, so that you must prepare well enough to make every moment count.

Verses 7 and 8, which describe the result of our penances, contain the central thrust of this passage. It will be well to accent them strongly.

John 12:20-33

General sense —

Some people not of the Jewish faith seek Jesus, but John does not mention that they actually met him. His earthly ministry was only to his own. Yet he does speak to them, as to all of us, by his use of "anyone;" by the Father blessing his entire life and work; by his reference to "the judgment of this world;" and by his power to draw all people to himself as he is lifted up.

"The Book of Signs," as John's Gospel is sometimes called, serves not only to encourage our faith but also to show our Savior for what he is: the ultimate sign, or sacrament, by which we see how much it is our Father's delight to be with us, his children.

For your reading —

The strength of this beautiful passage is, of course, in the words of Jesus. We ought always to read his remarks slowly, pausing after each verse.

If the crowd thought they had heard thunder, in verse 29, your voice ought to have spoken with some gravity in verse 28.

Verse 32 is the climax of the passage. Speak it strongly, then taper off as the Evangelist adds a note at the end to explain what Jesus meant.

PALM SUNDAY

NOTE – For Palm Sunday, the first and second readings are identical for cycles A, B and C. See cycle A for general sense and reading hints.

Mark 14:32 - 15:47

General sense —

Mark's account of the Passion comes the closest to what might really have happened, in the opinion of most scholars. Its primitive, stark reality, unedited for any stately effect, is the crowning revelation of Mark's Man of Mystery. The Christ proceeds through the dark passage which must precede the glory of the Messiah. "The hour has come" and he must face it alone, innocence intact.

The frequent use of Old Testament citations establishes God's part in the carrying out of his will through a plan older than history. This gives the story we read today its theological character, and thus excludes any "rescue" of Jesus by his Father.

For your reading —

In most places nowadays the Passion is read by several people who re-enact the roles of its characters.

Those who share in this privilege will also share in the discipline of presenting each role in as lifelike a fashion as possible. Voices must be changed and modulated to suit each moment.

The supreme tribute to your individual and collective skills will be when some of the congregation put down their texts to listen to you.

EASTER SUNDAY — PRINCIPAL SERVICE

NOTE – For Easter Sunday, the first and second readings are identical for cycles A, B and C. See cycle A for general sense and reading hints.

Mark 14:32 – 15:47

General sense —

Some think this is the end of Mark's Gospel, that the remaining twelve verses were added later, to replace the true ending, which had been lost.

The central insights of this passage are two: the fundamental Christian statement that Jesus was raised, as the Cross yielded to the Easter triumph, in verse 6; and the fright of the women in verse 8 at their proximity to this as yet unexplained miracle.

It is typical of Jesus' always exquisite courtesy to women that they would enjoy the privilege of being the first recipients of the Good News of Easter.

For your reading —

Your hearers are so anxious to share this great message as

a part of today's joy that you must read it like the announcement it is.

Keep your voice loud and clear, in harmony with the colorful, festive atmosphere which fills your church. The response of the young man (or angel) in verse 6 is the high point. Make it the high point of your reading, too.

The mysterious ending is read in a somewhat more subdued voice, reminding us all of our fear of the overwhelming nearness of mystery.

SECOND SUNDAY OF EASTER
Suggested theme for today's readings —
The power of the risen Jesus removes all our doubts.

Acts 3:12-26

General sense —
Peter seizes an opportunity here. He has just made a lame man walk, and to the amazed crowd he quickly shows the continuity of the present Church with the God of the Old Testament. He runs through the Passion story, stressing Jesus' innocence, then he issues, in the last ten verses, the proper call to conversion, based on the people's Old Testament faith, to which he refers time and again.

What the author of Acts intends here is to leave a record of a sermon molded to the plan of the book. That plan is to show the intense fervor of the Spirit-filled apostles, as well as the great strides the early Church is making through the power of the risen Jesus.

For your reading —
Since this is a speech, read it like one. Keep your voice up, ringing out this message of encouragement.

Its language serves to remind us that we are sons and daughters of a rich and ancient heritage, descendants one and all of the great Old Testament figures who spoke so eloquently of the Lord.

Modulate your voice in verse 22 as you quote Moses in that verse and the next.

The last two verses, the direct appeal, should be a strong conclusion to this message.

1 John 5:1-6

General sense —
In previous chapters, the Apostle has shown what he means by the love that is rooted in faith. Now he expands on the nature of this faith that gives love its meaning. The love of God, he says, consists just as much in obedience to his commandments as it does in the love of the brethren.

For your reading —

Read slowly, deliberately, and with the affection which must have moved John to set down this simple yet eloquent testimony to an active faith.

There are no complex sentences here, so that if you are careful to pause after each sentence, your presentation will be most effective.

NOTE – For this Sunday, the gospel reading is identical for cycles A, B, and C. See cycle A for general sense and reading hints for the Gospel.

THIRD SUNDAY OF EASTER

Suggested theme for today's readings —
The joy of Easter is God's forgiveness of our sins.

Acts 4:5-12

General sense —

Peter and John stand before the court, accused of healing a cripple in the name of someone other than the Old Testament God. Their arrest, at the moment when salvation is being proclaimed to Israel, begins the tide of opposition which will scatter the Christian community far and wide. (See Ch. 8, verse 1b).

In God's plan, the time is now ripe for the Gentiles to hear the message. The conversion of Paul and of the Roman centurion Cornelius follow, as Peter begins to see his destiny, in Ch. 10, verse 34. The stage is nearly set for the worldwide spread of Christianity.

For your reading —

In verse 8, as the Spirit fills Peter with the courage to state his mission before a hostile court, let your own voice mirror that divine enthusiasm. Lead up to the climax, "the name of Jesus Christ of Nazareth," then, in the same verse, lean on "by *him*."

It is in the same name of the Risen One that our own Easter celebration includes our salvation.

1 John 1:1 - 2:2

General sense —

John skips his usual personal identification here, which suggests that the letter we read today was a part of his oral Gospel, which he presumes that his hearers know about.

The substance of the apostolic testimony is the truth of what has been seen and experienced. And the joy that Jesus promised — and gave — finds its constant fulfillment in their ministry, as John says (with a smile, no doubt) in verse 4.

For your reading —

Read this short passage in a leisurely, calm tone. There are great truths here, but the affectionate pen of this loving old gentleman colors them not so much with rabid enthusiasm as with quiet insistency.

Pause frequently — after each verse, so that your hearers will not miss any of this beautiful testimony.

After you have read verse 10, gentle your voice for the personal address in the last two verses, 1 and 2. John intends no tirade; his is the voice of a father and counselor, reminding us of the revealing of God's forgiveness for our sinfulness.

Luke 24:36b-48

General sense —

It is time to leave. The mission on earth is finished; the everlasting joy of the Spirit awaits fulfillment.

Jesus' appearance is radically changed (verse 44 says, "while I *was* with you"); he stands before "startled and frightened" men, who think they see a ghost.

Just as we might today, they murmur, in their incoherent joy, "I don't believe this is happening." Imagine them, stunned to silence, watching him eat!

The final six verses inaugurate the apostolic preaching tradition: Jesus must suffer, then rise again — a message to be announced to the ends of the earth.

For your reading —

Verses like verse 38 are not easy to deliver in a realistic, human way. It makes the most sense to accent "troubled," and "questionings." Questions would never rise anywhere else but in hearts, it seems clear. So "hearts," therefore, needs no accent.

Pause a bit after verse 43. The demonstration is over; now comes the commissioning to preach. Read these last six verses in the grave and important tone Jesus lent to them, as you conclude.

FOURTH SUNDAY OF EASTER

Suggested theme for today's readings —
Today, what we are asked to have in common and share is not always our material goods, but also our gifts and talents.

Acts 4:32-37

General sense —

We read today of the ideal Christian Community. We cannot know whether this is genuine reportage or a later idealization. Regardless, we learn that goods were possessed in common, and that some people sold what they had, even, like Barnabas, spectacularly.

For your reading —

There are no strong modulations here. The single requirement asked of you is to read this passage with the joy it must have engendered in those who wrote it, and who either heard it or read it.

1 John 3:1-8

General sense —
John's teaching that we are children of God is fundamental with him. All is fulfilled in that concept: God's gift of our identification with his divine Son as brothers and sisters; our treatment by the world while we possess that identity; and the future fulfillment of our hope as we live the Christian life.

For your reading —
Speak gently — how could you not, as you pass on these loving words, full of affectionate hope, in verses 1 through 3?

Verses 4 through 6 are more serious. John wants no one to forget the price of living like children of God. Be very reflective of John's earnestness as you render to your hearers these cautions.

John 10:11-16

General sense —
In Jesus' time, all the sheep tended by the villagers were kept in a common corral, or fold. The owners, who called them out each day to go to pasture, had free entry into the fold. Anyone not belonging there could be discovered instantly. The sheep would heed no voice but the shepherd's.

Having developed this down-to-earth analogy in the verses which precede today's reading, Jesus now explicitly identifies himself with the shepherd who risks his life, as many did, for his sheep. Then he masterfully extends the analogy to his divine sonship and to a future world Church, in verse 16.

For your reading —
Be firm and strong throughout this reading. Jesus announces great truths, with worldwide implications for the future which we know only today, after the fact.

Pause after verse 13, as he emphatically restates his principal thesis, applying it now to his vision of the future.

FIFTH SUNDAY AFTER EASTER
Suggested theme for today's readings —
The Good News of Jesus is that God has sent him to love us visibly.

Acts 8:26-40

General sense —
In this short story, a cast of only two, Philip and the eunuch, account for all of the action. The point of the episode is twofold: Philip's anxiety to tell someone of the "good news" of Jesus, and the eunuch's desire to hear it and to act on it.

It's still Eastertime. The joy and peace of the season are reflected in the whole atmosphere of this little gem.

For your reading —
Read with a light, upbeat tone. It's a happy time. The early
verses set the scene, from 26 to 34. At verse 35 the climax begins
to build, as Philip delivers the message. Let your voice reflect the
excitement of the eunuch's conversion, as he readily becomes a
believer.

Pause after verse 31. Give Philip a second or two to get up
into the chariot, as the story changes from setting the scene to
the business of the encounter.

The exciting verse is 38, when the eunuch commits himself
to his newfound faith. Pause for a second after it, then continue
to the end. Try to communicate your sense of wonder that this is
happening.

1 Letter of John 3:18-24

General sense —
Here is an old man of about ninety years, who has simplified
his life down to one word: love. In this idea he has, like so many
people his age, found the source of all other virtues. He preaches
it in season and out. It is his sustaining force, and he wants it to
be ours.

For your reading —
Imagine yourself speaking in gentle accents to someone you
love very much: your spouse, your children, your dearest friend.

This is not an easy reading. Some ways to keep it from becoming a sleep-producing, monotonous drone:

1. Read it leisurely. Pause after each sentence.
2. *Lean* a little on words like:

"deed" and "truth" (18);
"God is greater" (20);
"whatever we ask" (22);
"love one another" (23);
"Spirit which he has given us" (24).

3. Put into your reading the love you love to express toward
your own.

John 14:15-21

General sense —
Jesus sits at his last supper, and he knows that his life on
earth is over. There is no more anger at the establishment, no
more rage against its religious hypocrisy, no more challenging
its leaders. He is alone with his own. Nothing matters any more
except his love for them, and what his Father will do to reward
their fidelity. It is his deathbed speech to his family.

For your reading —
Proceed quietly. Imagine that this is your last opportunity
to speak to your own of the time when you will meet again in

heaven. You know what heaven will be like, and you are anxious to share it with them, to give them strength for the horrible three days they will experience before you see them again.

There is no better way to read well than to pause after every sentence. This is an important and very consoling message that Jesus passes on. Go slowly. Don't let anyone miss a word.

SIXTH SUNDAY AFTER EASTER

Suggested theme for today's readings —
We are ambassadors of the love of God through our generosity to others.

Acts 11:19-30

General sense —

Not a great proclamation here, but three bits of history: the founding of the Church at Antioch; the invention of the word "Christians;" and the first collection for the Famine Relief Fund. The Universal Church is a little over twenty years old. Herod is just beginning his attacks on people like James and Peter.

For your reading —

Perhaps you are an elderly disciple, reminiscing about "the old days," when the Church was in its early growth. You will be happy to turn this page of history with a smile, reading it not too slowly. It is as if you were improvising, as the memories come back to you.

The important phrases are the personal touches we can all identify with today: verse 21, on conversions; verse 23, remembering a sermon, and the last few verses, about the relief fund, still with us today.

Stress those important ideas. They are the links between us and history, human realities that never change.

1 Letter of John 4:7-21

General sense —

This reading follows a few verses after last Sunday's. Once again this beloved old gentleman speaks of what he knows best: the love we should have for one another, as it relates to and is drawn from our faith.

For your reading —

There is hardly a more difficult passage all year. Unfortunately, it is far too long — not because it is tedious or repetitive, but because it is simply too rich for us to absorb its depth.

Dividing it into three segments may help make it as understandable as we can for our hearers.

1. Verses 7 through 10 throb with the beat of John's theology: God is love. Caress these incomparable lines, pausing after verse 8 and after verse 10.

2. Verse 11 through verse 16 describe the working out of God's love in our lives through the giving of the Spirit. Continue in the explanatory mode. You are speaking not so much to ears as you are to hearts. Be careful to take them along with you as the thought develops.

3. Verses 17 through 21 round out the idea of how the love among us will be the source of our eternal glory. The passage ends with John's little summary in verse 21. He wants to be sure love is something we will never forget.

John 15: 9-17

General sense —

Scholars disagree on whether Chapter 13 through 17 of St. John's Gospel were actually spoken as one long discourse at the supper table on Holy Thursday evening, or whether they are a collection of his sayings put together later.

It doesn't matter. Only Jesus matters. Only his words are precious, not the exact time they were spoken.

For your reading —

Earlier today we read John's exhortation to mutual charity. In this passage we hear from its source.

There seems to be a natural pause after every verse. Each verse could stand by itself as a complete reading. Revelations abound: Jesus' love for us is equal to God's love for him (9); he speaks not for his pleasure but for ours (11); he calls us not servants but friends (15); he has shown us his Father without reserve (15); it was he who chose us and sends us forth (16); he does not ask, but commands, that we care for one another (17).

The pause you make after each of these divine disclosures is the only way you can give them the eminence they deserve. Your own devotion to your calling as a reader will be your best ally in placing this message in their hearts.

ASCENSION DAY

For Ascension Day, readings are identical for cycles A, B, and C. See cycle A for general sense and reading hints.

SEVENTH SUNDAY AFTER EASTER

Suggested theme for today's readings —

Our unity in Jesus and our charity for one another speak as loudly as any prayer.

ACTS 1:15-26

General sense —

Matthias replaces Judas as the twelfth Apostle. His election is so quickly and simply done that we find ourselves wishing for such efficiency today. It takes more than a hundred and twenty people these days to make any sort of decision at all, it seems.

For your reading —
Your principal effort in this reading may well be to read this story as carefully and straightforwardly as it deserves. Raise your voice at verse 16, as you quote Peter's speech directly. All the way through verse 22, you are giving a speech too. Let the people know you are making yourself heard.

Then, at verse 23, you may resume your narrative tone. Verse 24 is a prayer. Make it sound like one, then return to conclude the narrative with the final verse.

1 Letter of John 5:9-15

General sense —
John now concludes the letter we have been reading from for the past five Sundays. In this excerpt he makes his two final points: the Father testifies himself that Jesus is his son; and our acceptance of Jesus in faith will earn us eternal life and assure us that we "have obtained the requests made of him." Or, as another version of the Bible puts it, "we know that we have already been granted what we asked of him."

It is a fitting close to the joy of the Easter season. We move now into the final week before the coming of the Spirit of Jesus at Pentecost.

For your reading —
Pause after you read verse 10. Then begin verse 11, the key verse, by saying, in the strong terms of an announcement, "THIS, is the testimony:" then lean on each word of the announcement itself, through verses 11 and 12.

Verse 13 resumes John's loving tone, as he urges us to confidence. Though your voice remains softer and more personal, you must communicate a deep sense of urgency to these last two verses, 14 and 15.

Pause for a beat after "obtained" in verse 15, to stress the fact that God, through Jesus, has already granted our prayers even as we speak to him.

John 17:11-19

General sense —
Those of us who have visited the sick know how easy it is to pass into a prayerful mode after we have spent some time sharing ourselves with someone.

As Chapter 17 of John's Gospel begins, Jesus has told his friends what he wants them to hear about his mission. Now, the love he feels for these good men moves him to recommend their future destinies to his Father's goodness. His humanity recalls for a moment that he and his Father are one. He asks two favors: that his people may also be one, and that his own joy may be in them.

For your reading —
We are brought up short when we try to fathom why the simple words of Jesus are so utterly beyond our comprehension.

So it is today. You are privileged to pass on these sacred and reverent lines to your hearers. Almost embarrassing in their intimacy, they make us feel as if we were eavesdropping.

Read them as slowly as you dare. Let every thought be lingered over. Pause often, even after every verse, or even in mid-phrase, as with "consecrate them - in truth."

I can advise you no further. Our hearts are involved here. You must speak of your love for this profound mystery.

PENTECOST SUNDAY

For Pentecost Sunday, readings are identical for cycles A, B and C. See cycle A for general sense and reading hints.

TRINITY SUNDAY

Suggested theme for today's readings —
God speaks in the depths of the human heart when he reveals himself to us.

Exodus 3:1-6

General sense —
The episode of the burning bush comes immediately (no one knows how many years) after the prologue to the life of Moses in the preceding lines of Exodus. We tell today of his call to lead God's people out of their slavery.

Like ourselves when we think we hear a divine invitation, the young man is baffled, unsure and a bit afraid, but he is still drawn to this mysterious voice. With no idea where he is going or what he is to do (again, like us), he hears and answers. His life's work has begun.

For your reading —
The story unfolds on it own terms; God simply takes charge. Your sharpest emphasis would be raising your voice at the call, "Moses! Moses!"

Be sure to read very solemnly, and somewhat more slowly, the commands of the Lord as he introduces himself.

Finally, as Moses hides his face in fear, you conclude your reading almost hastily, glad to close such a bizarre incident, so full of the unspeakable presence of God.

Romans 8:12-17

General sense —
The three manifestations of God which we name the Trinity all appear here, in this bit of teaching by the great Apostle, as he teaches the intimacy of our Christian sonship and the central-

ity of the spirit sent by Jesus, which we have celebrated this past week of Pentecost.

For your reading —

As you bring this message to your hearers, be aware of the intensity of expression Paul invests in these simple phrases.

There are many "mental periods" for your voice to enunciate. After "debtors" in verse 12; after "sons," in verse 14; after "himself," in verse 16; after "heirs," in verse 17; and after "Christ," in verse 17.

If you mark your study text with these periods, your reading will sound pretty much like the Apostle originally conceived it.

John 3:1-16

General sense —

Nicodemus comes after dark, only to find that he has measured Jesus by the old signs: wonder works and miracles. But those signs are passé now. What Jesus demands for entrance into the Kingdom of God is a new sign: interior conversion, born, as John tells us elsewhere, not of woman but of the Spirit.

In this passage Jesus explains the nature of conversion and the teaching that all God requires for it is our consent.

For your reading —

The key words, by which Jesus boldly disavows the old teaching, are "born anew," in verse 3, and its explanation, "of water and the Spirit," in verse 5. Everything springs from that, so that if you lean strongly on those phrases, with one of our "mental periods" after each, your reading will make the sense it should.

Verse 16 says it all, as far as Jesus is concerned. That verse climaxes your reading with one of the sentences used in our weekly liturgy. Speak it like the major announcement it is — strongly, loud and clear, so that no one will miss it.

NOTE – For propers 1, 2 and 3 after Pentecost, please refer to the readings for the 6th, 7th and 8th Sundays after Epiphany, respectively. The readings overlap because of the variations each year in the date of Easter.

PROPER 4

Suggested theme for today's readings —
God's commands are not found in books of rules but in our hearts.

Deuteronomy 5:6-21

General sense —

The Ten Commandments, or the ten "words," as they were sometimes called, have been given earlier in the Bible, in the Book of Exodus, by a different writer. But both versions date from much more ancient times as lists of vices or sins. Three elements make this list important: Moses' calling together of "all Israel," in verse 1 of this chapter; the permanency and relevance of God's Covenant "not with our fathers but with us," in verse 3; and God's solemn declaration of his identity in verse 6.

For your reading —
You might want to begin your reading at verse 1, to provide your hearers with the background for this important passage.

The most difficult responsibility you face here will be to keep your voice as solemn and majestic as you can, and to pause after each Commandment, giving all of them the equal importance they deserve, as we do when we recite them interspersed with prayers at a Eucharist.

2 Corinthians 4:5-12

General sense —
The greatness of Paul's ministry is more than himself, more than all his natural human troubles along the way. In verses 8 and 9 he masterfully turns every problem into a triumph.

His life has a twofold aspect, as do all of ours: the carrying in ourselves of the death of Jesus, while we share with and pass on to others the life of Jesus.

For your reading —
Typically of him, the Apostle's ideas tumble forth so rapidly that you must be careful, in your preparation, to locate them and give them their due importance.

For example, stop for a moment after verse 6. Paul begins here a new idea: our human frailty.

Verses 8 and 9, the series of paradoxes, is the author's next idea: though we have problems, we can overcome them by our attitude. Read these four contrasts with a breath after each, to make his victories clear.

The last three verses, 10 through 12, provide the theological foundation for our winning out over weakness and trouble: it is all for a purpose, which is the working of the Spirit of Jesus in us, toward life.

Mark 2:23-28

General sense —
This episode demonstrates that the general principle of human need takes precedence over the Law. David, Jesus explains, was excused from the Law as anyone would have been in his situation.

It doesn't matter whether it is the Sabbath or not.

Jesus closes with his justification of the disciples' violation by his own authority, apart from any external circumstances. It is part of the gradual revelation of himself so typical of Mark's Gospel.

For your reading —

Be aware that you must modulate your tone of voice to suit the conversation. At the end, read the final two verses with the assurance Jesus must have felt as he revises the ancient Law in just a few words, to the embarrassment of the Pharisees, who thought keeping the rules was all that mattered.

PROPER 5

Suggested theme for today's readings —
Our fallen human nature is the cause of our troubles and the object of God's redeeming love.

Genesis 3:8-21

General sense —

This is the Fall of man — from innocence to knowledge, from freedom to toil, from grace to sin, from life to death. With this fateful episode he begins a journey back to the unity of God's Kingdom which will last to the end of the world.

For your reading —

You are to read today a dialogue between primitive man and his Creator. It needs to be invested, through your voice, with the drama proper to its importance.

If you make the words attributed to almighty God stand out, both by pausing before you say them, and by reading them at a somewhat slower speed and higher volume, your efforts to make this monumental episode as real as the day it happened will be successful.

2 Corinthians 4:13-18

General sense —

Paul, stung deeply by misunderstanding and shocked by the sinful behavior of his beloved Corinthians, goes beyond mere fraternal correction in this letter. His own weakness, he argues in our reading today, is an example of the fallibility of all preachers. Yes, he remembers, I have had my down days, too, just as you have. But, he urges, let's look at the reward rather than the task, and fix our eyes on our common goal: "the eternal weight of glory."

For your reading —

Your voice need not be dropped until the last word of verse 13, as you say, "and so we *speak*." That word introduces the remainder of the passage (and much more after it, which doesn't concern us here).

In verse 14, lean on the two phrases, "us also," and "us with you." Paul is here expressing his faith that he looks forward to heaven as much as his hearers do.

Drop your voice in verse 15; make a strong sentence out of

"for it is all for your sake." That is a very key phrase.

Now pause, as you end verse 15, because verse 16 ties the writer to his readers, as he lets them know everything is for their benefit.

Make a "mental period" after "compassion" at the end of verse 17, and after "unseen" in the middle of verse 18. That makes Paul's comparison clear, as it should be.

Mark 3:20-35

General sense —

We begin today a series of eight successive Sunday readings, devoted to Mark's account of Jesus' early Galilean ministry.

The episodes we are to read signal a basic change in the Master's relationship with his disciples. From now on he will pay less attention to the crowds and more to the formation of the men who will preach his Gospel.

Today's passage begins that change. Harried by the growing resistance to his work, he flares up in exasperation when he hears the murmured accusations that he is a tool of Satan, and again when his well-meaning family comes to "take care of him," thinking he is out of his mind. The Spirit is at work in him; to deny that, he warns, is to incur eternal punishment.

For your reading —

Once you remember that Jesus is annoyed by the events depicted here, your voice will have a certain edge to it which will communicate to your hearers the atmosphere of this passage. Read it strongly throughout.

In verse 23 Jesus begins to speak. Mark that with your raised voice. Renew your voice again at verse 28, where Jesus rails against anyone who thinks his mission is not of the Spirit.

Finally, let him loudly disown his family for the sake of the Kingdom. It is a powerful climax, but it will lose its force unless you can get across to your hearers the reality of Jesus' moment of impatience with the way things are going.

PROPER 6

Suggested theme for today's readings —
Our hope is in the Kingdom which God's fatherly love has prepared for us.

Ezekiel 31:1-6, 10-14

General sense —

Nearly six hundred years before the coming of Christ, the prophet sings a song of profound hope in the God who will not suffer our enemies to overcome us. The breathtaking imagery which illuminates his lines focuses today on an image peculiar to this ancient culture: the divine curse.

In this passage he reminds the Pharaoh of Egypt that although his nation towers like a great cedar in the forest, its arrogance will destroy it, and it will lie dead across the ground, used only by the birds and the animals.

For your reading —

Take your time with the almost camera-like image of this great tree. Let you imagination soar as you draw its picture in words, in the first half of your reading.

Verse 10 signals a total change, as the Lord tells Ezekiel that he will, through Egypt's conquerors, lay waste the nation signified by this proud cedar. Your voice goes down a pitch as you solemnly intone the bad news.

As verse 11 ends, lean hard on the curse itself: "I have cast it out." Repeat the curse just a strongly, in verse 12. Remain in this very heavy and dark mode until the end. Read more slowly than usual, so that no one may miss this warning against our pride, of which the towering cedar of Egypt is a symbol.

2 Corinthians 5:1-10

General sense —

We resume our reading of Paul's second letter to Corinth where we left off last week. He explains in more detail the divine promise of eternal glory. He offers hope and consolation to us who still struggle "at home in the body and away from the Lord."

For your reading —

Be careful, as you read today, not to pile one idea on another, by going too rapidly. Your aim, as was Paul's, is to elucidate very clearly how the single idea of hope draws all the sentences into one theme.

Verse 5 is a strong affirmation of the source and author of our hope. It should be your climax to the first paragraph. Slow down here, because it marks the end of Paul's doctrinal preface. Then pause for a moment.

Verse 6 begins his application of hope to our own situations. He speaks with friendliness; he is smiling as he identifies our troubles with his own. He urges us to be of good heart, or, as we would say today, to "hang in there."

Your ability to read with a smile in your voice will be a great help in encouraging us, your hearers. We need God's Word always to comfort us.

Mark 4:26-34

General sense —

As we pursue our Marcan readings, Jesus narrates one parable after another, striving to make clear to his disciples what the Kingdom of God is like. In keeping with his desire to instruct them, he explains everything privately.

For your reading —
This is not a difficult passage; the principal areas of concern are the pause after verse 29, which ends the first parable, and a similar pause after verse 32, at the conclusion of the second parable.

Then you close, as you explain to your hearers (it would be well to look out at the congregation as you do this) why Jesus spoke in this fashion, and what he did after each speech he gave.

PROPER 7

Suggested theme for today's readings —
Although the Lord can speak in the midst of a storm, he usually comes only to calm the storm.

Job 38:1-11, 16-18

General sense —
The mysterious ordeal of Job is almost over. His friends, at first speechless with horror at his plight for seven days, have all had their say, analyzing and rationalizing his problem endlessly without any solution.

Now, out of the raging whirlwind, comes the Lord himself, to close the case. Unanswerable, he makes evident to the point of absurdity Job's — or anyone else's — human inability to know anything about God's designs for us, or why he does what he does.

For your reading —
The perfect setting for the reading of this passage would be a rather loud wind machine running in the background, as God speaks out of the whirlwind.

You must try your best to simulate the splendor of the presence of the Lord, uttering his questions with the ring of authority and majesty.

The best way to do this with our frail human voices (except for those gifted with the proper timbre) is as follows:

Speak slowly, pausing at the end of each question, and loudly enough so that you adequately represent the momentous significance of what is happening. Maintain that tone right through to the end of the reading.

2 Corinthians 5:14-21

General sense —
Paul continues today his reflections on our mission as Christians. In this passage he justifies and ennobles all our strivings. It is the love of Christ which drives us. His sacrifice identified him with our sinfulness, so that we "might become the righteousness of God."

For your reading —
Verse 16 provides a conclusion to the logic of the first two

verses. "Therefore," reasons Paul, and your address becomes more pointed, to drive home his thinking.

Stop after the first "point of view" in verse 16. There is a semicolon in the text. A period would be better.

Verse 19 is the end of more reasoning. Stop after you read it, then slow down as the Apostle applies it to us: "so *we* are ambassadors for Christ."

Read verse 21 very carefully: "for our sake he made him to *be* sin who *knew* no sin."

Finally comes the strong climax: "we are to become the righteousness of God." It is the foundation stone of our Christian faith and hope. Make it that important, through your voice.

Mark 4:35-41

General sense —

As we have been reading for the past two weeks, Jesus is weary from a day of preaching in parables, then explaining everything to his not-yet-enlightened disciples. Now he asks for a boat ride across the lake, and there he performs a miracle. Since they have left the crowd behind them on the shore, this one is just for his own, whose formation he has been busy with.

His reminder of the need for faith during a storm is a lesson in discipleship under stress. It is for us as well as for the apostles, even to their (and our) complaint that he is asleep and needs to be waked up.

For your reading —

Raise your voice at verse 37; a "great storm of wind" is at hand — a terrifying experience in a small boat. The voice of the disciples in verse 38 is an urgent message, and should be read with some alarm.

Verse 39 is a solemn command: "Peace! Be Still!" It demands the importance which properly suits the story's climax. And as you read of the "great calm," taper your voice as though you had quieted the storm yourself.

Jesus' words in verse 40 are quiet and gentle. As you conclude, let your voice mirror the bewilderment of the disciples as they wonder about this man of mystery who can calm a storm.

PROPER 8

Suggested theme for today's readings —
Whether financial, material or spiritual, our kindness to others is the very soul of our spiritual life.

Deuteronomy 15:7-11

General sense —

We read today a portion of the code of customs, particularly the religious observances, set down in the Second Discourse of Moses to the people.

The reference here is only to the sabbatical year, when all debts were forgiven and cancelled. But the prescriptions of charity laid down could well be the admonitions of St. John so many years later, of him who had learned Jesus' lessons of kindness to our neighbor so well.

For your reading —
Stop and drop your voice after "open your hand to him," in verse 8. That is the heart of the instruction and one of the key phrases in the reading.

The second important stop is "freely," in verse 10. The temptation not to give and the accusation of sin are negative; "freely" reinforces the mandate to give from the heart.

The third and final emphasis comes in verse 11, summarizing the teaching. After "I command you," slow your tempo; make it sound like a carefully enunciated, not-to-be-forgotten order.

2 Corinthians 8:1-9, 13-15

General sense —
Most of us read letters like this every day, as this or that organization solicits funds. This passage from Paul is cross-cultural. How well it links that long-ago civilization with our own!

Paul is quick to add, of course, that "this is not a command," as he begins his appeal for the Corinthian Relief Fund. He cites the generosity of the Macedonians, "even though they are not rich people." He knows that the love of the Christians at Corinth will be just as genuine.

The words and logic which this message uses throughout are still a basic strength of church fund-raising programs nineteen centuries later, whether printed in a handsome brochure or spoken from a pulpit. Human nature never seems to change.

For your reading —
There are no particular points of emphasis here. As in all "sales pitch" letters, the smoothness and sincerity of the presentation are what count. Paul is asking in absolute earnest (stirring in a bit of flattery) for what no church can do without: operating money.

If you make yourself just as earnest, your reading will pass on to your hearers the importance Paul gives this important matter.

Mark 5:22-24, 35b-43

General sense —
Jesus, model of courtesy and accessibility, raises a little girl to life, by special request, as his early ministry in Galilee nears its close.

The tour has not been very successful. There were many

fruits of the Master's work, of course, but as we would say today, it was pretty much a public-relations failure. The scorn of the people and their lack of faith (as in verse 35) have stunted the growth of any general effect on the community at large. We will see more of that rejection as we pursue Mark's Gospel in the coming weeks.

But a new phase of Jesus' ministry now begins, in which the Twelve will play a much more active role.

For your reading —

In verse 23, raise your voice as you echo Jairus' plea for his daughter.

Verse 35 portrays the rather sarcastic tone of the untrusting, which you will reflect in your voice.

Verse 41 announces the climax of the little drama. Raise your voice again, as Jesus calls the child to life.

PROPER 9

Suggested theme for today's readings —
The price of our calling is often trouble and sorrow, but our faith sustains us.

Ezekiel 2:1-7

General sense —

Ezekiel has just opened his book of prophecy with a stunning vision of the "chariot of God." Now at the heart of his vision he sees what he judges as the glory of the Lord. As we begin our reading, from that glory a voice speaks.

This is Ezekiel's call to his vocation, his life's work. He is, as Jesus will tell his disciples almost six hundred years later, to go among a rebellious, stubborn people, and speak without fear of them, whether they hear him or not.

For your reading —

Please lean strongly on verse 1. It is a call for attention; our hearers should immediately perceive it as such.

The general tone of your reading should be, as we say today, loud and clear. It is a proclamation rather than a story. The voice of the Lord dominates the entire passage. Make sure that your voice simulates his as closely as you can. Be *strong!*

2 Corinthians 12:2-10

General sense —

A remarkable passage, as the Apostle praises himself to defend his ministry. To prove his care for the people at Corinth, he must boast — even though, as he concedes with a shrug and a wry smile, it will gain him nothing. Let his opponents brag about anything that shows *their* concern, he insists.

For your reading —
In verses 2, 3 and 4, Paul is revealing something very extraordinary, an experience hardly to be believed, for which he has no words. Let the awe-filled wonder he felt come through in your voice. Speak slowly, quietly, as if you were storytelling around a campfire. (Be careful about speaking too softly to be heard!)

Pause after "Man may not utter," as the vision ends. Now, as Paul steps back into character, your voice goes with him, through verses 5 and 6.

In verse 7 comes the price Paul had to pay for his privilege. Read it, as well as verses 8 and 9, as if it were a complaint. Remember that Paul is recalling a very painful part of his past.

Verse 10 ends the passage with Paul's unquestioning acceptance of his personal troubles. His upbeat conclusion is an act of faith. The similar acceptance of the troubles you and I have overcome through faith should glow here through your voice, as we all rejoice together in our humanity.

Mark 6: 1-6

General sense —
As we remarked last week, the rejection of Jesus is becoming more evident, Jesus acknowledges it, and like so many of us who set out utterly convinced of the importance of our mission, he finds it difficult to accept. How often have you and I said in frustration, "How can they not understand what I'm trying to do?"

For your reading —
In verse 2, drop your voice after "astonished." A moment's reflection on our own conversations must convince us that the word "saying" is never important. It might, as in this verse, just as well be left out. You will do well to slide over it quickly and get to the important part, namely, what was said.

There ought to be an edge to your voice down to the end of verse 3. These are complaints tinged with sarcasm.

Verses 4, 5 and 6 are read in a somewhat lower tone, as the moment of Jesus' discouragement gives these last three verses a downhill flavor. He is down for a moment, as we all are, but he keeps on going.

PROPER 10
Amos 7:7-15

General sense —
Amos the shepherd, called by the Lord to remind the nation of its violations of the social order, sees here the homely figure of a plumbline to signify God's fidelity.

Suddenly the text is interrupted to speak of Amos in the third person, which means that there was a later addition to the story. The priest of Bethel is rude and sarcastic. "O seer," he says, meaning nothing of the kind, as he orders Amos to leave the country. Whereupon Amos, humble enough not to hide anything, reveals his true origin.

For your reading —

As always, raise your voice when the Lord reveals himself with an important announcement, in this case the renewal of his fidelity in verses 8 and 9.

Verse 10, the message Amaziah sent to the King, begins the priest's scornful words to Amos. Then, when in verse 11 he takes some previous words of Amos completely out of context, let your voice become harsh and accusing.

Turning now directly to Amos, the priest officially gives him his notice of deportation. Stern words, they should be sternly delivered.

Finally, in verses 14 and 15, you are Amos' defense attorney as he pleads, through your voice, for his vocation. Drop your voice after "herdsman," and after "sycamore trees."

Stress the references to "Lord," because by them Amos asserts that his calling is indeed an authentic one.

Ephesians 1:1-14

General sense —

We read today Paul's hymn to the plan of God, which is our election and salvation — the mystery hidden from all eternity.

Baptismal references abound here: our sonship; the forgiveness of sin; our incorporation into Christ; the seal of the Spirit. All point toward the happy fulfillment of God's will for us: our guaranteed possession of the Spirit "to the praise of his glory."

For your reading —

Be aware right from the start that you have been assigned a difficult reading. One magnificent statement follows another, as we move through this insightful, exalted hymn.

Read it like the proclamation it is. There are no obvious places to ease up or to conclude a thought. The whole passage reads as if Paul had received this revelation in a vision.

Keep your voice elevated, strong, reassuring. Don't let anyone miss a word.

Mark 6:7-13

General sense —

Jesus' formation of his Apostles has now proceeded far enough so that they can be sent out on their own. The Master and his teaching have not fared very well; perhaps the Twelve will do better. Much time went into their preparation. Some wonder if we are presented in this passage with not so much an account of their mission adventures as with a preparation for Jesus' self-revelation to them as the Messiah.

For your reading —

This simple and straightforward episode has no particular places for emphasis. And in that lies your challenge here — to make it as interesting and attractive as you can, by whatever modulations in voice or tone may suggest themselves to you.

It is well to slow down for the final phrase, which sets forth the reason why the Savior sent them out: "they anointed with oil many that were *sick,* and *healed* them."

PROPER 11

Suggested theme for today's readings —
Jesus' reconciliation of our sinfulness with God our Father is a source of hope and comfort.

Isaiah 57:14b-21

General sense —

In far-off Babylon the Israelites are in exile. The Babylonians, true to the prophecies, have leveled Jerusalem and deported the people. Look up the Book of the Prophet Jeremiah, chapter 52, verses 28-30, where you will see that there were about forty-six hundred people exiled. They were away for forty-nine years, from 587 BC to 539 BC.

Second Isaiah (chapter 40-66) is called the Book of the Consolation of Israel. The nation's early glory is past; its future will reveal its true Messianic eminence. Every divine promise is on the verge of fullfillment. The Israelites, not to be allowed to return home for another whole generation, needed to hear these words of comfort and hope which we read today.

For your reading —

Stress strongly the thematic command in verse 14: "Build up, build up." "Prepare." "Remove every obstruction." All these indicate the dropping of your voice, as at a period.

By verse 16 the tone is softening a bit. God has been perceived as angry for the reasons in verse 17.

But in verses 18-19, he reaches out to the people with a healing hand, climaxed by the invocation of his own peace. Drop your voice at the first "peace." Then hesitate for a beat before the second, to accentuate the repetition of the word.

Finally, verse 20 comes like an afterthought. Read it in a lower tone — everyone knows the truth described in it, as you conclude.

Ephesians 2:11-22

General sense —

To understand this passage is to be aware of the vast and

ancient gulf between Jew and Gentile. Symbolized by the wall around the Temple's inner court, the system of separation permeated every phase of Jewish life. As God's holy people, they were to keep themselves from every defiling influence.

Now, through Paul, comes the Good News of reconciliation between Jew and Gentile and their uniting in Christ. Jesus has "broken down the dividing wall of hostility, abolishing in his flesh the law of commandments," and the epoch-making change God's power has effected in those (the Gentiles) who had been estranged.

For your reading —

Verses 11 and 12 describe the plight of the Gentiles. Drop your voice after "promise" in verse 12, so that you can give the proper emphasis to "no hope" and "without God."

Verse 14 is the key: "for he is our peace." This, with verses 15 and 16, contains the strength and meaning of the entire passage.

Pause after verse 18, as Paul now applies the results of Christ's reconciliation. Verse 19 through to the end is a proclamation. This is what lends significance to all the previous verses.

Finish strongly, accenting, for best effect, the final three words: "in the Spirit."

Mark 6:30-44

General sense —

Jesus, now alone with the Twelve, at least for the moment, leads them away for a short retreat. But it is not to be. The crowds press in, and Jesus spends with "the sheep without a shepherd" what the Apostles had hoped would be time with them alone.

Toward evening the Twelve can contain themselves no longer. They want the privacy they came here for. And here, in a most unlikely and unexpected surprise, Jesus begins to reveal himself to them, in the miracle of the loaves. Their awe at this Man of Mystery deepens.

For your reading —

This episode is so smoothly and matter-of-factly told that it reads itself.

Verse 33, containing the Apostles' first disappointment, should be read rather more quickly, to portray the hustle and bustle of a suddenly-appearing throng.

Verse 35 sounds a note of weariness and complaint, which your voice ought to mirror clearly.

The remainder of the passage will speak for itself, as you narrate, in the same simple way as the Evangelist, this revelation of the power of God in Christ.

PROPER 12

Suggested theme for today's readings —
We must respect the Spirit of God in others.

2 Kings 2:1-15

General sense —

This is a story, colored by its cultural ambience, of two leaders and the passage of spiritual power from one to his successor. Historically, Elisha was a lesser man than Elijah, and lived in the reflected glory of his master.

Culturally enriched by the miracles and wonderworks common to ancient accounts of religious leaders, this episode is more practically seen as a testimony to the importance of invoking the Spirit of God on all our work, and of our respecting that Spirit in other people.

For your reading —

It's a bit disconcerting to realize that the story you have been assigned to read is a bit of wide-eyed wonder at two great celebrities of the day. Things haven't changed much, it appears.

Read it, then, simulating the naive but genuinely felt excitement of the moment. Our respect for the Word will help us to respect these simple people and their faith that a prophet of the Lord is an important person indeed.

The text consists mostly of the very human conversational modulations we all use every day. It will be a good exercise of your story-telling ability.

Ephesians 4:1-7, 11-16

General sense —

This is the third of eight successive Sunday readings from Paul's letter to the Church at Ephesus, one of the Seven Churches of Asia.

In this passage the Apostle, having concluded his essay on the Plan of God, now advises us that those called to partake of these great mysteries must live a life worthy of that calling. His counsel seems quite up-to-date: he talks of unity in diversity; of the pluralistic gifts of the Spirit; and of our growth to maturity in Christ — all of which exhortations we still hear today from our preachers and authors.

For your reading —

In verse 2, by dropping your voice in three places, you will give the gifts of the Spirit their importance: "you have been called." "lowliness and meekness." "in the bond of peace."

The next "mental period" will be in verse 6: "God and Father of us all."

This passage is one of the classic examples of Paul's "tumbleweed" style, as ideas pour forth one on top of another.

The mental periods, as we call them, are here so frequent that it would be confusing to list them all.

Let your judgment and your experience be your guide as you go over these lines in practise. Make them a living, hard-hitting encouragement to better living.

Mark 6:45-52

General sense —

Jesus has just multiplied the loaves and fishes (the first of two such miracles); no wonder the disciples had to be made to leave the place without him.

Imagine their fright, then, between three and six o'clock in the morning, with their boat bucking a strong headwind, when they saw Jesus approach them on the surface of the waves. He almost passes by, then speaks with them, and as he gets into the boat the winds die down. A rather scary experience.

Mark cannot forget that they have still not penetrated the mystery of this Man. Had they understood who it was who had multiplied the loaves, their hardened hearts would have known him out on the water. He has not revealed himself sufficiently yet. There will be more parables and signs.

For your reading —

When you reach the second half of verse 48, lend to your voice the eeriness of the spectral figure of Jesus walking on the water.

As verse 49 blends into verse 50, raise your voice as the men cry out in terror, then soften it as the Master reassures them.

Pause a beat before you read of their astonishment, in verse 51b, then end quietly.

PROPER 13
Suggested theme for today's readings —
Our life in the Spirit is a constant source of nourishment.
Exodus 16:2-4, 9-15

General sense —

Anyone who has read the Book of Exodus has heard the consistent motif of the murmuring in the desert.

This time the Lord rewards his people by making them aware of two natural phenomena still available today to the desert tribes: the honeyed manna from the area's tamarisk thickets, and the exhausted quail on their long flight back to their northern summer homes.

These events do not have to be miracles: all the earth is made for man. What God's goodness does (in this episode, for example) is to point out its blessings to us. They were there all the time.

For your reading —

The substance of verse 3 has been uttered by thousands of armies, of pilgrims, and all other kinds of people, from time immemorial, whenever they find themselves stranded in a place not of their choosing. Place no special emphasis on it as you read; its only purpose is to set up the action which will follow.

In verse 9, proclaim Moses' call to assembly by raising your voice, and do the same with the Lord's words in verse 11.

End strongly with Moses' declaration that the discovery of the manna and the quails is truly a sign of God's loving care for us.

Ephesians 4:17-25

General sense —

Paul's principles for spiritual renewal begin with the typical Jewish rhetoric of the day: the Gentiles are simply no good at all. We don't usually condemn a whole people today in such general terms. It ill befits the charity of Christ which is in us by the Spirit.

But we do urge one another constantly, as the Apostle does in this passage, to be "renewed in the spirit of our minds."

For your reading —

Three strongly accentuated verses appear here. The first is verse 20, which is the point of the contrast between bad ways of life and better ways.

The second is verse 22, the command to "put off your old nature;" and the third is at verses 23 and 24, as you accent Paul's urging to be "renewed in the spirit of your minds and put on the new nature." As we would say today, it's turning over a new leaf.

All these are to be the key stress points of your reading. They will unify it and make the message of today's lines a clear and understandable one.

John 6:24-35

General sense —

For the next four Sundays we will attempt to understand some of the wonders of John's longest continuous story except the Passion: the mystery of the Bread of Life in Chapter 6 of his Gospel.

Today Jesus reveals the nature and source of something more lasting than his miracles and his feeding them with ordinary food. It is the heavenly bread of God his Father.

For your reading —

Read this passage as straightforwardly as it appears. Your lifelong familiarity with conversational modulations of speech will serve you well.

Verse 35, the conclusion, is the climax of Jesus' revelation:

his identity with the bread he has described. Read it more slowly, each word weighted with the meaning he intends us to remember always.

PROPER 14

Suggested theme for today's readings —
"The good land" in which we dwell today is bounded by our faith and our fidelity.

Deuteronomy 8:1-10

General sense —

This passage follows by a chapter or so the giving of the Ten Commandments. Moses here reminds the people that during their ordeal in the wilderness they were still the apple of the divine eye. Through a triple deliverance — from hunger, from sore feet and ragged clothes, and from their desert existence, he announces that "it will be a good land he has given you."

For your reading —

This entire passage contains but one idea — fidelity. There are no transitions or contrasts, no changes in mood, and no conversation.

Read these lines, then, as a proclamation to your hearers of the unfailing generosity of God. Keep your voice strong and confident throughout. There is no bad news here — simply a reminder of how forgetful we all are of the good things in our lives.

Ephesians 4:25 – 5:2

General sense —

Paul comes now to some homely admonitions, which follow naturally from his culturally-derived low opinion of the Gentiles: don't be like those people. He warns the Christians, however, in a friendly and positive way, to be imitators of God, "as beloved children."

For your reading —

Drop your voice after "members" in verse 25. That is the key to the Apostle's reasoning.

Do the same after "labor" and "work" in verse 28. That emphasis establishes the contrast with what a thief's hands were doing before: they stole instead of doing honest labor.

Finally, the last two verses, verses 1 and 2 of chapter 5, ought to be spoken more gently. Drop your voice after the counsel to "walk in love." The rest of the verse merely explains what that would entail in practise.

John 6:37-51

General sense —

With not very much luck, Jesus here tries to talk to the

Jews. (When John uses the word 'Jews' he is showing his annoyance with their hostility to the Master.) If they would only respond to the grace of God, they would believe, and not be continually distracted by pointless objections. It is only the believer who attains eternal life, not by the old way, as in verse 49, because the manna was only for a particular situation. Jesus' way is, as the priest says at our Eucharist, "to feed on him in your hearts, by faith."

For your reading —

You have been assigned today a rather long and difficult passage. If you take it in segments, your reading will make good sense and be better understood by your hearers.

1. Verses 37 and 38. Jesus utters his message, to do his Father's will.
2. Verses 39 and 40. Jesus explains what it is to do his Father's will: the gathering in of all nations through faith.
3. Verses 41 and 44. As the crowd heckles him, the Savior dismisses their objections by recalling the centrality of God's call to everyone.
4. Verses 45 through 47. The ancient prophecy is fulfilled in Jesus, and this is the way it works: through him.
5. Verses 48 through 51. Jesus' identity with our eternal life and with the sign of the bread.

Each of these segments marks a slight change of emphasis and a different facet of the story. Be sure to pause after each segment before you begin the next.

PROPER 15

Suggested theme for today's readings —
As Christians, we believe that living our faith is "living in the way of insight."

Proverbs 9:1-6

General sense —

The Book of Proverbs is an anthology — a selection — of many ancient volumes of wise sayings, brought together in this form about five hundred years before Christ, just after the Israelites' return from their exile in far-off Babylon.

The authors of Proverbs, seeking to adapt the religion of the past to a changed condition in the life of the people, here equate the seeking of Wisdom to the joys of the Lord.

For your reading —

You are reading today an invitation to a tired and disillusioned people to live "in the way of insight."

Verse 4 should be stressed, as it puts the invitation in words. Verse 5 repeats it in more attractive detail.

The entire passage is delivered in a joyful, upbeat tone, befitting its message.

Ephesians 5:15-20

General sense —
Paul continues his detailed admonitions on everyday Christian living. His advice, shaded today with a touch of the usual elitism, is against too much partying and not enough time for prayerful song and thanksgiving.

For your reading —
Your reading of this brief passage is virtually assured of being your very best. No particular problems present themselves. Announce it in a leisurely, clear way. Let everyone be assured that the way to good Christian living is about the same today as it was in those days so long ago.

John 6:53-59

General sense —
Jesus, having identified himself as the Living Bread, now takes his stand against those who lack the faith which brings understanding of his gift. He repeats what he had already said in the verses immediately preceding this passage, which we read last week.

As we will see next Sunday in the conclusion to this four-week reading of John's Eucharistic chapter, the violent opposition to his announcement did not cease. But he is firm and clear: this is the way it is to be.

For your reading —
Verse 53 ends with what should be a period. Drop your voice here; verse 54 simply re-echoes 53, only the other way around.

Make sure that verse 53 through 58 are all perceived by your hearers as separate and distinct statements. Jesus keeps repeating the same idea over and over again, to drive his point home with unmistakable clarity.

Speak each verse strongly, and pause for a beat after each one, as Jesus might have done.

The final verse is read separately also, in a lower voice, merely as a conclusion citing the occasion of Jesus' announcement.

PROPER 16

Suggested theme for today's readings —
Our fidelity to God's love is a reflection of his faithfulness to us.

Joshua 24:1-2a, 14-25

General sense —
Moses' successor, Joshua, now old and dying, has gathered all the tribes of Israel together at Shechem for the periodic ceremony of the renewal of their Covenant with the Lord. It includes

a narrative of their deliverance from Egypt; the Covenant stipu-
lation of fidelity; and the blessings for fidelity with the curses
and threats if faithfulness were not observed.

The passage we read today is part of Joshua's final discourse
before he dies, in which he urges them once again to be faithful,
and delivers the usual sanctions if they fail.

For your reading —

Drop your voice in verse 14 after "faithfulness." It concludes
a thought.

Do the same after "dwell" in verse 15, because the next words
strike a contrast and so must be separate.

Verse 17 needs a "mental period," or dropping of the voice,
after each phrase, except after "sight."

Verses 19 and 20 sound strange and out of place here. They
were probably added many years later as a legal binder which
made the people "witnesses," or accessories, as we would say
today, to the crime of infidelity. Read them without changing
your voice.

Verse 25 ends with a description of what happened after
Joshua's speech: the ritual animal sacrifice which sealed the Covenant, and the recording of the day's "minutes."

Ephesians 5:21-33

General sense —

The opening lines of this passage are not generally well received by many women of this day and age of sexual equality.
The wife was expected, in Paul's day, to be subject to her husband;
he owed her love and respect.

In a concept unique to the New Testament, Paul here uses
married love as a model for Christ's love for the Church, which
designates a selfless giving of self.

For your reading —

In verse 26, drop your voice after "sanctify her," which states
the purpose of love and therefore marks the end of a thought.

In verse 29 make a "mental period" after "cherishes it," and,
a few words later, after "the church."

Your own experience will take you through the remainder of
the passage without difficulty.

John 6:60-69

General sense —

This passage ends Jesus' talk on the Bread of Life; sadly, it
seems to have reduced the number of his followers. But the Apostles show that his intensive training of them has not been in
vain. Not until Pentecost will they know him in his fullness, but
they are growing in maturity. They have seen and they believe.

For your reading —

Verse 60 is an unbeliever's complaint. Let your hearers know that. The same clarity on your part is applied to Jesus' rebuttal in verses 61 through 64. The tone is insistent and argumentative throughout, and should be read strongly.

At verse 64b, lower your voice a bit as the Evangelist adds a comment of his own.

Verse 65 comes with a note of finality. The Master has spoken; there will be no more on the subject.

In verse 67, sound a gentle note as Jesus turns to the Apostles. He really doesn't want them to leave.

Simon Peter's heartfelt avowal of faith, in verse 68, raises your voice once more for a strong finish.

PROPER 17

Suggested theme for today's readings —
In our struggle with the powers of evil in the world, God's care for us will be our strength.

Deuteronomy 4:1-9

General sense —

This prayer is part of Moses' discourse on the greatness of Israel as God's chosen nation. It was given near the end of the people's forty-year wanderings in the wilderness, as they were preparing to enter the promised Land of Canaan.

In his address Moses has recalled the places and events of their travels. Now he turns directly to his people and reminds them, in the words we read today, of the responsibilities which their divine election confers on them.

For your reading —

In verse 3, do not drop your voice after "Baalpeor." In the same verse because you have already mentioned the name of the place once, make a "mental period" after "followed." It is the followers who were destroyed; that's the important word.

In verse 6 there is a "mental period" after "them," and another after "peoples."

In verse 9 drop your voice after "diligently." What follow are merely the reasons for being diligent.

Ephesians 6:10-20

General sense —

Today, in the last of our eight readings from Ephesians, Paul concludes his magnificent essay on the Plan of God and our part in it. His summary of the Christian life in practise envisions the cosmic power of evil we must confront daily. The struggle is not against a human enemy but, as we would say today, "the system:" the sense of futility we sometimes feel in our efforts to face a controlled world whose governing powers are so often beyond our influence.

For your reading —

"Put on the whole armor of God," urges Paul, and we emphasize that idea by a "mental period" after "God" in verse 11.

To show the contrast, in verse 12, between earthly evils and the larger ones we cannot control, drop your voice after each of these powers: "against the principalities." "against the powers." "against the world rulers of this present darkness."

Maintain a firm and confident tone until the next "mental period," in verse 17, after "Sword of the Spirit."

In verse 19, as Paul himself asks for prayers, drop your voice again after "and also for me."

The same "mental period" applies after "in chains" in verse 20, with an added drop of your voice after "ought." Since the Apostle is already speaking, that final word becomes secondary. Paul is saying, "Help me to do what I *ought* to do."

Mark 7: 1-8, 14-15, 21-23

General sense —

Today begins the final quarter of the Church year. During these thirteen weeks which remain before Advent, we take up the Gospel of Mark. Jesus confronts and supersedes the Old Law; he works miracles; twice he predicts his Passion and death. He speaks of children, of the price of discipleship, of the love of riches, of scandal, of the end of the world. And at the last, facing his death, he asserts his kingship over all the universe.

Jesus' confrontation with the Pharisees, as they try to maintain the old ways, is our text today.

For your reading —

In verse 2, the word "defiled" ends a thought. Your voice marks it with a "mental period."

The same holds for "elders," in verse 3, as it does after "themselves" in verse 4.

The contrast between worship with the lips and with the heart in verse 7 ends with a "mental period" after "far."

Look up at your hearers in verses 3 and 4, as Paul adds a footnote for those who may need it.

Jesus' scorn is made evident by the words of verses 6, 7 and 8. Be sure you mark that by raising your voice and taking on the stern warning tone in which he speaks.

PROPER 18

Suggested theme for today's readings —

Our years of waiting for God's coming demand that our faith be practical and workable.

Isaiah 35: 4-7a

General sense —

We read today a plea by the prophet to the faint of heart, who have grown tired of the years of waiting. These lines are also a part of the readings for Advent, full of the joy of restoration, as the Lord saves Zion.

For your reading —

There are passages in the Bible which stir us to recall what a privilege it is to read them to our hearers. This is one of them. All of us are hungry for the bright, upbeat words of hope and encouragement spoken here.

Read these happy lines in a strong, firm voice. Make a stop after "be strong" in verse 4, as you begin. It is a call to courage.

Happily, the punctuation in this passage, with the exception in verse 4, lends itself well to the spoken word. Communicate its joy to those who hear you.

James 1:17-27

General sense —

Of uncertain authorship, this epistle reads rather like a written instruction or lecture. Its concern is that our faith be worked out in our lives, rather than remain abstract and theoretical.

Typical of that central concern is today's passage, which urges us to be "doers of the Word."

For your reading —

This selection ought to be delivered calmly, reminding us of the things we already know, as would happen at an early morning service on a weekday, in the quiet of a little chapel.

Whenever there is a reference to doing, as opposed to merely hearing, accent that idea with your voice, so that the principal theme of James' letter may be made clear to all.

The last two verses, 26 and 27, summarize what has gone before. Raise your voice as you come to them, so that you may finish strongly.

Mark 7:31-37

General sense —

A handicapped man is cured today. Mark reveals to his readers part of the secret of Jesus which is the driving force of his Gospel: even though the signs — the astonishment, the "doing all things well," — say unmistakably that the Messiah has come, Jesus is not ready himself to reveal that truth. There is much more to be done before his fame reaches the ears of those who would put him down.

For your reading —

The first "mental period" occurs in verse 32, after "speech" as the description of the man's handicaps ends.

The word "Ephphetha" needs a drop in your voice also. It stands as a complete thought by itself.

Do not stress "saying" in verse 37. The important phrase is "beyond measure." That is where your voice signals the end of a sentence by dropping, as if at a period. "Saying" is only a link between that phrase and the next, which is the praise of Jesus' work. It has no other value at all.

PROPER 19

Suggested theme for today's readings —
Our Christian lives of faith mean good works rather than good words.

Isaiah 50: 4-9

General sense —
Today's six verses mark the third Song of the Suffering Servant. The sacred writer personifies Israel as the persecuted one, waiting for the good time of the Lord to come, yet not open to the saving Word that is being fulfilled by suffering.

The persecution becomes more violent and personal, as in verse 6. But the servant has the help of God, and the adversary will fade away like a moth-eaten garment.

For your reading —
The first three verses, 4 through 6, contain a bit of self-satisfaction that the speaker has been faithful despite adversity.

Raise your voice as verse 7 begins, when the writer uses courtroom terminology to state his case and express his hope.

The reading ends firmly on this positive note.

James 2:1-5, 8-10, 14-18

General sense —
We read from this letter for the second of four Sundays. "Be doers of the Word" is the continuing theme. It is herein exemplified by hospitality to strangers and by a remarkably up-to-date comment on people who wish others well but do nothing for them.

The letter is not opposing faith to works, but living faith to dead faith.

For your reading —
Read these practical, down-to-earth prescriptions in a clear and confident tone. To make the reading forceful, words to accent are "Jesus Christ, the Lord of glory," in verse 1, and "Listen, my beloved brethren," in verse 5.

The climax to the passage, the point of these precepts, is in the last few verses: James' sharply pointed analogy about well-wishers. Read it like the summary it is — with strong conviction, ending your reading with finality and authority.

Mark 8:27-38

General sense —

On this passage hinges the entire Gospel of Mark. It climaxes Jesus' self-revelation with the disciples' first recognition of him as the Messiah, and it is the first allusion to his coming Passion.

The incident of which we read today happens at Caesarea Philippi, the source of the Jordan River and an ancient shrine hallowed by memories of the pagan emperors. Did Jesus lead his disciples here to demand — and receive — a faith that ran counter to all that this place stood for?

For your reading —

When Peter declares the faith Jesus has been training him to accept, in verse 29, accent his statement strongly: "*You* — are the Christ."

Drop your voice after "killed" in verse 31, to separate the importance of Jesus' death from the importance of his resurrection.

Be stern as you read Jesus' rebuke of Peter in verse 33. Make his just anger evident in your voice.

Verse 36 indicates a drop in your voice for a "mental period" after "world," as does verse 37, after "give." Both of these emphases make clear the magnitude of our human dignity. It is worth more than all the world's goods.

Finally, in verse 38, drop your voice after "Son of man also." No need to stress "ashamed." You've already done that earlier in the verse.

PROPER 20

Suggested theme for today's readings —
True wisdom is conducting our lives by the standards of Jesus Christ.

Wisdom 1:16 – 2:1, 12-22

General sense —

The Book of Wisdom is among the Episcopal Church's apocryphal books, because it was not in the Hebrew Bible but only in the Greek. It was written by a Greek-speaking Jew, probably to strengthen the faith of the Jewish community at Alexandria, the great intellectual and scientific center of the ancient Mediterranean world.

Today's passage sets forth the erroneous philosophy of the wicked in the form of a speech. Since God and virtue are mentioned, the addressees are assumed to be Jews who have abandoned their faith.

For your reading —

Announce these lines the way the author intended them: as a warning of danger. Surrounded by the pagan society of Alexandria, the Jews needed a reminder of their heritage and a challenge to virtue.

Verse 1 of chapter 2 should be spoken with irony and sarcasm. Make your voice heavy with it.

The sarcastic quote continues throughout, from verses 12 through 22. It is life as the godless see it.

At verse 20 the quote ends. In verses 21 and 22 the man of Wisdom now speaks for himself. After you have made an obvious pause at the end of verse 20, indicating a change in tone, the last two verses are read in a rather sad and pessimistic voice.

James 3:16-4:6

General sense —

The sacred author here contrasts real wisdom with its opposite, then proceeds to exemplify what we would call today "street smarts" as typical of worldly wisdom.

For your reading —

Verse 16 is negative, verse 17 positive, as well as more gentle. List the rewards and qualities of wisdom one by one, dropping your voice after whichever ones seem to make sense to you. But be sure, as in the reading of any list, to isolate the individual importance of each item by a little pause.

Verse 1 of chapter 4 suddenly picks up the tempo, as the author turns to the hostilities in the community. Raise your voice here; insist, in verse after verse, that you know these people with all their faults.

In verse 5 drop your voice after "in vain." That's the key phrase.

Keep your voice elevated throughout, and finish with a positive air. The passage is intended, as we say, to disturb the comfortable. Be sure you communicate that.

Mark 9:30-37

General sense —

The disciples, as Jesus predicts his Passion for the second time, either have no idea of what he is talking about, or they are, as we say today, blocking out anything that sounds like bad news.

And on top of that, they still think they have free passes to his Kingdom, and will be in some sort of rank there. But they are too ashamed to admit that to Jesus.

For his response, the Savior gives the same answer we still hear today. We are to be like children; we are to be "last of all and servant of all."

For your reading —

In verse 31, as always, do not make anything of the phrase, "saying to them." That is only a connective. The word to stress (by dropping your voice) is "his disciples." Then take a breath and just slide through the connective. More important words follow.

Drop your voice after "silent" in verse 34. In verse 35, do not drop your voice as you read "and he said to them;" get right to what he said. Never stress the connective. The same holds for a similar phrase in verse 36. Its only another connective.

PROPER 21

Suggested theme for today's readings —
The best cure for the urge to complain about our lot is to do a good deed for someone.

Numbers 11: 4-6, 10-16, 24-29

General sense —
The Israelites (and the rabble, or foreigners among them, for this was by no means a homogeneous group) struggle through the wilderness. Fatigue, hunger, and now resentment against their leader, eat at their souls.

The dust of the desert has set nerves and tempers on edge. Even Moses is not above adding to the general griping a few complaints of his own. Finally, the council is formed to ease his load. The sagging esprit de corps picks up a bit, despite a petty wrangle over who should prophesy where.

For your reading —
This is not an easy passage. Emotions flare as the "rabble" complain. You must read these verses, 4 through 6, with the same petulant voice Moses heard.

In verse 10 the Lord's anger "blazed hotly." And Moses appears even angrier. His voice drips with heavy sarcasm through verse 13, as should yours.

As verse 13 ends, pause a moment, because Moses now ceases his anger to beg prayerfully for some help. Be sure to note that transition as you read. Verses 14 and 15 might have found Moses down on his knees.

The last segment, verses 24 through 29, reveal in a calm way the resolution of the conflict. You raise your voice only at the alarmed young man in verse 27, and when Joshua pushes the panic button in verse 28.

End strongly as Moses cuts through the trivia in verse 29, and concludes the episode.

James 4:7-12

General sense —
In this last of our four readings from James, the Apostle urges a spirit of humility and penance, and concludes with a brief appeal for fraternal charity.

For your reading —
The structure of these lines lends itself well to clarity of expression, as the moral pleas come in sentences which are short and to the point.

Verse 11 changes the subject from humility and penance to the obligation of charity. Pause after verse 10 and wait a beat before resuming your reading.

Drop your voice after "judges," when you say "judges the law."

In verse 12, there is a mental period after "you." It brings the central idea of these last two verses home to your hearers.

Mark 9:38-48

General sense —
The fifth of our readings from Mark's Gospel encourages all who do good, however minor, even to the gift of a cooling drink, and follows with a severe warning against scandal.

For your reading —
Your first inflection here will be the dropping of your voice after "water to drink," in verse 41.

Otherwise, the short sentences and the readily recognizable admonitions throughout the passage will help you to read them with the proper sense.

Since scandal is a subject with which Jesus deals quite severely, adjust your tone of voice in verses 42 through 48 to the text, as you spell out these dire warnings.

PROPER 22
Suggested theme for today's readings —
Our respect for one another is a sign of our dignity as children of God.

Genesis 2:18-24

General sense —
In his own profoundly mysterious way, in the "deep sleep" of our habitual unawareness of his presence, the Lord gives man a helper "like himself." The prior creation of the animals in this passage emphasizes by contrast the true role of the woman.

Two ideas we might have thought were fairly new have their origin in this long-ago milieu: woman is man's complement, not his service appendage; and her similar nature corresponds to his own.

For your reading —
At verse 21, lower your voice as we witness Adam's deep sleep. This will provide a strong contrast to the rather matter-of-fact creation of the animals. More importantly, it will evoke for your hearers the profound silence in which the Lord performs his wonders in us.

Verse 23, Adam's realization that his helper is someone special, is his proclamation of the might of the Lord and his gratitude for the divine action. Your heightened voice here will add to the importance of this epochal event in our human history.

Hebrews 2:9-18

General sense —

We begin today seven readings from the Epistle to the Hebrews. Writing to Jewish Christians, the author warns against apostasy from the faith and demonstrates the priesthood of Christ as the abolition of the Old Covenant.

Today's reading proclaims that the exaltation of Jesus was preceded, and authenticated, by his identification with us through humiliation and suffering.

For your reading —

In verse 9, lean on "because;" it establishes the reason Jesus was glorified, and it is the key to the sentence.

As you end verse 11, drop your voice after "brethren." The next word, "saying," is to be glided over almost imperceptibly. It is not important. Only what follows is.

Drop your voice after "likewise," which establishes Jesus' identification with us.

Verse 18 ends the reading with a strongly-worded summary of that divine oneness with us. Make that your most important verse as you conclude.

Mark 10:2-9

General sense —

Jesus here takes moral authority into his own hands, as the Messiah is entitled to. His announcement of the inviolability of the marital bond supersedes the more flexible Mosaic Law of verse 4.

For your reading —

Drop your voice after "heart" in verse 5. It concludes the reason for the Old Law precept.

Beyond that, this reading should present no difficulties. It is plainly worded, clear and familiar to us. Be sure to slow down a bit for the last verse. It represents Jesus' final and definitive statement on the matter, a conclusion he draws after quoting twice from the ancient Book of Genesis.

PROPER 23

Suggested theme for today's readings —

We demonstrate our fidelity to God by renouncing whatever does not lead to him.

Amos 5:6-7, 10-15

General sense —

Amos, an Israelite of the eighth century before Christ, was by his own word no prophet but a shepherd and a handyman. Called to prophesy by the Lord, he saw the Israelite society of his day as full of social injustice and in serious violation of the Mosaic covenant of the brotherhood of all.

A rough-hewn man from the country, his harsh and severe words bitterly flay the oppression of the poor by the rich.

For your reading —

Amos is angry; his straight talk is often echoed today by those who feel about our society as he did about his. Put some of that anger in your voice as you read. Maintain a firm and resolute tone.

The references to "the gate" allude to what we would call a Small Claims Court at the entrance to the city, where cases were heard daily.

At verse 14, after Amos has spent some of his anger, soften your voice as he urges his hearers to make an effort to remember the presence of God.

Lean on the phrase "it may be" and the word "gracious" in verse 15. It is the sum of Amos' hope that things will get better.

Hebrews 3:1-6

General sense —

As Jesus reveals himself, during these weeks of our readings from Mark, the author of Hebrews continues his theology of the priesthood of Christ.

Today's passage cites the fidelity of the savior and his pre-eminence over Moses.

For your reading —

Drop your voice after "Jesus" in verse 1, as the author introduces his principal subject.

There should be a comma in verse 3 after "Moses," because it interrupts the story to offer a comparison. Observe that pause with your voice.

Pause before "as a son" as you conclude. That drives home the superiority of Christ over Moses.

Mark 10:17-27

General sense —

In this passage, Jesus' encounter with a young man flatly contradicts the common Jewish attitude that wealth is a sign of God's approval. As deeply as the Master is moved by the good life of the young man, the principle remains: voluntary renunciation is the door to the Kingdom.

For your reading —
In verse 17, the word which draws the picture is "knelt." Drop your voice at that point. Be sure, as usual, to glide through the phrase "and asked him;" get to the important words, as the quote begins.

Verse 21 is important — a beautiful picture to be lingered over for just a second or two: "Jesus, looking at him, loved him." We do that all the time to those who are precious to us. Observe the "mental period" after "loved." Let your audience treasure those words which mean so much to all of us.

Verse 23 changes the tone somewhat, as Jesus turns and reflects on the incident. He speaks strongly here, repeating himself to stress his point.

Finish in a very firm tone. Jesus settles the question with his reference to the almighty power of God.

PROPER 24
Suggested theme for today's readings —
Suffering is a safe prediction for every human life. What counts is how we deal with it.

Isaiah 53:4-12

General sense —
We hear today the classic prophecy of the Passion. In the writer's mind is a portrayal of the ideal Servant of God. He is the perfect Israelite, whose consecration to God's will, even in the midst of pain and suffering, takes away the sins of many. Six centuries later the prophecy was fulfilled in the divine Israelite, Jesus Christ.

For your reading —
It would be well to accentuate at least two of the three qualities mentioned in verse 4 — either "stricken" or "smitten by God," plus of course the one which ends the sentence.

In this reading the phrases and sentences are simple ones. The punctuation is all there and need not be changed. What is of paramount importance, then, is the tone of voice you assume.

To convey the atmosphere of these somber enumerations of suffering, you must read more slowly than usual. Frequent pauses, at least after every sentence, will help in setting the scene, and in accenting, by isolation, the importance of each of the trials of the Servant.

If you are satisfied simply to recite this passage, only its "downbeat" tone will come through, and as a result you (and we hearers) will hear not much but a dreary monotone.

Hebrews 4:12-16

General sense —
It is a theological commonplace to assert that the Word of

the Lord judges us, critiques our life. Here the sacred author points out the dynamic power of the Word to give life and to be effective in penetrating our inner selves.

Nevertheless, our compassionate high priest, Jesus Christ, human in all but sin, understands our weakness and gives us confident access to Mercy.

For your reading —

Drop your voice after "sword" in verse 12, as the description of the Word passes on to its dynamic qualities.

There is also a "mental period" after "open and laid bare" in verse 13.

In verse 15, make a stop after "as we are," before you add the exception mentioned.

There is another vocal stop indicated after "help" in the final verse 16. The help we received outweighs our need.

Mark 10:35-45

General sense —

Jesus has just forewarned his disciples for the third time of his future Passion. The sons of Zebedee continue to misunderstand (or block out bad news). So Jesus gently explains one more time that place and rank mean nothing in the Kingdom — only the unconditional commitment to service.

For your reading —

Verse 35 is an excellent example of oral punctuation departing from what appears in print. The verse should be read aloud thus: "And James and John the sons of Zebedee came forward. (and said to him) Teacher," and so on. The key word is the beginning of their address: "Teacher —"

In verse 39, lean on the twice-repeated "will." Jesus is stating a future certainty.

Pause after verse 40, as the story shifts its center to the other ten disciples.

In verse 42 the same principle applies as in verse 35 above. Like this: "And Jesus *called* them to him. (and said to them) "You know," etc.

Drop your voice after the first "you" in verse 43, to bring out the contrast with Gentile custom, and also after "serve" in verse 45, to accent the contrast there.

PROPER 25

Suggested theme for today's readings —
Our troubles are often the result of our blindness in not realizing God's unfailing love for us.

Isaiah 59:9-19

General sense —

These are the discouraging days, after the Israelites' return from their exile. They have been away from their homeland for more than a whole generation. It is as if today someone had been gone since the 1930's. Jerusalem was destroyed; the sacred Ark of the Covenant was lost, never to be found again. The Promised Land, the great reforms they had begun so well, their royal heritage — all were ground into the desert under the terrible hammer of the Babylonian army.

The lines we read today powerfully and vividly evoke, in a community confession of guilt, the haze of defeat and ruin, then end in a trumpet blast of hope.

For your reading —

As you read, you are drawing a picture of despair almost unequalled in the Bible. Your voice will show that by its edge of sadness and gloom, while still maintaining its volume.

At verse 12, pause. Here begins the confession of guilt. Your voice now becomes penitent and sorrowful. The event is nearly three thousand years old, but you are reading what is in the hearts of yourself and your hearers today.

In verse 15b we turn to the Lord. From this point on, our destitution recognized, we accept his full redeeming power. Let your voice ring out at the end with the hope and trust we all live by.

Hebrews 5:12 – 6:1, 9-12

General sense —

The author of this letter impatiently urges his readers — who he says should be teachers by this time — to get back to fundamentals, then ends with a word of encouragement.

For your reading —

Verse 12 is the important word here. A good place for a "mental period" drop in your voice would be after "again."

At verse 9 of the next chapter the tone softens considerably, as if the writer regrets his impatience. Pause before you begin it, and read these last four verses gently, not to crush anyone but to help those who have neglected their faith.

Mark 10:46-52

General sense —

The miracle of the blind man is told in Mark's matter-of-fact style. There are no healing gestures; Jesus, for a change, does not object to being hailed as a royal descendant; the blind man sees, in Jesus, that real royalty stoops to serve.

The cure is done, and the Savior passes on hearing none of the usual astonishment at his exquisite courtesy.

For your reading —

Stop after "Timaeus" in verse 46. His name is what matters,

not where he is sitting. Where else would anybody sit but by the roadside?

In verses 47 and 48 be sure to raise your voice as you cry out with the blind man. Drop your voice after "cry out." Glide through "and say" as if it weren't there.

Verse 49 is another instance of gliding through. Stop after "blind man," because the next word is "take heart." "Saying to him" is only a minor connective.

In verse 50, put some excitement in your story, as the blind man throws off his mantle and springs to his feet, as if he were already cured. Speak a little more quickly here. The blind man's voice rises and tightens as he begs his favor, then you conclude with Jesus' calm and gentle answer before he passes on.

PROPER 26

Suggested theme for today's readings —
True worship of the one God is expressed in one command-ment: to love one another.

Deuteronomy 6:1-9

General sense —
Today's reading announces the basic Jewish creed, called the Sh'ma, still recited daily by devout Jews and taught to their children. Its words, in verses 4 and 5, mark an epochal departure from the multi-god worship of the ancient people, as Israel rejects all others for the one true God.

For your reading —
This is a proclamation. The important thing is not this or that pause or inflection, but the tone of your voice.

Verses 1, 2 and 3 build up to the climactic declaration which follows. Pause after verse 3 to mark the end of this brief preface.

Verse 4 should be the strongest of all, the key verse of the entire passage. Let it ring out.

The ensuing verses instruct the people how to receive those majestic words. Your voice becomes a bit lower but just as firm, as you conclude this proclamation.

Hebrews 7:23-28

General sense —
This passage describes the priesthood of Jesus, unbound by time, always redemptive, whose one sacrifice constitutes him our perfect intercessor forever.

For your reading —
Drop your voice after "permanently," in verse 24. That word is more important than its synonym which follows.

Make another "mental period" after "all time," because it echoes the idea of permanency expressed above.

In verse 26 you could drop your voice again either after "fitting" or "have." Use whatever emphasis makes the best reading for you.

The remainder of the reading should present no difficulties.

Mark 12:28-34

General sense —

Whether Jesus, in his word to the scribe in verse 34, was saying that the Scriptures had been correctly understood, or was simply consoling an old man near the end of his days, is of course not made clear.

Nevertheless this is a favorite passage for older people, as Jesus recalls the lines so dear to every good and devout Jew for centuries, in verses 29 through 31.

For your reading —

Your reading today is a fairly easy one, with no particular variations from the tone indicated by the text.

In verses 32 and 33, the scribe's enthusiasm at hearing Jesus quote what he already knew should show in your voice.

PROPER 27

Suggested theme for today's readings —
Our love for God is shown in our hospitality to others.

I Kings 17:8-16

General sense —

Today's reading is typical of many stories told in ancient times of holy men, to enhance the authority of the prophetic word by a prediction (verse 14) and its fulfillment (verse 16).

Its historic value is real enough for Jesus to cite it many years later, not for the prediction and fulfillment, but to show that the Lord can work his good deeds through the most unlikely people.

For your reading —

The land was in its third year of drought, which accounts for the poverty of the widow, as well as her conviction that this would be her last meal. But notice, and bring it out in the tone of your voice, that her hospitality to a stranger is willing and immediate.

As Jesus would say in his own time, "Your faith has saved you."

Verse 12 expresses the widow's discouragement, which your voice should pick up, as well as the immediate contrast of Elijah's strong and reassuring words in verse 13.

In verse 14 Elijah quotes the Lord. Proclaim these words in a somewhat elevated tone. Then return to your storytelling for the last two verses of the fulfillment of the prophecy.

Hebrews 9:24-28

General sense —

Jesus' sacrifice was sufficient till the end of time. What our priests offer is a remembrance of that sacrifice. The author uses the analogy of an unrepeated death to bring out his point, then concludes with a reference to the Lord's second coming.

For your reading —

Drop your voice after "heaven itself" in verse 24, to make clear the contrast between heaven and a sanctuary made with hands.

Beyond that, these brief lines will speak for themselves and assist you in doing your very best.

Mark 12:38-44

General sense —

Jesus never had a problem with sin; his exquisite courtesy erased it time after time, with the balm of forgiveness.

His chief opponent, we are ashamed to say, was organized religion. His antipathy toward the Jewish religious establishment is made clear in the first half of today's reading.

His Passion is almost upon him, yet he still has hope for Israel in the widow's gift of her mite, to which he proudly alerts his disciples.

For your reading —

The opposite human qualities of hypocrisy and generosity are manifest now and then in every one of us. Be sure you make a clear and evident pause after verse 40, to separate the two incidents here.

PROPER 28

Suggested theme for today's readings —

Whatever our troubles, we are sustained by our Christian hope.

Daniel 12:1-4a

General sense —

This book is not by Daniel but about him. In the latter chapters, he has four visions. Today's reading is a part of the fourth, designating, through the image of war, the end of the world. But the hope is always there, in that the Lord, as we say, will be "the judge of the quick and the dead."

For your reading —

This is something of a proclamation. The author is quoting the Lord himself. As such, it deserves an elevated tone in your presentation. These are important words for our future.

The passage ends with a note of mystery, as Daniel is ordered to keep secret whose names are in the Book of Life. Read this verse, 4, with the note of finality and mystery it indicates.

Hebrews 10:31-39

General sense —
We end our series of readings from Hebrews on a note of encouragement. The author reminds us of all the good we have done, and urges us to "hang in there," as it were, for the coming of the Lord. At the end he identifies with all who have not "thrown away (our) confidence."

For your reading —
This reading would more properly begin with verse 32, so that the positive tone of it will remain intact.

The principal change in the tone of your voice will be after a pause as you end verse 38. Read verse 39 in an upbeat, reassuring way. And drop your voice after "have faith." It is of equal rank with "keep their souls." A comma after "have faith" would reduce it to a less important idea.

Mark 13:14-23

General sense —
We conclude today the series from the Gospel of Mark we have been reading for the last twelve weeks. As the Church year once again draws to a close, we hear Jesus speak of the end of the world.

For your reading —
Jesus speaks today in a tone of the utmost seriousness and authority. He sees sacrilege coming to the holy city and to the Temple, "where it ought not to be," he adds.

Stop for a beat after verse 17, as Jesus' compassion appears. Begin verse 18 in a more quiet tone, to vary your reading.

Conclude in the strong voice in which you began. The Savior's dread prophecy, as far as his hearers were concerned, could come true at any moment. Let that urgency show through in your voice.

PROPER 29

Suggested theme for today's readings —
We end the Church year with sorrow for our sins and thanks for our blessings.

Daniel 7:9-14

General sense —
We read today part of a dream of Daniel. He dreamt of four beasts, symbolizing the four pagan empires of the times: the Babylonians, the Medes, the Persians and the Greeks. He witnesses their destruction.

Stories like this one are part of the "mystique" of the ancient Israelite nationalism. Perhaps, in their context, we would call them today something like "special effects," created to reinforce and enhance, by a Messianic dream, the glorious destiny Israel felt herself called to in the design of God.

This passage tells of the fourth beast, picturing the celestial court scene at which the beast, representing the Greek empire, was condemned and destroyed.

For your reading —

As you proclaim this passage, let your voice reproduce the vivid colorations of the heavenly scene. Your sense of wonder should take dramatic note of each marvelous detail: the whiteness of snow, the blazing fire, the multitude around the throne, the suspenseful opening of the book, and the fiery consummation of the beast.

In verse 14 comes the climax, as your voice sounds the praise of the victor throughout the universe. It is a strong ending to a highly arresting vision.

Revelation 1:1-8

General sense —

The pages of this obscure and mysterious book teem with symbols, numbers, expressions and categories of thought which seem strange to our Western ears.

"Apocalypse" means in Greek "an uncovering." In this book we take it to signify a revelation, or uncovering, of "what must soon take place," God's ultimate purpose: the second coming of Jesus Christ; the consummation of history; the final victory over Satan; the universal judgment; and the establishment of the heavenly Jerusalem.

Today's passage opens the curtain to these wondrous events with the salutation and solemn introduction.

For your reading —

Make your reading as solemn and profound as you can manage. It is a remarkable sequence of ideas, truly cosmic in its impact.

Let your voice ring out. Pause after each sentence, especially at the end of verse 7, which underlines its gravity by repetition.

The Lord's words in verse 8 are intoned somewhat more slowly, as a fitting conclusion to another Church year. Keep your voice ringing like a bell throughout!

John 18:33-37

General sense —

These lines could well be thought of as the last words of Jesus, though they were not historically. He speaks of his Kingdom and appeals to all those who are "of the truth," as he implicitly calls on Pilate to take a stand on the side of truth and life.

For your reading —

Be sure, with your voice, to mark the contrast between the firm but dispassionate words of Jesus and the cynical sarcasm of the bored and impatient Pilate. Raise your voice when Pilate speaks; put an edge on his contemptuous attitude.

In verse 37, Jesus concludes his earthly ministry with a summary of his mission. Give these words the solemn finality they convey, as you conclude.

Year C

FIRST SUNDAY IN ADVENT

Suggested theme for today's readings —
Our expectancy of the Lord's coming is what keeps life interesting.

Zechariah 14:4-9

General sense —
Zechariah's prophecies mainly concerned the rebuilding of the temple after the Exile.

Here the theme of a later writer, added to the book, is the convulsions of the earth at the coming of the Lord, contrasted with the security and peace which stem from his presence.

For your reading —
These highly imaginative vignettes of the Messianic age to come are to be rendered in the mode of an announcement, in keeping with this beginning of Advent, as we look forward to the coming of the Lord.

The verse which rings with the truth of this season is verse 9. Read it as your strong ending; it speaks of the spirit of our Advent hope with perfect clarity.

1 Thessalonians 3:9-13

General sense —
Paul affectionately greets his beloved Church at Thessaly on the Aegean Sea. Grateful for their love and support, he prays for an early return to them, wishing for them the best of the Christian life.

For your reading —
These lines from a devoted and loyal heart will give you a chance to speak to your hearers with the quiet earnestness which so befits this season.

No particular emphasis marks any verse; it is a message of Advent joy and peace. Let your voice be animated, expectant, rejoicing.

Luke 21:25-31

General sense —
In deeply prophetic language, Luke sketches here the final apocalyptic vision of the Second Coming. He speaks of signs and cosmic upheavals, ending with a quick and obvious parable.

Nothing looks deader than a fig tree in winter. Yet when it blooms, summer is on the way.

So, in parallel, with the Son of Man and his Kingdom. Only after Christians weather the winter of troubles will the final achievement of Jesus' mission — world redemption — be near. Advent looks forward to it, as a lasting sign.

For your reading —

Tell your story solemnly; read verse 25 through 28 as gravely and authoritatively as you can.

Feel free to begin verse 26 with "people" instead of "men."

Verse 29 is a parable. Change, after the usual pause, to a softer tone: less severe, quieter than the first four verses. Read as if Jesus, having spoken of the doom and foreboding, suddenly turns and sees the fig tree. He uses it as an example, and everything becomes clear.

SECOND SUNDAY IN ADVENT
Suggested theme for today's readings —
Our own "glorious Jerusalem" will be the arrival of the Lord in our midst.

Baruch 5:1-9

General sense —

This book, existing only in Greek and thus not a part of the Hebrew canon, presents vignettes from the history of the Exile and reflections on that history.

The strikingly beautiful allegory we read today is the sight of a future glorious Jerusalem — a foreshadowing and guarantee in the mind of the prophet of the great event to come: our salvation.

For your reading —

What lovely images your reading draws for us today! We are Jerusalem; our Church "stands on the heights;" turned to the East, we face the glory of the rising Sun of Justice.

Announce these visions as if you were an eyewitness of their splendor. Pause after verse 4, as you begin in verse 5 the direct address.

At verse 7 the tone changes again, as your voice now reflects the wonderful deeds of the Lord himself.

Verses 8 and 9, though part of the Lord's acts, conclude your reading on a gentler note.

Lines like these are a not-very-often privilege for us to deliver, reminding us of what a calling it is to be a reader.

Philippians 1:1-11

General sense —

Paul's love for both a fellow-worker and for one of the

Churches he was responsible for are features of this brief but affectionate and joyful letter.

There were then no "bishops and deacons" as we understand them today. The elders of the community acted as its guardians or overseers; it is they the Apostle includes in his greeting.

For your reading —
Deliver these lines with a smile, reflecting the happy bond of gratitude between the Apostle and the Church at Philippi. He knew they had continued his work, and were preaching the Gospel for which he had been imprisoned.

Emotions run deep in this greeting. Lean on them in nearly every verse, and make them a sign of our Advent joy.

Luke 3:1-6

General sense —
This is the first appearance of John the Baptist in this third Gospel. The reference to Tiberius Caesar is the most precise dating in all the Gospels, and anchors the beginning of Jesus' ministry to the year 27. "In the wilderness" combines geography and theology, following the Old Testament tradition of a spirituality of the desert, where so many good things had happened to the Israelites.

For your reading —
The portion of this passage which quotes the prophet Isaiah is to be read in a higher tone of voice, as an announcement. No need to shout it, but it was originally written to attract attention.

Accent especially the final verse, 6, which is what applies to us today relevant to the coming of our Savior at Christmas.

THIRD SUNDAY IN ADVENT
Suggested theme for today's readings —
As we wait for the Lord's coming we are reminded of our human frailty.

Zephaniah 3:14-20

General sense —
In the turbulent seventh century before Christ, this fierce nationalist calls down the anger of the Lord on a wayward nation. Israel's enemies have distracted her from her true destiny, but a bright Messianic future glows at the end of her tunnel of trials.

We read today of that future. Jerusalem's most important citizen, her Savior, will come into her midst in a great festival of joy.

For your reading —
This, just a week or so before Christmas, is what Advent is all about: a coming, in joy and gladness.

Read these glowingly optimistic lines with your heart and

voice attuned to their message of encouragement in the midst of our daily trials.

Verse 14 is difficult: you must raise your voice as if you had just traveled across the mountains with great news. Command your hearers' attention as you begin.

The tone remains on this high plane until verse 20. After a pause, lower your voice for this intimate summons to come home, investing your voice with all the joy which that concept has always had for you, as you end with our final victory.

Philippians 4:4-7

General sense —

These few lines sketch for us the happiness we all strive for. Their smiling turns of phrase evoke for us the image of the people we know and admire for their beautiful dispositions.

In the midst of our Advent expectancy, Paul reminds us that to wait for redemption is the authentic Christian experience, full of the peace and joy of God's unceasing care for us.

For your reading —

You have but a few seconds here to call out this happy news. Make the most of your time by the modulation of your voice, somewhat in the following fashion:

Verses 4 and 5 are the good tidings we await next week. Your voice is at its most joyous.

Verse 6 is read in a more informative tone, as Paul sums up our daily dispositions.

Finally, verse 7 is a direct address. Raise your eyes to your hearers, to wish them the gift of peace, in the words our celebrant uses after our Holy Eucharist. Speak these parting words gently and affectionately.

Luke 3:7-18

General sense —

The Evangelist here summarizes the preaching of John the Baptist. A flinty man he is indeed, hard to know. He chops away at our compromises, our shifting allegiances, our broken promises. But he is good for us. He is a scholar of the truth.

For your reading —

Be a bit edgy as you read the first three verses, 7 through 9. John is coming on strongly.

Verses 10 through 14 are the practicalities. Recite them clearly — they are for us as well as for the people who first heard them.

From verse 15 through 17 John finally reveals the One who is greater than he. Read these lines more slowly; they are the heart of the message. They speak of the One you and I are expecting as well, next week.

The last verse, though sounding rather matter-of-fact, is intended to set up the next episode in Luke's Gospel.

FOURTH SUNDAY IN ADVENT
Suggested theme for today's readings —
In our silence before the mystery of Christmas, we know the Prince of Peace.

Micah 5:2-4

General sense —
Micah was the last of the great prophets of the eighth century before Christ. He, like Amos his contemporary, could be called a "non-professional" prophet. Of poor and rustic origins, he had the resentment of the common man against the oppression and injustice which is so often their lot.

Here he foresees the future king coming from Bethlehem, as did Jesse and David.

For your reading —
This passage is so brief that you need but one tone of voice throughout: strong and clear. Otherwise, you will lose your hearers' attention.

This is an important prophecy. End it on a rising tone, as its vision extends, in true Messianic terms, "to the ends of the earth."

Hebrews 10:5-10

General sense —
The superiority of the sacrifice of Jesus over the old animal offerings consists in this: that it was consecrated by obedience. The old ways are not repudiated but bettered. Our Father "prepared a body" for his Son; the Son hallowed it by offering it freely, to carry out his Father's will, for our salvation.

For your reading —
The infinite value of such a total self-offering by Jesus reminds us of whom we welcome at Christmastime. Jesus has already made his presence known in a human way since the beginning of Advent; today, as you read his theological introduction, as it were, your tone is more solemn and serious.

No special problems present themselves here. If you keep your mind on the central idea that the whole point of Jesus' life on earth was to do his Father's will, you will read with understanding, as you lean on verse 10, which sums up the meaning of Christmas.

Luke 1:39-56

General sense —
Our familiar Morning Prayer canticle illuminates this pass-

age on the Visitation. The whole passage is rich in Old Testament allusions, deeply emotional and prophetically convincing. God's fashioning of Mary is a resplendent cameo of humanity's hope fulfilled. Loneliness receives fruitfulness, poverty grows to riches, littleness blossoms into blessedness for all generations.

For your reading —

You will read the first two and a half verses, through 41a. Suddenly Elizabeth, like many other saints throughout the ages, is transported by the nearness of Jesus. Your voice should leap with the babe in her womb, rising as you read through verse 45, to reflect Elizabeth's thrill of recognition.

Mary, after your pause at verse 36, speaks more slowly, quietly, with great deliberateness and humility. It seems well to honor this hymn by reading it in its entirety, as we do in our Prayer Book. Maintain your even pace to its end, as the Virgin pours forth her deepest feelings.

Verse 56 rounds out the passage with the end of the Visitation episode, so that your reading will conclude on a quiet and reflective note.

NOTE – Readings for Christmas service I, II and III, first Sunday after Christmas, second Sunday after Christmas, are the same for all three cycles, A, B and C. See cycle A for general sense and reading hints.

THE EPIPHANY

NOTE – The readings for the Feast of the Epiphany are identical for cycles A, B and C. See cycle A for general sense and reading hints.

FIRST SUNDAY AFTER EPIPHANY

NOTE – For this Sunday, the first and second readings are identical for cycles A, B and C. See cycle A for general sense and reading hints.

Luke 3:15-16, 21-22

General sense —

Luke here presents John the Baptist's Messianic preaching. The people, echoing Isaiah's prophecy of ages before, were "on tiptoe of expectation," says one Bible version; "full of expectation," says another. "A feeling of expectancy had grown among them," says the Jerusalem Bible. John had done his job as precursor by exciting such interest in Jesus.

The references to the Spirit are typical of Luke, whose Gospel is often called "the Gospel of the Spirit."

Fire was a common Old Testament backdrop for divine wonders.

For your reading —
The first two verses set the scene for the last two. Be very definitive in verse 16, when John "answered them all," then deliver his message with great conviction.

In verses 21 and 22 you announce a great theophany, or divine manifestation. Verse 22 is a solemn one, as Luke virtually skips over Jesus' baptism to get to the climax of his account, never even mentioning John's name.

Speak the Father's words with strong emphasis as you conclude.

SECOND SUNDAY AFTER EPIPHANY
Suggested theme for today's readings —
The manifestation of God's presence in our lives appears in our service of others.
Isaiah 62:1-5

General sense —
If the visitation of the Magi only two weeks ago is still fresh in our minds, we might fancy these solemn words of praise coming from those noble travelers as they stand by the crib of the Christ Child.

But that would be centuries in the future, from the prophet's place in history. He rejoices that after the long, frustrating years since the Exile, God's silence at last gives way to this affectionate song of recognition.

For your reading —
Be joyful here: praise and happiness abound. The Messianic prophecies are designed to give hope and encouragement to a tired and worldly people. As such they speak to us, as well as to these Israelites of old.

This rather short passage has no particular climax or emphasis. The names "Forsaken," "Desolate," and "My delight is in her," are all typically Israelite, based, as are most ancient names, on the personification of events.

1 Corinthians 12:1-11

General sense —
Paul devotes three entire chapters of this letter to the gifts of the Spirit — how to recognize them, their value, and their exercise. The gifts are symbolic of the supreme gift of the Lord, foretold by Isaiah in our first reading.

All gifts, the Apostle begins here in this first of the three chapters, come from the one source, the Spirit of God. All conform to our Christian faith, and upon their usefulness to the Church depend their value. In the classic next chapter, 13, he installs charity as better than all the other gifts. The third chapter, 14, deals with practical rules for handling our gifts.

We will continue our readings from these three chapters for the next seven weeks.

For your reading —

Today, with the Apostle, you are a teacher. You address your hearers directly, in verse 1; you compassionately excuse their excesses in verse 2; then you provide an authentic criterion of true faith in verse 3.

Maintain a smooth, clear tone as you continue your explanation, all the way through the rest of the passage. There are no particular climaxes; every verse is important. It is vital that you stress Paul's constantly repeated references to the Spirit, as the principal and only source of our gifts. That is his main message here. Make it yours as well.

John 2:1-11

General sense —

The story of the marriage feast at Cana, continuing today's theme of the gifts of God, tells us much about Jesus. It records his first public miracle; it stands on his respect for his mother; and it establishes his disciples' belief in him.

But how much more deeply does John's prophetic vision consecrate this touching moment! In the Book of Signs, as this Gospel is often called, it is the first. It opens the eyes of the disciples to something greater than the Baptist had foreseen. And through this episode John writes history: the "sign" of Cana is a sign in the fullest possible sense — one of the sacraments (or signs, or gifts) by which our faith links this Jesus of the wedding feast to the Savior we witness daily in the life of the Church, as the perfect gift of God our Father.

For your reading —

This story is so quietly and matter-of-factly told that it is almost impossible to convey the richness of its meaning. In most places, we hope and trust, the homilist or preacher will elucidate that significance for our hearers.

Pause after verse 7, at the miracle itself; and after verse 10, to prepare for John's theologizing of the incident which concludes the narration. And be sure to do your best to dramatize the conversational modulations in verses 3 through 5. They add much to the development of the story.

THIRD SUNDAY AFTER EPIPHANY

Suggested theme for today's readings —
The Word of the Lord touches our hearts and judges our life.
Nehemiah 8:2-10

General sense —

If Ezra's reading of the Law took from morning until midday, let us give thanks for our shorter readings. And let us, as we read verse 7, rejoice that thirteen people do not stand with us to explain the text as we go along.

The point of the passage, it seems clear, is to underscore the great respect the ancients had for the Law, as evidenced by their tearful dismay at its severity.

Verse 10, as you conclude, resounds with praise for the Word, despite the Levites' rather clumsy attempt to quiet the people down and send them away.

For your reading —

It may seem futile to pass along hints on your presentation here, when quite probably most of your preparation time will be consumed in mastering the pronunciation of all the names.

Nevertheless, verses 2 and 3 vividly outline the solemnity of the scene, and should be delivered with a good sense of their importance.

The last phrases of verse 10b will stimulate your hearers' reflection. Lean on them forcefully as you conclude.

1 Corinthians 12:12-27

General sense —

Paul's colorful analogy of our bodies and the community of faith constitutes our reading today. We are incorporated into the Body of Christ, as through our Baptism we share in the life of the risen Lord.

For your reading —

One of the multitude of teaching passages in Pauline literature, the instruction we read today is best delivered in a mode which is enthusiastic and filled with new insights. The author has truly hit upon the perfect figure of our oneness in Christ.

Modulate your voice with great flexibility as you read verses 15 through 21. Imagine all the gestures a speaker would have to make in explaining the analogy.

Your voice then reverts to the calmer, more explanatory mode of the last six verses, as the implications of the comparison are clearly developed.

Accentuate the final verse, 27; speak it slowly as the analogy is ended.

Luke 4:14-21

General sense —

Jesus reads from the Law, as did Ezra centuries before him. So singularly does it pierce the heart, as it was meant to do, that its hearers cry out — Ezra's in dismay, Jesus' in disbelief and anger.

Luke writes here of attitudes which will typify Jesus' public ministry to the end: his rejection by his own people and the appreciation of him by outsiders.

For your reading —

You have for your — and our — reading pleasure today a dramatic incident. Opportunities abound for your heightening the tension.

Pause after verse 17b, as Jesus opens the book, and after verse 19, to let Isaiah's words sink in.

After verse 20, re-create the deathly silence by your pause, as all eyes are fixed on Jesus.

That pause will give verse 21 its proper impact, as you solemnly conclude.

FOURTH SUNDAY AFTER EPIPHANY

Suggested theme for today's readings —
We are responsible for the exercise of the gifts God has given us.

Jeremiah 1:4-10

General sense —

The prophetic mission of Jeremiah, born and raised in Jerusalem, close to the temple, endured for forty years. Intimate with royalty, he was friend and confidant to those in power during Israel's most turbulent times, as the mighty kingdom of Assyria fell to its successor, Babylonia.

Today we read a personal note: the dawning of this man's prophetic vocation. Twenty-six centuries later, our own dialogue with the Lord, complete with human excuses and divine encouragement, forms our calling as disciples in almost the very same words.

For your reading —

Verse 6 is a human rationalization familiar to us all. Be sure to make it a prominent one, because its importance is further accented in the next verse, 7, as the Lord repeats his command to take up the work he has selected for us.

In verse 9, pause a bit before you read it, to reinforce the dramatic gesture the Lord makes to confirm Jeremiah's (and our) calling.

Finish by announcing the specific orders of the Lord clearly and strongly.

1 Corinthians 14:12b-20

General sense —

Genuine prophecy exhorts, warms, comforts, corrects. Of all of the gifts of God, prophecy best fulfills, as Paul puts it, the "building up of the Church."

The Christians at Corinth eagerly desired what they thought was a better gift, that of speaking in tongues. The Apostle responds, in today's passage, in terms which label the gift as dangerous, unwieldy and impractical — what we might call today an "ego trip."

For your reading —
One of Paul's finest gifts is to write as he would speak, so that a passage like this can be read either as a letter of instruction or a brief talk in front of a group of friends.

Your treating it as a talk will be more effective, because it will add to the words the conversational voice modulations which will give it life and energy.

Pause briefly before verse 20, then deliver the little summary there as a word to the wise.

Luke 4:21-32

General sense —
We continue this week the reading of the incident in the synagogue at Nazareth. Jesus has read from the Scriptures; now he sees in the stories of Elijah and Elisha their true meaning: God's Spirit speaks to whom he wills. He does not, as Jesus' hearers were used to thinking, limit himself to speaking to those skilled in theological disputation. Jesus has offended their pride. But when the decisive moment comes, on the brow of the hill, no one will touch him. And he moves on, speaking with authority.

For your reading —
As you deliver this argumentative speech by Jesus, your voice must be the faithful transmitter of its importance. Jesus is saying that God chose two completely unknown, obscure people to help.

Immediately, in verse 28, the realization that God has visited and assisted two Gentiles changes the whole picture. Let your voice reflect their anger here, through verse 30.

The last two verses are now read calmly, the authority of Jesus now asserted and secure, as he goes on his way.

FIFTH SUNDAY AFTER EPIPHANY
Suggested theme for today's readings —
Every one of us receives a call from the Lord to a particular mission only we can accomplish.

Judges 6:11-24a

General sense —
The Book of Judges deals not with lawyers or magistrates, but with leaders who inspired and led this or that tribe against Israel's constant enemies, in the early days not long after Moses.

Gideon was one of these leaders. In today's passage he receives a strong conviction, like Moses and Joshua before him, that God is calling him. Like us, he tries to get out of it, but a miracle of consuming fire changes his mind and brings him peace.

For your reading —
This is an assignment to a mission, and as such deserves to be read in a strong and resolute fashion, to impress on your hearers the authority of the Word of the Lord.

From the start through verse 18, be alert to the conversational modulations involved in the divine call, the unwillingness of Gideon, and the insistence of God that his plan be carried out.

Verses 19 through 21 simply narrate the sacrifice, and are read in a storytelling tone.

After a pause, verse 22 conveys the point of the story. Gideon's recognition of the Lord and his peace of mind strike a strong contrast between the man's excitement and the Lord's gift of peace.

1 Corinthians 15:1-11

General sense —
In response to some at Corinth who thought of the body as a hindrance to the activity of the soul — an ancient Greek and Platonic idea — Paul here declares that in Christ, the bodily resurrection has become the basis of the Christian message of hope.

For your reading —
Verses 3 through 7 are read with assurance, as the Apostle certifies the bodily resurrection of Jesus by listing his many appearances.

As he reflects on his own unworthiness, your voice should descend a bit for verses 8 and 9.

In the last two verses the firm conviction of his own self-worth returns, with verse 10 being the strongest affirmation of the whole passage.

Luke 5:1-11

General sense —
Vocation stories abound, in both Old and New Testaments. It is edifying to hear of a divine call, to know that the Lord's delight is to be with the children of men, as he nominates us for his service.

Today we read of the call of Peter, who was to be the leader of the Apostles. Like any vocation, its human qualities are familiar ones. The surprise of it, in the midst of ordinary human circumstances; the self-doubt and the skepticism; the astonishing sign; and the final acquiescence, all make this the beginning of a very special life.

For your reading —
Suddenly, at verse 5, the human element explodes, in Simon's doubt. After a calmly narrative opening, raise your voice to echo Simon, and keep it high through verses 6 and 7.

Now Simon is humbled, and the tone changes to reflect his

embarrassment and remorse, in verse 8, as well as in verse 9, which explains verse 8.

Jesus' peaceful words, and the disciples' total conviction, round out the episode as you close firmly but quietly.

SIXTH SUNDAY AFTER EPIPHANY (OR PROPER 1 AFTER PENTECOST)

Suggested theme for today's readings —
A good interior life makes for a happy life in the world.

Jeremiah 17:5-10

General sense —

No one knows whether these few nuggets of wisdom came from the pen of Jeremiah or not. This passage, and many others like it, are simply there, with no sound argument for or against their authenticity.

But the sentiments expressed here are a part of Jeremiah's constant devotion to the primacy of our interior life. We still hear these truths today: trust in the Lord; God sees into our hearts; we are rewarded according to our deeds.

For your reading —

This reading is a quiet summary of some age-old verities about our lives. Deliver it calmly, as if you were counseling someone. Reassure your hearers that God is the sole refuge of our sometimes deceitful hearts.

1 Corinthians 15:12-20

General sense —

Last week Paul spoke of the resurrection of the body, which some at Corinth had doubted. Today he avows that to believe anything else is to render the whole Christian apologetic an empty charade, leaving us "still in our sins."

For your reading —

Paul makes one hard-driving thrust at a single point: to deny the resurrection of the dead is fatal to all faith. Let your conviction be as strong as his. Keep your tone of voice clear and insistent throughout.

Verses 16 through 19 are the key to the message, as the Apostle directs the argument toward us. These verses are to be read a bit more slowly.

Feel free to substitute "people" for "men" in verse 19, or simply to omit "men" entirely.

Luke 6:17-26

General sense —

We continue our reading of the Gospel of Luke with his introduction to what we call in Matthew's Gospel the Sermon on the

Mount. Luke's version is less than forty verses long; Matthew's is one hundred and seven verses. Luke has only four Beatitudes to Matthew's nine, and the woes which balance them are exclusive to Luke. Luke represents a more literary style as compared to Matthew's catechetical approach. The cures in verse 9 exemplify the poor being accepted into the Kingdom of heaven.

For your reading —
Begin very expansively, in broad tones, as you set the scene for this event.

The opening in verse 20 is especially solemn. It is indicated, as elsewhere in the Gospels, by Jesus raising his eyes and turning to his disciples.

Pause after each blessing in verses 20b through 22, to give them equal importance. Then lower your voice and speak more gravely as you enumerate the woes.

SEVENTH SUNDAY AFTER EPIPHANY (OR PROPER 2 AFTER PENTECOST)

Suggested theme for today's readings —
The way of the Gospels rarely agrees with the way of the world.

Genesis 45:3-11, 21-28

General sense —
Joseph reveals himself alive and well, to the shame and remorse of the brothers who had mistreated him years before. He theologizes the event as he relates it to God's providence. Then he loads them down with presents, telling them to go home and bring the good news of his success to their father.

For your reading —
Joseph's is a long and complex story. Not everyone agrees that he is as saintly as he appears to be. Today we read just a portion of that story: its climax, in truth, after Joseph had dealt with his brothers incognito, for some time.

The key to the passage is the providential explanation of the events, in verses 4 through 11, where Joseph speaks as if he were God himself, forgiving all and promising great things for the future. Read these words in a higher tone of voice, as befits their importance.

Deliver the next five verses, 21 through 25, in a storytelling mode. When the news nearly kills Jacob in verse 26, your voice rises to reflect the old man's joy, through to the end.

1 Corinthians 15:35-38, 42-50

General sense —
Paul defends the resurrection of the body this week with a description of its manner. He uses the analogy of nature, which

requires passage through death for any life to exist. Then he draws a fine series of contrasts between our earthly and heavenly bodies, to prove his point.

For your reading —
The writer speaks quite emphatically and to the point. Be insistent here, in keeping with that mood.

The chain of contrasts in verses 42 through 50 deserves your most careful attention. Too much reading speed here can make all the comparisons a meaningless blur, unless you draw them carefully, with pauses after each verse. As usual, we end on a strong note in verse 50, which ought to be reflected in your tone of voice.

Luke 6:27-38

General sense —
Jesus expands today on the meaning of the Beatitudes he gave us last week, in his Sermon on the Plain (the Sermon on the Mount, in Matthew). As happens so often in the Gospels, Jesus' ways seem so upside-down to us, what with the injunctions to love our enemies, blessing those who curse us, and expecting nothing in return for our goodness. But that is his way.

For your reading —
How many people turn off their spiritual hearing aids at such subversive talk? We don't know, of course, but the fact remains that here are indeed some hard lessons. Jesus just piles them on, and there is no reason why, as lectors, we shouldn't do the same. Read with great conviction, especially at verse 35, where Jesus begins to reveal the rewards of Christian behavior.

As he does this, in verses 36 through 38, strengthen your tone, so that no one will miss these consolations. The final sentence is one to take home and think about, and so should be read after a slight pause.

EIGHTH SUNDAY AFTER EPIPHANY (OR PROPER 3 AFTER PENTECOST)

Suggested theme for today's readings —
Fidelity and a sincere heart are keys to a good life.
Jeremiah 7:1-7

General sense —
We read today one of the many calls to reform throughout Israelite history. This temple discourse of Jeremiah, probably toward the end of the seventh century before Christ, urges us to join sincerity to our practise of worship, in order to reap our reward of everlasting life.

For your reading —
In verse 2, it may seem well for you to substitute "people" for "men."

The tripling of the expression "the temple of the Lord," in verse 4, illustrates the superstitious and magical significance attached to the temple in the popular mind. Read it as the prophet himself sees it: words that are merely deceptive, uttered in a somewhat sarcastic tone. As is demonstrated, it is our virtue which makes the temple holy.

No other problems seem to be present here. It is just that we all need the reminder that our worship means very little without a good life to back it up.

1 Corinthians 15:50-58

General sense —

This passage concludes the presentation of Paul's thesis on the resurrection of the body, which we have been reading for the past several weeks.

Today he solemnly announces a mystery, a truth of divine revelation: the transformation of our bodies and the final victory, in Jesus Christ, over our death. His use of the first person suggests that like many others of his day, he considered Christ's Second Coming to be imminent.

It is good for us to hear that our steadfast labors are not in vain.

For your reading —

Be sure to raise your voice at verse 51, as the Apostle shares his good news. The excitement of it all happening "in the twinkling of an eye" is an attractive and colorful analogy. Let that novelty be evident through your voice.

Speak in a joyous, upbeat fashion throughout, particularly at Paul's exclamation and his description of the final victory over death.

Verse 58 is a direct turning to your hearers, as you pass on the final encouragement to be faithful. Make as much eye contact as you can with them, as you conclude.

Luke 6:39-49

General sense —

This passage ends Luke's version of Jesus' Great Discourse. Whether it was on the Mount or on the Plain is secondary to its important precepts for living. We read here a series of maxims for living, familiar to us but a revelation to Jesus' hearers, accustomed to the cold prescriptions of the Law.

For your reading —

The conversational modulations Jesus uses in his examples here present a challenge to you as a storyteller.

In verse 46 Jesus' patience with our tepidity and slothfulness wears a bit thin. Let your voice sharpen that edge, as he goes on to present the analogy of the man who built his house with a good foundation, as compared to someone who did not.

LAST SUNDAY AFTER EPIPHANY
Suggested theme for today's readings —
The glory of God is a frightening yet challenging vision. But he always comes in love.

Exodus 34:29-35

General sense —

The Covenant has just been announced to Moses, and now he comes down from Mount Sinai. But he is a new, strange being to his people; he must wear a veil over his face so they will not be frightened by his appearance.

Incidentally, the Hebrew text used a word for the radiance of Moses' face which also translates as "horn." St. Jerome used that meaning for his Latin translation of the Bible (called the Vulgate) and many artists since then, including Michelangelo, have portrayed Moses with horns.

This is a climactic end of our Old Testament readings for the season of Christmas and the Epiphany. The Lord has truly shown himself to us as he did to Moses, so that our hearts shine with radiance as we prepare for the season of Lent next week.

For your reading —

This is an episode filled with wonder. Verse 29 carries some of that wonder. Slow your speed as you describe how Moses' face shone, both in this verse and in verse 30, as well as in verse 35.

As you read these lines, let a hushed sense of wonder be your constant tone.

1 Corinthians 12:27 – 13:13

General sense —

These sublime lines portray the loftiness of the Pauline theology and his repeated insistence on the principal theme of charity. They conclude with a masterful linking of our charity with our maturity and with our final end. The charity urged here bears no relation to either philanthropy or to humanitarianism, as we see in verse 3. It is no less than the most difficult and demanding of all Christian virtues: the effort to be kind to all people at all times.

For your reading —

From verse 27 on, you have worked on the introduction to what follows. Now, as verse 1 comes, pause, then read more slowly, more carefully. These are words of immortality which it is our privilege to read only once every three years, as Cycle C comes around.

Treasure each line. Remember that many of your hearers chose this passage as a wedding-day reading, and have fond memories of its meaning for them.

Pause before verse 11, at which point begins the analogy of our human growth as it points toward our final destiny. Your tone here becomes a bit lower and more personal, as the author searches his memory.

The final verse, 13, should also be read after a pause, because it sums up the entire passage.

Luke 9:28-36

General sense —

Except John, all the Evangelists include the Transfiguration in their Gospels. Each of the three accounts — those of Matthew, Mark and Luke — follows immediately Jesus' description of the cost of discipleship, which confirms the Savior's teaching that glory is preceded by suffering.

Reminiscent of Jesus' baptism and the transfiguration of Moses in our first reading, the Father ratifies his son's mission, in the climactic line of the episode. We must listen to what Christ says of the price of salvation.

For your reading —

Several changes in tone contribute to dramatizing this passage so that it will attract your hearers and provide food for their reflection.

Verses 29, 30 and 31 are read with mounting intensity, as the Transfiguration takes place. Verse 32, in a storytelling mode, brings the disciples into the scene.

Verse 33 should reflect Peter's hasty, excited reaction; then, in verse 34, the disciples' fear.

The final two verses resound with the voice of the Lord and the quickly spoken conclusion of the scene.

ASH WEDNESDAY

NOTE – The readings for Ash Wednesday are identical for all three cycles, A, B and C. See cycle A for general sense and reading hints.

FIRST SUNDAY IN LENT

Suggested theme for today's readings —
Each Lent we offer ourselves to the Lord as the first fruits of his love for us.

Deuteronomy 26:5-11

General sense —

This is the prescribed ritual offering of the annual harvest's first fruits to the Lord. It is a solemn act of faith, performed in and by the community, sharing a common heritage and tradition.

The use of the first person identifies deeply with the ever-present Israelite sense of history: my father was Israel, therefore I am Israel.

For your reading —

This is one of the occasions when the reading may well be extended back to the beginning of the chapter. Starting your reading at verse 1 will give your hearers a fuller sense of what is going on.

Verse 5 through 10 contain the ritual prayer of thanks and offering, and should be read in a higher voice, as if you were intoning a public prayer for all the people.

Lower your voice from verse 10b through to the end, as the prescribed ritual concludes.

Romans 10:8b-13

General sense —

Paul describes here the new way of righteousness. It is not, we learn from verse 5 onward, the observance of the Law only. What matters is the Word of faith in our hearts. "If you confess," in verse 9, is the foundation of the new way. Paul urges the basic Christian apologetic, uttered from the heart, acknowledging not only the act of Jesus but our Father as its source.

For your reading —

We begin our Lent with the avowal of what it takes to be a Christian. To complete the idea here, it might be well to start your reading at verse 5 with Paul's comparison of the old and the new.

Verse 9, as we have said, is the basic statement. Read it more slowly and emphatically, to stress its importance.

The last verse, 13, is also a key one, equally deserving of emphasis.

Luke 4:1-13

General sense —

Each Lent we take up the Gospel of a different Evangelist. This season we hear from Luke. Writing primarily for Gentiles, he is the literary one: worldly, educated, compassionate. He catches mannerisms, psychological reactions, hidden motivations. He is constantly aware of the workings of the Spirit in us.

The temptation episode is typical. Twice in the first verse he refers to the Spirit. In the narrative, he makes it clear that Jesus is fully human, against those who considered flesh to be evil. He re-lives the desert experience of the ancient Israelites in the wilderness, and he portrays Jesus as subduing the hostile powers, becoming a new Adam living in harmony with the world.

For your reading —
   If you raise your voice slightly here at the words of the devil, while speaking the responses of Jesus in a lower tone, you will be successful in creating a dialogue between the two, and thus make for an interesting and absorbing reading.

SECOND SUNDAY IN LENT
Suggested theme for today's readings —
Our fidelity to the Christian life can often involve trouble and sorrow.
Genesis 15:1-12, 17-18

General sense —
   Two principal threads of the Old Testament heritage are woven here, for the first time. Both are promises; both are ultimately fulfilled — one in Abraham's descendants, and the other in the land they will inherit.
   The Covenant, made at Abraham's request, is one of many in the early days. It is sealed with all the awesome signs of divine intervention common to Israelite storytelling, in verse 12.

For your reading —
   This passage is a moving tribute to the faith of the patriarch Abraham. Most of it consists of dialogue, demanding your best effort at reproducing its variations in tone.
   For example, Abraham argues, while the Lord calmly sets out his plan. So profound is the author's sense of salvation history that not even four hundred years of oppression can interrupt that design.
   Verse 5 is to be stressed; it is the divine way of reducing Abraham's fears to nothing.
   Other key verses are 12, setting the scene; 17, where, instead of the human partners in a contract walking between the halves, as was customary, the Lord himself passes through, signifying that the Covenant is his alone to keep.

Philippians 3:17 – 4:1

General sense —
   With smiling affection, Paul begins the closing lines of his letter to the Church at Philippi. These people are his pride and joy, far removed from the worldly. He reminds them of their shared hope and encouragement.

For your reading —
   If you can attract your hearers' attention by speaking these brief lines with a smile in your voice, you will make the most of your few seconds at the lectern.
   Pause before verse 20, to strike the contrast between the ways of some people and the Christian way.

In verse 1, Paul refers not to his Lord but to his brethren as his beloved. Be sure to make that clear by the inflection of your voice as you conclude.

Luke 13:31-35

General sense —
Jesus has made for himself a reputation for honesty which annoys those in power. Friends warn him of reprisals, but his steadfast resolve to go to Jerusalem for what he knows will happen there is stronger than any fear.

What Jerusalem does stir up in the Savior, however, strikes a far deeper chord: his love for the city and for what it represents, along with his sense of frustration that his mission will not be accomplished without his being consumed.

For your reading —
The murmured warnings to get out of town, contrasted with Jesus' determination to ignore them, should be reflected by the changes in your tone of voice.

Pause before verse 34, as a sudden wave of sadness comes over the Master. Put that sadness in your voice until the last half of verse 35, as Jesus utters the prophecy.

THIRD SUNDAY IN LENT

Suggested theme for today's readings —
In the wanderings of our personal Exodus, we bear fruit as good Christians.

Exodus 3:1-15

General sense —
The timeless epic of the Exodus, model for all of our goings out of ourselves for a larger purpose, begins with the lines we read today: the call of Moses to be God's servant.

To accomplish this mighty end, God, in need of a leader, chooses him with marvelous efficiency. The miraculous burning bush, the sanctification of the ground, and his repeated announcements of his identity with the God of Moses' forefathers, all serve to stun this reluctant shepherd into one of history's most amazing conversations.

For your reading —
You are reading today a memorable passage indeed. The action begins in verse 2, with your voice rising somewhat to signal the sudden appearance of the angel.

Verse 4, in which occur the opening words of the Lord, deserves special emphasis, as he calls out Moses' name.

As the conversation goes on through the rest of the reading, you will establish its reality if you use a slightly higher voice and speed for Moses, and a lower voice for the Lord, delivering his words more slowly.

In verse 14, the expression, "I am who am," is basic to God's self-identity, and should be read with great emphasis.

1 Corinthians 10:1-13

General sense —

Paul alludes here to some lessons of history. The tribulations inflicted on the unfaithful Israelites in the wilderness are a warning to Christians. Despite their deliverance (verse 1) and the food and drink the Lord gave them, they fell into idolatry. God is faithful, but our cooperation with that fidelity consists in not desiring evil.

For your reading —

Pause a beat before verse 6, as the writer begins the application of history to the present circumstances.

Pause again before verse 12, the official warning and lesson. Verse 13 changes the tone somewhat, to a more gentle address. It makes for a consoling conclusion to this passage, typifying the compassion and respect the Apostle always shows for his people.

Luke 13:1-9

General sense —

Jesus, continuing his travels, speaks today of the necessity of repentance, and of his faith in his Father's mercy, typified by the fertilizing of the fig tree (Israel) in the hope that it will ultimately bear fruit.

For your reading —

In verse 2, speak strongly and argumentatively, as Jesus does, ending at verse 5 with the sharp point of his two examples. Death can happen to anyone at any time, regardless of whether we have led good, bad or indifferent lives.

Verse 6 begins a parable, to be read in your very best storytelling voice. Be attentive to the usual conversational modulations here.

FOURTH SUNDAY IN LENT

Suggested theme for today's readings —

Our Lenten penances are our Passover to better Christian lives.

Joshua 5:9-12

General sense —

This is the great event itself — the actual Passover. Under the command of Moses' designated successor, Joshua, Canaan is in their possession at last. "The reproach of Egypt" is no more, neither is the manna, for the people may now eat of the fruit of their land.

For your reading —
The significance of this event is such that it needs only these few understated lines to provide us with food for meditation.

Verse 9 sums it up, as you read it with particular emphasis. The humiliation of the Egypt experience is past.

For the rest of this short passage, it will be well to deliver it with a note of triumph in your voice. It is a turning point in history.

2 Corinthians 5:17-21

General sense —
We are encouraged, as we pass mid-Lent, by this appeal to reconciliation through Christ. If we are in Christ, we are a new creation, we are his ambassadors, and we are his righteousness, or, better, goodness — the goodness of God to all we meet.

For your reading —
The notions here expressed are few but powerful. Read this brief passage slowly and meaningfully, especially verse 19, where all our sins are forgiven and we are entrusted with reconciliation based on that forgiveness.

The last two verses, 20 and 21, are also important enough to be given particular emphasis.

In verse 21, God made Jesus to *be* sin. Be sure to accent "be," so that the full meaning of Jesus' life and sufferings will be abundantly clear.

Luke 15:11-32

General sense —
The immortal tale of the two brothers, more popularly known as the prodigal son, has no parallel in revealing the true nature of the reckless abandon with which God loves us. We are all the prodigal; we are all the good but jealous other son. Now Jesus tells this parable that we may be like the good father, whose love reaches out to the prodigal even before he comes home (verses 18-19).

For your reading —
How to deliver these consoling and cleansing lines? Simply tell us our story. Jesus needs no backdrop of time or place: "A man had two sons." Every one of us has two sons. The Older lives too carefully, then resents the good fortune of others. The Younger lives too carelessly, then is filled with remorse.

There are places here that your experience will urge you to emphasize: verse 17, where the prodigal comes to himself; verse

20, where the father cannot wait but runs out, with open arms and no questions asked; and verses 22 through 24, where your voice rises with the deeply-felt joy of reconciliation.

Verses 25 through 30 are read in a rather irritated mode, with the petulancy of the jealous older son.

Finally, in the last two verses, the father's healing words are delivered in your most gentle and reassuring voice; they are truly addressed to our heart.

FIFTH SUNDAY IN LENT
Suggested theme for today's readings —
The Lord is always there to help us through our troubles, because he has made us his own.
Isaiah 43:16-21

General sense —
The Lord is Deliverer and Redeemer. He will make for us a path through our troubles. The glories of the past (verse 18) are not to be lingered over; the whole passage of our human time is one great redemptive act, making every moment a new creation. God has formed us for himself.

For your reading —
We read today a proclamation of the wonders of the new Exodus. Your rendering of its content will be in an upbeat, victorious tone of voice.

No special points of emphasis occur here. If you can sense, through your reading of the rest of chapter 43, the event of Israel's final liberation and its meaning for us as the Lenten season winds down, you will do this passage the justice it deserves.

Philippians 3:8-14

General sense —
"Christ Jesus has made us his own." So the Apostle reflects, twenty years after his conversion, in these illuminating lines. It is more than intellectual knowledge; it is true communion, ever deepening as he strives to "attain the resurrection from the dead," "pressing on toward the goal."

For your reading —
Our goal this Lent has been, in the last analysis, a deeper knowledge of Christ, aptly described here by Paul. Read this excerpt with his own earnestness, not stressing any particular verse but always aware of its depth and of its constant reference to Christ as the goal of all Christians.

In verse 9, drop your voice after "Christ," because what follows it merely explains it.

In verse 11, the same "mental period" holds after "resurrection," to bring out the contrast between resurrection and death.

Luke 20:9-19

General sense —
Jesus has arrived in Jerusalem, to live his last days on earth. His teaching has roused organized religion, from skepticism to open hostility. "God forbid!" they shudder, at the merest hint that his Kingdom might go to others. But the Master stands firm, and only their fear of the people prevents his immediate arrest.

For your reading —
In verse 16, the phrase "God forbid!" deserves special emphasis. After the calm narration of Jesus' parable, the people suddenly realize that he is applying it to their rejection of him.
Pause after verse 16, as Jesus sees into their hearts, then looks them in the eye. Verses 17 and 18 are read with firmness. The result of the people's anger in the final verse does not need special accenting; it is the natural consequence of what Jesus said, and makes a predictable conclusion to the incident.

PALM SUNDAY

NOTE – For Palm Sunday, the first and second readings are identical for cycles A, B and C. See cycle A for general sense and reading hints.

Luke 22:39 – 23:56

General sense —
Luke's account of the Passion, like Matthew's and Mark's, is the longest continuous narrative in the Gospels, and the first to take definite shape in the early Church.
Matthew and John teach us of Jesus, as Son of God; with Mark, we look on in sorrow as the mystery of Jesus is revealed. But Luke invites us to be another Simon of Cyrene, walking with him; another Peter, full of weakness; another Good Thief, in prayerful hope.

For your reading —
In most places nowadays, the Passion is read by several people who re-enact the roles of those who lived it first.
Those of you who share in this privilege also share in the discipline of presenting each role in as lifelike a fashion as possible. Voices must be changed and modulated to suit each moment.
The supreme tribute to your individual and collective skills will be when some of the congregation put down their texts to listen to you.

EASTER SUNDAY – PRINCIPAL SERVICE

NOTE – For Easter Sunday, the first and second readings are identical for cycles A, B and C. See cycle A for general sense and reading hints.

Luke 24:1-10

General sense —

All four Gospels record the doubt and hesitation of the disciples. The Resurrection was, understandably, totally foreign to their experience or expectations, despite Jesus' predictions.

But the women, in Luke's version, were sure. Even though he makes no comment but writes only of what they saw at the tomb, this Evangelist does so with the insights of faith: "they remembered his words" (verse 8). One of the treasures of Luke's Gospel is that he treats women with the same dignity and respect with which he deals with men. Nowhere is this more evident than here, in this moment so critical to posterity.

For your reading —

Everyone knows what you are going to read: the Gospel of the Resurrection. The effort here will be to make it sound new and startling and joyous.

Some ways to accomplish this might be: 1. to stress the drama in verses 4 through 7, reading them in the same tone of excitement the women must have felt; 2. letting your voice fall a bit with disappointment as the reading ends with the unbelief of the Apostles; and 3. reading in an unhurried fashion, pausing after each verse, especially the first three, as the drama of this remarkable day begins to take shape.

SECOND SUNDAY OF EASTER

NOTE – For the second Sunday of Easter, the Gospel reading is identical for cycles A, B and C. See cycle A for general sense and reading hints.

Suggested theme for today's readings —

When we admit the Spirit into our lives, the results are often amazing.

Acts 5:12a, 17-22, 25-29

General sense —

This passage begins with signs and wonders and ends with the second persecution of the Apostles. Jealousy, in verse 17, is the clear motive of the anger of the authorities — and who could blame them? This new movement stood directly opposed to four thousand years of tradition and teaching. And imagine, in verse 29, the Apostles' claiming that they were obeying God rather than men! They add insult to injury. But the work of the Spirit was just beginning.

For your reading —

The strength of this matter-of-factly told incident lies not so much in its words as in its demonstration of the power of the Spirit, who had transformed these fearful men into zealous preachers.

If you read with the conversational modulations dictated by the text, you will transmit through your voice the utter bewilderment of the council at what is happening, and the quiet assurance of the Apostles.

There is a good example of this contrast in verses 28 and 29. Let your voice take on both the irritation of the council and the confidence of the Apostles' answer.

Revelation 1:9-19

General sense —

John, Apostle and Evangelist, in an ecstasy of prayer, is ordered to write what he sees, then to send the book to the seven Churches in Asia.

This remarkable introduction to the Book of Revelation radiates awe and mystery. The frequent use of the word "like" tells us that words are inadequate to convey what John saw. All he knows is that Christ in glory appears, presenting himself as the source and governor of the life of the Church.

For your reading —

If the divine voice is like a trumpet (verse 10), it seems only reasonable that your voice should rise to transmit that quality to your hearers.

Verses 12 through 16 are to be read with the tense excitement of who is telling an amazing story to eager listeners.

In verses 17 through 19 the Lord identifies himself in more detail; his voice softens somewhat, as should yours, as you conclude.

THIRD SUNDAY OF EASTER

Suggested theme for today's readings —
Often, our sudden awareness of the Lord's presence can change our lives.

Acts 9:1-19a

General sense —

With the conversion of the rabid persecutor Saul into the Apostle Paul, the early Church achieves its first major milestone. The Spirit was there; the believers were legion; the Apostles were working wonders. And as the brilliant apologist Stephen gave his life, this man Paul rose up to be the Great Popularizer, who not only preached but wrote and traveled tirelessly to bring Christianity to the Gentile world.

For your reading —

This story is dramatic enough to stand on its own. It needs little embellishment, as long as you let this spectacular episode speak for itself.

A sub-plot arises with verse 19, as Ananias enters the picture. Pause a bit here, to establish the temporary change of scene.

There is an important climax in verse 17, as Saul receives the Holy Spirit. Lean strongly on Ananias' words to Saul, and on the scales falling from his eyes. Conclude with eye contact with your hearers as you read the final verse to close the incident.

Revelation 5:6-14

General sense —

This is the second of five passages from this remarkable book, in which John's vision of the Lamb of God continues from last week's reading. The Lamb sits at the throne of God and among the elders, linked here with God and with the Church. He receives, for his earthly sacrifice, the praise of the entire physical universe "from every tribe and tongue and people and nation." Every creature gives him glory as this mighty cosmic liturgy unfolds.

For your reading —

The voice of wonder must be your constant tone as you speak these stirring lines. Remember that it is a vision, a glimpse of a heavenly liturgy reserved for the eyes of John only.

Verse 9 should be proclaimed in an uplifted voice, as should the chorus of voices is verses 12 and 13.

Keep your tone high, to impress your hearers with the unspeakable grandeur of this scene.

John 21:1-14

General sense —

How many times would we have to read this mysterious Gospel to penetrate its depths? The risen Lord appears out of nowhere, shows his care for his disciples, and shares a meal with them on a quiet morning on the lakefront.

Why had they not already tried their nets on the right side of the boat? Why didn't the others recognize him as John did? Why exactly one hundred and fifty-three fish? Why didn't the net break? Why didn't anyone ask Jesus who he was?

For your reading —

Read this entire passage as an intimate sharing, with your friends, of an unforgettable experience. No need to announce or proclaim here — just let the closeness of this man Jesus with those he loved speak for itself.

Frequent pauses, like after verse 3, after verse 8, after verse 12 and after verse 13, will heighten the interest even more and help make the story line clear.

FOURTH SUNDAY OF EASTER

Suggested theme for today's readings —

The Church's celebration of our great feasts is intended to be a foretaste of heaven.

Acts 13:15-16, 26-33

General sense —

The visit of Paul and Barnabas to Antioch gives the Apostle his first opportunity, on this initial missionary trip, to speak to a Jewish audience. Paul wastes no time in connecting Jesus with the God of the "sons of the family of Abraham," and with the fulfillment of the Good News prophesied of old.

For your reading —

Verse 16 sets the stage for Paul's remarks. Read it with a sense of anticipation, to create a bit of suspense for your hearers (remember that you are fundamentally a storyteller). Accentuate the comma after "stood up," by taking a quick breath. Then pause again after "hand," so that you can say, without stopping, the next two words, "said Brethren." The word "brethren" is said on a rising pitch, as Paul did, to obtain their attention.

Deliver these last eight verses in the mode of a speech, leaning especially on the whole point of the address in verses 30 and 31. These are Jesus' credentials.

The last sentence is a direct quote, as Paul indicates, and deserves a particular accent because of its importance.

Revelation 7:9-17

General sense —

The scene we read about today pictures the Church in heaven glorifying God, after its victory over persecution. The liturgy is celebrated together by all, as a whole world community. The numberless multitude reflects — and fulfills — the age-old promise given to Abraham, that his descendants would be as countless as the stars of heaven.

For your reading —

In order to catch for your hearers the utter grandeur of this vision, your voice must ring out strongly and clearly throughout.

The only place to soften somewhat would be at the final verse, as you close with the consoling words of the Lamb about the peace of our final destiny.

John 10:22-30

General sense —

The feast called today in the Jewish community by the title Hanukkah sets the scene for Jesus' last discourse in Jerusalem. With it the Evangelist concludes his section on Jesus as the Light. The writer has used several visits to the city on the great

Jewish feasts, to show their deeper significance with the coming of the Messiah.

For your reading —
    With your usual careful attention to the voice changes necessary in reading conversation, read this declaration of Jesus' stand on the issue of his Messiahship in as lifelike a manner as you can.
    In verses 25 and 26 there is an edge in Jesus' voice, born of his frustration that no one has understood him. Then he softens from verse 27 on, as he explains the security his followers will enjoy because of his Father's care.

FIFTH SUNDAY OF EASTER

Suggested theme for today's readings —
The practise of Christian charity is the finest praise of the Lord.

Acts 13:44-52

General sense —
    Luke deals here with the enthusiasm of the people for the Christian preaching, as against the jealousy of organized religion. Then, a milestone in history: the turning to the Gentiles, in verse 46. A whole new world is to receive the "light for the Gentiles," "to the uttermost parts of the earth."

For your reading —
    We know that no "whole city" could fit into one synagogue. Luke is trying not to count people but to make a point. But accent this expression when you read it, to show how deeply the new way has caught the people's fancy.
    Verses 46b and 47 are the climax of this passage. As you introduce it in 46a, do not accent "saying." The important words here are "boldly" and "necessary." Slide over "saying" to get quickly from "boldly" to "necessary."
    As you announce the big news, the turning away from the Jews, slow your pace, to stress its primary importance. Do this through verse 47.
    The rest of the passage, the result of these words on both Gentile and Jew, are read in a storytelling mode, so that the final verse, 52, makes an upbeat, joyful conclusion.

Revelation 19:1, 4-9

General sense —
    As we continue our reading of John's vision in Revelation during these post-Easter Sundays, we become aware that much of this book uses symbolic language which is obscure and difficult to understand. Today's passage comes after a rather somber account of the fall of the great Babylonian Empire in the preceding

chapter. Now the heavens resound, as we read today, with the praise of the Lord.

For your reading —
This is not a simple passage to read, because you must keep your voice somewhat elevated with the fervent cries of this huge multitude.

The best way to accomplish this might be to pause frequently, so that you avoid becoming monotonously shrill, pausing especially after verses 2, 4, 5 and 8.

John 13:31-35

General sense —
Jesus' command to charity, almost word for word with John's letters so many years later, is his solemn legacy. Delivered on the eve of his Passion, he joins it with his sufferings and with the disciples' future missions as the glorification of God.

For your reading —
You have only a few seconds to hand on to your hearers these memorable lines. Read them, therefore, with great care and deliberateness. Force yourself to pause after each verse, to heighten their impact.

Verse 35, as you conclude, is the most vital of all. Give it the meaning it deserves by your special treatment of it.

SIXTH SUNDAY OF EASTER
Suggested theme for today's readings —
Jesus is the Light of the world.
Acts 14:8-18

General sense —
Paul and Barnabas cure a lame man and are immediately called gods, even with gods' names, in a language they do not understand. When it dawns on them what is going on, they protest, in great dismay, that they are men, trying to call attention to the Good News of the Gospel.

For your reading —
In verse 10, raise your voice as Paul commands the crippled man to stand.

Verse 15a is the apostles' cry of distress; this should also be reflected in your voice.

These two climactic verses set the tone for the understanding of the passage.

Revelation 21:22 – 22:5

General sense —
The dreamlike vision which closes this remarkable book

climaxes, in the lines we read today, at the center of the heavenly Jerusalem: the Lamb who is its Light. The entire place shines with the Light who knows no sin, and all may gaze on the divine face, a privilege denied in this world.

For your reading —
These lines are a tonic for a jaded world. We see all kinds of "special effects" at the movies. But our spirits, looking through the eyes of faith, cannot help but be captured by this vision of the wonders God has prepared for those who are faithful.

Other than a pause after the last verse of chapter 21, to indicate a change in the scene, there are no particular points to emphasize here. Let the joy of our final destiny shine through your voice as you sketch this rapturous picture.

John 14:23-29

General sense —
Jesus continues his discourse at the Last Supper with a word about fidelity to his commandments, the giving of his peace, and an encouragement to faith.

For your reading —
The words uttered here are spoken to the heart. They are givers of life, so that your delivering them in clear and even tones throughout will be more effective in touching your hearers with their meaning.

As is customary, the importance of the pause in bringing out thoughts, as well as allowing time for them to sink in, cannot be overemphasized. This principle applies particularly here, especially after verse 26, when Jesus is about to offer his gift of peace.

ASCENSION DAY

For Ascension day, the readings and Gospel are identical in cycles A, B and C. See cycle A for general sense and reading hints.

SEVENTH SUNDAY OF EASTER

Suggested theme for today's readings —
The presence of Jesus is the driving force behind the Church's mission to the world.

Acts 16:16-34

General sense —
At Philippi Paul, working with Silas, heals a slave girl. They are arrested not for soliciting converts but for disturbing the peace. The authorities have no idea of Christianity, but think Judaism is being preached. Romans were not allowed to embrace the Jewish faith (verse 21). Paul and Silas are jailed, then somehow delivered. A later-added bit of folklore suggests a dramatic possibility, in verses 25-34.

For your reading —
Both the woman's cry in verse 17 and the command of Paul in verse 18 are to be read in the strong and clear fashion demanded by the text.

Verse 25 begins the tale of the miraculous delivery. Whether it is true or not matters very little. Give it the excitement it must have had for the ancient people who read it first.

Revelation 22:12-14, 16, 17, 20

General sense —
These are the closing lines of John's vision or dream of the heavenly kingdom. In this epilogue Jesus identifies himself, then twice proclaims his return to consummate the world's history.

For your reading —
As the Easter season ends, we prepare to welcome the Spirit next week at Pentecost. We read today the ultimate prophecy, from the last page in the Bible: Jesus will return.

The notion of coming should be your principal emphasis here. It occurs four times, and needs to be stressed to make it clear to your hearers that this is the central theme of the book.

Conclude with a strong "Come, Lord Jesus!"

John 17:20-26

General sense —
Jesus concludes his revealing of himself and of his innermost desires, just before he moves out of the Upper Room to begin his journey to Calvary. His prayer now extends to the Church of all time, beseeching his Father for the unity in love so necessary to verify his mission. His departure for his glorification becomes the first act of his everlasting presence within the Church.

For your reading —
Read these final words of Holy Thursday night with the gentleness and love they express so deeply.

There is no climax; there are no particular emphases, only the outpouring of an affectionate heart for his own — the summary of the meaning of a life for others.

Your reading speed should be even, never rushed, to communicate more clearly the intimacy of these sublime words.

PENTECOST SUNDAY

The Readings and Gospel for Pentecost Sunday are identical for cycles A, B and C. See cycle A for general sense and reading hints.

TRINITY SUNDAY

Suggested theme for today's readings —
The mystery of the Lord of heaven and earth sanctifies our Christian life.

Isaiah 6:1-8

General sense —

Isaiah is the prophet of "The Holy One of Israel." The sanctity of the awesome, unspeakable Lord dominates his theology. With his profound sense of this presence goes an intense awareness of our own sinfulness and that of every human creature. Our sin, cosmic in scale, affecting the whole universe, is never without forgiveness.

The sublime lines we read today in worship of the Trinity of God are the foundation of Isaiah's life and message.

For your reading —

Verse 3b is a hallowed one for us; we sing it at every Eucharist. Deliver it with awe in your voice — slowly, devoutly, to communicate to your hearers the mystery we adore.

Isaiah's plea in verse 5 is read in exactly that mode: a plaintive, earnest disclaimer of his worthiness.

In verse 8 the Lord asks a question to which there is only one answer. Read it in something of a mocking way, to set up for the devoutly enthusiastic response which concludes your reading.

Revelation 4:1-11

General sense —

The triple invocation of the Holy One in verse 8 continues the trinitarian theme from our first reading today. This is John's first vision of the future, where he glimpses the court of heaven, not by entering it but through one open door. The entire scene is cloaked in the absolute "otherness" of the Lord, in the day-and-night constancy of his rule of the universe.

For your reading —

These lofty, symbol-laden concepts are so far beyond our understanding that your reading of them must take on some of the awe John must have felt at their revelation.

Lean on the "holy, holy, holy" in verse 8, and on the praises of the Lord in verse 11. Those are the two high points of the passage, and the ones your hearers can most readily identify with.

John 16:12-15

General sense —

Even now, as Jesus lays down his earthly life and concludes his mission with us, there is much left unsaid. The ultimate revelation will be through the Spirit, to whom, under the Father,

Jesus now relinquishes his role as teacher and guide.

For your reading —
The Lord begins to turn his face from earthly things in these deeply felt words of promise to all of us.

In the few seconds you are granted at the lectern, you are to convey to your hearers the absolute serenity and assurance contained in these lines. Read them in a reflective, leisurely fashion, pausing after each verse for maximum effect.

NOTE – For Propers 1, 2 and 3 after Pentecost, please refer to the readings for the 6th, 7th, and 8th Sundays after Epiphany, respectively. The readings overlap because of the variations each year in the date of Easter.

PROPER 4
Suggested theme for today's readings —
The temple in which we worship is one of the best places to begin the cure of our ills.
1 Kings 8:22-23, 27-30, 41-43

General sense —
King Solomon, a basically good man who ultimately began to believe in his own glory, here utters his prayer at the dedication of the new temple he has built. It is a humble supplication, acknowledging the reality of the presence of God in heaven, rather than confined to the temple.

For your reading —
As the prayer begins in verse 23, raise your voice somewhat. Keep it on that higher plane throughout, remembering that King Solomon is speaking before a great assembly, not privately.

There are no particular points of emphasis here; the notion is to remind ourselves of the presence of God in our place of worship and of his rule over all the earth.

Galatians 1:1-10

General sense —
On the grounds that he was not personally commissioned by Christ, Paul's authority as an Apostle is challenged. The "Judaizers," who advocated the keeping of some Jewish practises, such as circumcision, for Christian converts, accused Paul of watering down the Gospel to accomodate the Gentiles.

This letter warns his people of these errors, stressing the new freedom granted in Christ. He comes quickly to the point.

For your reading —
Beginning with verse 6, there are strong words here. Paul is very sure of himself. Make your voice just as firm and decisive,

especially in verse 8, and speak with equal vigor as Paul repeats his scorn in verse 9.

Verse 10 should be read after a pause, as the Apostle defends his reason for insisting on his version of the Gospel.

Luke 7:1-10

General sense —

Jesus, though physically absent, here cures a servant, simply by his words. In Matthew's Gospel the centurion comes to Jesus himself; here, he sends two delegations, one of the elders and one consisting of his friends. Luke's typical sensitivity makes the sick slave "very dear" to the centurion, and in critical condition. And what a wonderful touch of Jesus' humanity that he marvels at the man's faith!

For your reading —

Be the storyteller here. Draw your hearers as you set the scene in verse 2. In verse 4 the elders of the Jews testify to this Gentile, the centurion, who even built their synagogue for them. Borrow their pleading enthusiasm.

In verse 6, see how this good man does not want Jesus to become legally unclean by entering the house of a non-Jew. His respect, then his act of faith in Jesus' word, based on his own experience as one in authority, reinforces his earnest desire to help his servant.

Pause after verse 8, to let your hearers imagine Jesus simply looking at the centurion's friends in wonder. Then begin verse 9.

Conclude with the happy ending to this incident in verse 10, as the friends return to the centurion's house believing, even as he did, that the slave would be well.

PROPER 5

Suggested theme for today's readings —
Jesus has overcome death.

1 Kings 17:17-24

General sense —

This is one of many holy-man stories, called "fioretti," or "little flowers," told to enhance a prophet's reputation and the authority of his words, as appears here in verse 24.

The widow's view of her son's untimely death as a punishment for her sins by the God whom Elijah represents in her house, is a common Old Testament mentality.

For your reading —

Raise your voice in verse 18, to echo the woman's distress, and again in verse 21 as Elijah prays for a cure.

Verse 24, as you conclude, should sound, by the tone of your voice, like a happy recognition by the widow of a true man of God.

Galatians 1:11-24

General sense —
This is the second of five readings from the letter of Paul to the Churches in Galatia.

Paul now sets down a sort of personal resume, to reassure the Galatians of his unusual background and present efforts.

For your reading —
Paul is insistent here, anxious to prove his case. Be insistent with him, through verse 14, then pause for a moment.

At verse 15 the tone becomes gentler, as Paul fondly recalls his apostolic origin.

The tone now reverts, at verse 17, to storytelling, through to the end of the passage, with a slight bragging note in verse 24.

Luke 7:11-17

General sense —
Almost all the Sunday Gospels this year are from Luke. We continue today with another of the miracles of the Lord, colored indelibly with the Lucan style. Last week Jesus marveled at a man's faith. Today he has compassion on someone bereaved. Luke notes, typically, that the dead youth was his mother's only son, and also demonstrates Jesus' unfailing courtesy to women.

For your reading —
This is quite a spectacle. A large crowd, relatives and mourners, follows the widow. Another sizable group approaches in the opposite direction, walking with Jesus. How dramatic the silence must have been, as everything stops, and Jesus murmurs just three words: "Do not weep."

Your storytelling ability is now your best ally. Draw this remarkable picture, accenting the words of the Lord.

Verse 16 is the official approval of a man of God, a tradition from Old Testament times. Lean on it, then verify it in verse 17 with the spread of the Good News.

PROPER 6

Suggested theme for today's readings —
Jesus' accepting and forgiving welcome to all people is our model in all our relationships.

2 Samuel 11:26 – 12:10, 13-15

General sense —
Almost parenthetically, we read today the key to our understanding of David's adultery with Uriah's wife: "But the things that David had done displeased the Lord." His wise counselor, Nathan, warns him of trouble, beginning with the child's death, but seasons it with God's forgiveness.

For your reading —

This is a simple narrative, broken only by a pause before and after verse 13, David's ready acknowledgment of his guilt. With that admission comes the divine absolution, almost in the same breath.

Nathan must then deliver the curse: the death of the illegitimate child. Conclude your reading on this note, which typifies the Old Testament mentality of connecting our troubles with our sins.

Galatians 2:11-21

General sense —

"The freedom we have in Christ Jesus," not only from circumcision but also from Jewish dietary laws, makes Paul see in Peter's actions an inconsistency and compromise which is against the spirit of the Gospel. So he rebukes Peter publicly, insisting that it is only by faith in Jesus that we are justified, or reckoned righteous.

In fact, he adds, the efficacy of Christ's surrender reshapes our life, by the influence of his living within us, so that our real life comes from this redemptive sacrifice. In faith, it is no longer we who live, but Christ who lives within us, as our principle of activity.

For your reading —

Up to and including verse 14, read Paul's account of his rebuke of Peter as a story, to set the background for the profound theological reflection which begins in verse 15.

At verse 15, slow your pace, and pause after each verse. If you attempt to rush through these last seven verses, your reading will be a jumble of unintelligible ideas, pouring out one on top of another, as Paul's thoughts so often do.

Read carefully, then, so that none of the richness of this reflection will be lost on your hearers. Verse 20 is one of Paul's classic and oft-quoted phrases, and is a good verse to emphasize.

Luke 7:36-50

General sense —

Luke seems to be of an impartial nature. Not only does he frequently present Jesus as a dinner guest (six times), but on three of these occasions his host is a Pharisee. Since this sect was a notoriously hostile one, accepting a dinner invitation meant a rather courageous act on Jesus' part.

Jesus not only accepts the sinful woman, but also reads Simon's thoughts, then negates the hosts's sarcastic answer to his parable with an exquisite instruction in Oriental etiquette.

We note in verse 47 that the woman loves because her sins

are forgiven — not, as is usually assumed, the other way around, since Jesus immediately adds that he who is forgiven little loves little.

For your reading —

This straightforward narrative is an interesting study of Jesus' relations with friends and strangers. He treats both the penitent woman and his worldly host with equal respect for their dignity. Yet he accepts the one and gently rebukes the other.

Observe, as you read, the conversational interplay in this situation, and be aware of all the voice changes which will make the incident come to life.

Your preparation for mastering all the nuances here should be painstakingly longer than usual. This is in no way an easy passage to deliver.

PROPER 7

Suggested theme for today's readings —

Every person deserves our respect as one redeemed by the sacrifice of Jesus.

Zechariah 12:8-10 – 13:1

General sense —

Like other prophets writing in the early years after the Babylonian exile, Zechariah insisted that the rebuilding of the temple was of the highest priority.

Today's reading looks to King David, a happy memory of centuries before, as a model of strength and vigor in Israel's future. Verse 10 is quoted in John's Gospel at the crucifixion of Jesus.

For your reading —

This prophecy bespeaks the undying hope Israel always had in their bright Messianic future. Read it in a calm way, treating the sudden switch to mourning in verse 10 as part of the story. The reference, most think, evokes the people's remorse at their poor treatment of the Lord, whose presence has loyally remained in their midst through all their trials and triumphs.

Galatians 3:23-29

General sense —

We continue our reading from the letter of Paul to the Churches in Galatia. This is the fourth of six assigned passages, all dealing with our freedom under the new law of Christ.

Today's three readings — from Zechariah, from here and from the Gospel, all stress the universality of redemption, with Paul's version of it expressed here in verses 28 and 29.

For your reading —

These lines ought to be read with frequent pauses, because

it is important that your hearers understand thoroughly the centrality of this message.

Paul is saying that the old rules keep us well enough, but only to prepare us until we have matured into faith in Jesus Christ. Verses 27 through 29 explain the meaning of this, and are the climax of the passage. Your reading, then, should conclude in a stronger voice, as you speak of the privilege we have been granted.

Luke 9:18-24

General sense —

Jesus, his Messiahship acknowledged by Peter, wants no acclaim from a crowd which misunderstands him. He repeats, in verse 22, the true nature of his destiny, a far cry from what they expected. On top of that, he presents the scandalous cost of discipleship, appealing to all people to follow him.

For your reading —

Be aware, in verse 18, of Jesus' very human temptation to wonder how he is doing, as we sense a note of loneliness, even of frustration, here. What Jesus seems to want is feedback from his own people. Read Peter's answer in an accented voice.

The tenor of the story changes abruptly at verse 21, as Jesus quickly disavows any false notions about himself. From this point on, verses 21 through 24, read Jesus' words in a somewhat higher, more emphatic tone of voice, as he reaches out to all people for all time with the essence of his doctrine.

PROPER 8

Suggested theme for today's readings —
Our discipleship is expressed in our joy at serving the Lord in others.

1 Kings 19:15-16, 19-21

General sense —

Elijah throws his mantle over Elisha, signifying the latter's call to serve the Lord. The well-to-do Elisha (twelve yoke of oxen!) gets so thrilled that he kills two oxen, then sets their wooden yoke on fire to roast them for his crew. With the yoke gone and the crew fed, he goes to serve the Lord unencumbered.

Such is the message today's readings bring to us: serve the Lord with gladness and alacrity.

For your reading —

The episode recounted today is told in the midst of a history of kings, to enhance the authority of the holy man Elijah.

The interest you create in passing on this vocation story to your hearers will come from two sources: your storytelling skill at reproducing the conversational exchanges, and your aptitude at awakening in the congregation a sense that they as well have been called to serve the Lord, each in his or her own way.

Galatians 5:1, 13-25

General sense —

The Apostle today passes on an instruction on the correct use of Christian freedom. If he does away with the Law, the Christian still may not abandon himself to earthly, material, Godless conduct.

Paul sets down in specific detail the comparison between spirit and flesh, and concludes with the Christian injunction to live together in charity.

For your reading —

There are strong words here; Paul is insistent, speaking from the heart. You will do well to deliver these lines in a vigorous, almost a speech-making mode. There is no way to say "flesh," and "bite," and "devour" gently, not to mention the list of the works of the flesh.

In verses 25 and 26, conclude, with the writer, on a gentler note, as he brings down to earth the ultimate application of life in the Spirit: care for one another.

Luke 9:51-62

General sense —

The rejection of Jesus sets him ever more firmly on the road to Jerusalem. He "sets his face" straight ahead; there will be no retaliation (verse 55).

Our call to serve unsparingly becomes Jesus' pre-occupation now, to the end of the reading, as he sets down the conditions for discipleship.

If you read the words of others in a slightly higher voice, and those of Jesus in a somewhat lower tone, you will communicate well the two-party conversations here. They serve to set Jesus' determination against the half-formed desires of those who would serve the Gospel at their own convenience.

PROPER 9

Suggested theme for today's readings —
Our dignity as Christians must always be seasoned with modesty and humility.

Isaiah 66:10-16

General sense —

The Book of Isaiah closes with this joyful hymn to the future of Jerusalem, blessed with the universal fullness of peace, contentment and love, the result of the coming of the Messiah.

All the people of God will be nourished by his presence. God himself, in a beautiful change of image in verse 13, will be the ultimate Comforter.

The hymn ends with the crackle of fire and the boom of thunder, common symbols of divine victory. The ancients always thought of any victory in terms of a killing judgment on defeated enemies.

For your reading —

On the warm summer Sunday on which these lines are read, you must make a special effort to give them the elevated tone they deserve. The pace is swift and unrelenting. The triumph of the Lord is described here in terms of fierce exultation, for the purpose of inspiring the sagging faith of the Israelites, who never saw the wonders performed for their ancestors centuries before.

At verse 15, it would be well to assume a tone of some sternness. Conclude your reading on this note of solid assurance, which suits so well the vengeful mind typical of the people of that time.

Galatians 6:14-18

General sense —

The last in our series of six readings from this letter is its conclusion, in which Paul takes pen in hand himself, having finished his dictation to a scribe, as was his custom.

After the severe words of the earlier chapters of this epistle, the final line speaks of reconciliation, as he addresses the people as "brethren."

For your reading —

You have but a few seconds to deliver this vital summary of what Paul's faith means to him. Make every phrase count, by your frequent attention to pauses, and by reading the three final verses with particular feeling and emphasis.

Luke 10:1-12, 16-20

General sense —

The mission band grows now to seventy, from the original twelve. Jesus sends them on ahead to prepare for his coming, giving them detailed instructions, even as to what to say. When they return joyfully he closes with a warning not to overrate external wonders but to thank God for their calling.

For your reading —

Beginning with verse 2, communicate to your hearers, by reading with great care, the insistence of Jesus that his directions be followed.

Verse 16 is a solemn one, as the disciples become his official ambassadors, even sharing in his authority.

Pause after verse 16 now, to indicate a time lapse, and to change the mood of Jesus from friendly direction to a serious warning against pride. Conclude your reading on this strong note.

PROPER 10

Suggested theme for today's readings —
Our discipleship originates in the interior voice of the Lord and culminates in our care for other people.

Deuteronomy 30:9-14

General sense —

God's message here constitutes a whole new kind of covenant. Covenants abound in the history of the Israelites, but this one is to be written on the heart. It penetrates to the interior of man, making each of us free and therefore responsible for our acts and our decisions. Later, philosophers of our modern age would name this condition existentialism.

Verses 11 through 14 represent a powerful summary of what existentialism means in our spiritual life.

For your reading —

In the first verse of this reading, the Lord sets down the happy future he has planned for his people, despite their historic infidelity to his covenants. Read these lines in a bright, happy tone.

Then comes the price, in verse 10: "If you obey . . . if you keep . . . if you turn," which you should read in a somewhat more serious voice.

The reason that there are no more excuses for not keeping the Lord's commandments now appears. The law is no longer a matter of rules as much as of individual conscience.

Verses 11 through 14 are common knowledge among us today. But they represented a completely new concept of morality when they were written. Deliver these lines, especially verse 14, as if they were still just as new, just as unheard of, as you conclude.

Colossians 1:1-14

General sense —

In this first of four Sunday readings from this letter, Paul greets the Church at Colossae in Asia Minor, an important textile center about a hundred miles east of Ephesus. He thanks God for their faith, pledges them his constant prayers, and reminds them of the author of their redemption and happiness.

For your reading —

The tone here rings with affection and good will, which

should be made evident through your voice and your manner of address.

Pause after verse 2, as the salutation ends and the body of the letter begins. From there until you conclude, maintain a light-hearted tone, as of one who cannot be there in person — Paul was not the community's founder — but is bonded in Christ to all who share his Gospel.

Luke 10:25-37

General sense —

As if to exemplify the covenant of the Lord in today's first reading — "the word is in your heart, so you can do it" — the Samaritan, without knowing the Law or even consulting it, knows what to do. Notice, in verse 37 of this classic parable, that the lawyer, even though the answer is obvious, cannot bring himself to mention the name "Samaritan."

For your reading —

As always, and particularly here, you are a storyteller.

This passage is neither speech nor proclamation, neither prayer nor pronouncement. Jesus simply makes up a story about the demands of discipleship.

There are demands being made of you as well. Conversational modulations include the rather haughty question of the lawyer, who expected a long, complicated answer; the self-righteous opinion in verse 27; and the line he thinks clinches his position, in verse 29.

Verse 30 begins Jesus' typically Oriental teaching methodology: the tactful, indirect mode of the parable. This is your prime storytelling opportunity. Render the verses as if you were seated in a small group of eager listeners. Everyone loves a story.

Pause at verse 36, as Jesus concludes, then asks the lawyer's opinion. Verse 37b, Jesus' arrow-sharp application, ends your reading as it points to all of us.

PROPER 11

Suggested theme for today's readings —
The life of faith brings with it many experiences and attitudes not understood by the world.

Genesis 18:1-10a

General sense —

Traditional Oriental hospitality invests this beautiful and very human scene with a special light. Our assigned passage ends just before the skeptical Sara cannot help but chuckle at the idea of conceiving a child, at her age. (Optionally, the reading may continue through verse 14.) Interestingly, the child delivered to her as promised by the Lord is called Isaac, which in Hebrew expresses a word for laughter. And Isaac was father to

Jacob, whose twelve sons founded the twelve tribes of Israel.

For your reading —

Simply told, the visit of the Lord to the patriarch and his wife seems rather unpretentious, until we realize how integral a part of our salvation history is its significance.

Read it, therefore, straightforwardly, with no particular emphasis, letting the details of the incident speak for themselves, while being attentive to the tone changes pertinent to the conversations.

Colossians 1:21-29

General sense —

The second of our four readings from the letter to the Colossians deals with Jesus Christ's act of reconciliation as exercised in the preaching of the Gospel. Beginning with verse 24, Paul explains his own part in this divine plan.

For your reading —

This passage is good news. It could be lines from a sermon preached today. Key words cry out for emphasis here. One is "reconciled" in verse 22. The triad of "holy, blameless and irreproachable" completes the same verse. Read these words one by one, accenting the commas between them. Lean on verse 26, another key concept.

Pause after verse 27, which ends Paul's theological justification and begins, in verse 28, the conclusion of the idea in this passage.

Luke 10:38-42

General sense —

Last week, the parable of the Good Samaritan exemplified a practical, effective way to live the Gospel. Today, looking into the home of Martha and Mary, the emphasis is on the primacy of faith.

Although variations in the translation of verse 42 are legion, the sense remains: Jesus is speaking about the importance of the underpinning of faith, no matter how many tasks demand our time and energy.

For your reading —

This incident goes by quickly, and the action strikes a deep chord of familiarity in us. Be careful not to trivialize it by a rapid, casual reading, as Jesus takes this little break from his hot and dusty travels to enjoy the quiet intimacy of a visit with some dear friends.

Deliver these brief lines with a feeling for the peace of the shady courtyard where the incident may have happened. Jesus speaks quietly and gently, leaving the two sisters, as well as ourselves, to ponder the mystery of the tension which always pulls between action and contemplation.

PROPER 12
Suggested theme for today's readings —
Our faith establishes our identity with Jesus Christ.
Genesis 18:20-23

General sense —

How striking to see primitive, almost prehistoric, man, as he grapples with questions no one can answer even today: who is responsible for evil? What norm does God use in the exercise of his mercy?

Abraham plea-bargains down to as few as ten good people in a wicked city. Paul, in the second reading, can say only, "because you believed." And Jesus himself, in today's Gospel, simply insists: ask, and ask again, even though our generosity, good as it is, is small potatoes compared to his Father's.

For your reading —

This is more than a story; it is a drama. The primitive theology of this ancient record pictures God as having to "come down" to inspect the city, then become involved in an Oriental-style haggle over the price of his mercy.

Your storytelling skills are all on display here as your voice rises and falls with the rapid-fire, courtroom-style exchange between the zealous defense counsel and the divine prosecutor.

Make the most of this exciting interplay, then pause after verse 32 to signify the end of the conversation. Then read the final verse, the anticlimax, in a quiet tone as you conclude.

Colossians 2:6-15

General sense —

Our faith establishes our identity with Jesus Christ, through whom we receive life from God. Not to ten good people, as we learned in our first reading, but to each single individual. God has extended his mercy, in making us alive, forgiving our sins, cancelling the law's bonds in us, and disarming Satan's principalities and powers for our protection and salvation.

For your reading —

Verse 6 strikes the keynote here of a reading strong in faith, positive in reassurance, always victorious in the power of Christ. Read it with the vigor with which Paul defends his people from the false teachings of the day.

Verse 13b and 14 deserve special emphasis: God has made us alive, forgiven all our sins and cancelled our debts to him.

Luke 11:1-13

General sense —

Luke's version of the Our Father is shorter than Matthew's, because they arose from different liturgical traditions. The doxology, "for thine is the Kingdom," etc., used in Protestant churches, is not found in most manuscripts.

Jesus, returning to the importance of faith as brought out in today's readings, compares his Father to a lazy man who will answer us only as we persist in faith-filled prayer.

For your reading —

To respect the importance of the Lord's Prayer, pause between the petitions in verse 2, 3 and 4.

When you have finished reading Jesus' parable, in verse 8, with due attention to the changes in tone which make good conversation, pause before verse 9. Here, Jesus turns directly to his hearers, to insist that they ask boldly for help.

Verse 13 begins another direct appeal to Jesus' audience. It is his clinching argument, preceded, to set it off, by a pause after verse 12, and a strongly delivered conclusion to your reading.

PROPER 13

Suggested theme for today's readings —
The true Christian can never be a pessimist.

Ecclesiastes 1:12-14 — 2:18-23

General sense —

The author of this interesting book tests all of life's pleasures and finds them lacking. He rails against a God limited by human insight and experience, e.g., justice leads to life, wickedness to death. Instead, unwilling to limit the divine prerogatives, he sees God's unaccountable ways, full of sovereignty and independence, always with the power, in absolute freedom, to give.

For your reading —

Every line of this passage breathes the sighs and murmurs of our own experience. No one should be unmoved by its familiarity. Read it as if you were confiding in a kind and patient counselor. For such we are to one another.

Pauses here will make these reflections even more poignant, for example, before verse 18, before verse 20, and before verse 22.

Colossians 3:12-17

General sense —

This little gem could very well be an early baptismal instruction, in its brief description of the community life the new Christian embraces. The virtues are there, but the garment of mutual love, modeled after God's great universal love, is the keystone of the entire structure. Notice the trifold repetition in verses 9 (just before this passage), and in verses 13 and 16, of the phrase, "one another." All our responsibilities are mutual.

For your reading —

Speak with an eager and deeply felt joy as you render these happy lines.

Verse 14 is the center of the piece, holding it together not only theologically but as a reading. Be sure to pause after it, as it is a climax to the admonitions of the first two verses.

Luke 12:13-21

General sense —

Jesus tells here the parable of the rich fool, who stands somewhere between the mournful resignation of today's Old Testament reading and the happy community life encouraged by Paul. The rich fool stores up his goods and rejoices in a man-made contentment. No melancholy brooding on his lot — no going about in naive, smiling poverty.

The principal idea here is not to frighten us with the thought of sudden death. Jesus would never descend to that "cheap shot" sort of thing. Rather, he urges us to see things in the light of our future destiny, then behave accordingly. The only real abundance is the riches of God.

For your reading —

Verses 13 through 15, in which Jesus refuses to be involved in a family dispute, have a worldly harshness to them. Jesus comes on to the man sternly, rather out of character, rare for the Master. Read these verses mindful of the Lord being caught rather by surprise that worldly goods are considered so important.

Immediately Jesus regains his composure, telling us how God views our attitude toward riches. These verses sparkle with conversational variations, as the Savior acts out the parts himself. They are a fine challenge to your ability to be a storyteller.

PROPER 14

Suggested theme for today's readings —
Our faith is rewarded by our glorious destiny with the Lord.

Genesis 15:1-6

General sense —

The Lord, in the course of promising Abraham a great posterity, shows today how small we think — the patriarch's worry over one heir — and how big are the plans God has for those who love him. "Fear not, little flock," comforts Jesus in the Gospel, and in today's reading from Hebrews we hear the rewards of a trusting faith.

For your reading —

As attentive as you must be to the varying conversational

inflections here, the climax of this reading arrives in the very last verse, 6. In almost the same words used by Jesus centuries later, Abraham's faith has healed him.

Pause, then, to give Abraham a moment, after verse 5, to ponder what God has told him, and to make the grace-filled effort to entrust himself to whatever the Lord has said.

After such a moment of silence, your rendering of the final verse should have a significant impact on your hearers, who will understand it better because they are people of faith too.

Hebrews 11:1-3, 8-16

General sense —
This passage opens with the two aspects of faith — not really its definition — which join our assurance of future good things with our confidence in the significance of the unseen realities of the present.

The writer then sketches a portrait of how faith influenced the lives of people who lived before the coming of Jesus Christ.

For your reading —
Notice how frequently the writer uses the expression "by faith" to tie together all his examples. This is your cue to lean on that phrase when it occurs, so that your hearers will perceive its centrality.

Verse 16 is a strong one, a line telling us of God's delight in being with us. It forms a fitting climax to your reading, as you end on this proud note.

Luke 12:32-40

General sense —
Luke collects here the sayings of Jesus on our own personal destiny as a reward for our faith, which is today's general theme for all the readings. Our anxiety about tomorrow can be eased by our zeal in always being ready for the coming of the Lord.

For your reading —
This is an eloquent plea for our awareness of the presence and work of the Spirit in us. It deserves a robust, assured delivery which leaves no doubt as to the wonderful status we enjoy as children of God.

The very first verse, 32, is the attention-getter. If it were read so that all who hear it would take heart, then the Kingdom of God on earth would truly begin to appear in your parish.

PROPER 15

Suggested theme for today's readings —
No Christian can be a worthy disciple of the Lord without some self-sacrifice.

Jeremiah 23:23-29

General sense —

In the verses which precede today's passage, Jeremiah has denounced bad prophets. Their moral conduct, he says, is evil. They do not truly prophesy but only flatter popular passions, and are therefore liars and victims of their own imaginations. A final criterion, in today's reading, is their reliance on dreams. Dreams are not always a good means of revelation; in today's opening verses they offend God's "otherness" by making him too humanly close.

For your reading —

In Jeremiah's day, to be a prophet was to be respected and listened to — an open invitation, as it is today, for charlatans to hoodwink the gullible and attain an importance in the community not otherwise possible for them.

These are angry lines, to be read with a certain edge of impatience, in a somewhat stronger voice than normally.

Hebrews 12:1-7, 11-14

General sense —

The words "discipline" and "disciple" are of course closely related etymologically. Here, their relationship arrears theological as well as linguistic. Every discipline the author describes is a part of being a good disciple. Our sufferings, our sacrifices, all "seem painful" at the moment, as do our efforts to understand the discipline of the Lord, in verse 6.

For your reading —

The "cloud of witnesses," our fellow Christians, spurs us on. This reading is a strongly worded, no-holds-barred, truth-in-packaging exhortation on what it means to be an earnest Christian. Read it vigorously, moving along to pile up the responsibilities involved in this struggle.

At verse 12, the address turns directly to the people. Pause before reading it; the generalities have ended and it is time to act, so that the last three verses will be as earnest and appealing as you can make them.

Luke 12:49-56

General sense —

Jeremiah urged the discipline of honesty, Hebrews the discipline of the Christian ethic. Now Jesus urges on us the no-looking-back discipline of this countercultural movement he has founded. He presses us to see the signs of the times which forecast trouble, even within our families, as a result of our convictions. It is one of the few glimpses we are allowed into the depths of Jesus' being. The urgency of his mission stabs him like a sword which for all time will divide the eager from the contented.

For your reading —

This is so urgent and demanding a passage that you must defuse its impact somewhat by pauses. Read the first three exclamations, in verses 49, 50 and 51a, then slow the pace and read through verse 53 in a solemn mode, foreseeing trouble to come.

At verse 54, Jesus' anger rises again. He turns to the crowd and raises his voice to be heard. These last three verses are a stinging indictment of so many people who are keenly aware of worldly things but never glance into themselves. Be sure your hearers, through the strength of your voice, catch the mood of our Savior here, as you conclude.

PROPER 16

Suggested theme for today's readings —
Our security is in the Lord and what he asks of us today, not worrying about the future.

Isaiah 28:14-22

General sense —

In the late eighth century before Christ, about 721, Samaria is about to fall to the invading Assyrian army. Israel seeks alliance with Egypt to withstand this threat to all of Palestine.

No, says Isaiah. Power politics like this is false security. The rulers of Judah are inviting destruction, putting their trust in lifeless idols (verse 15) instead of letting God lay a foundation of unquestioning trust which will void the "covenant with death." Trust is a pervading Isaian theme.

For your reading —

It is possible that few of your hearers will understand the significance of this warlike alarm.

Nevertheless, read its message with an appreciation that our trust in worldly values can often go sour. It would be better to deliver it straight through without special emphasis, since the tone does not change.

Hebrews 12:18-19, 22-29

General sense —

Our third Sunday reading from Hebrews strikes a contrast between the assembly of Israel, gathered for the giving of the Law in a rather intimidating situation, and the gathering in heaven, made available by Jesus, of those of the new law, or covenant.

For your reading —

The call to the renewal of our lives by adopting the freedom of the new Covenant is continued in today's second reading.

Read the first two verses here in a rather stern and forbidding mode. Then, verses 22 through 24 exemplify a much happier assembly, as should your more gentle tone of voice.

Verses 25 through 27 explain what went before; then, after verse 27 and a pause, the final two verses address the people directly, with a strong emphasis on the brief final verse as you close.

Luke 13:22-30

General sense —
The extent of the number to be saved is a perennial human problem. Jesus excludes no one who puts forth effort, except if they come along too late. Each one must get to work at it now. No one has an absolute right to the possession of the Kingdom.

For your reading —
If you stop after the question in verse 23, you will bring it up to date and more efficiently catch your hearers' attention.

The rest of this mysterious discourse of the Savior is better left unstressed at any particular point. Every verse is important, as Jesus links us with the patriarchs of old, then concludes by leaving the question of who among us will be saved where it belongs — up in the air: God's secret.

PROPER 17

Suggested theme for today's readings —
The lack of self-importance is one of the marks of the true Christian.

Ecclesiasticus 10:12-18

General sense —
This book is also known as Sirach, from the signature of the author, a respected teacher and a man of culture and wealth, who wrote this apology for Judaism about 180 B.C. The title "Ecclesiasticus" calls attention to the fact that although the Church adopted it, the synagogue did not. It is not a part of the Jewish Scriptures, hence it is designated in some churches today as apocryphal.

Today's passage is a heavy indictment of human pride.

For your reading —
These homely lines speak of what dwells in each one of us: the urge to think we are immune from human ills and mortality.

Your reading comes so close to home with us that it need not be declaimed or announced. Simply put forward its maxims, in a calm and assured manner, letting your hearers apply each admonition to themselves as they will.

Hebrews 13:1-8

General sense —

We conclude today our four readings from this epistle. The author, in closing his letter, urges on everyone the general maxims we all like to end our correspondence with: behave yourselves, be good, be careful, and so on.

Your leaders, he concludes, are examples of faith. They have passed on, but Jesus Christ is the same forever.

For your reading —

Our first reading today dealt with pride, this one with simplicity of life, and the theme of the Gospel will be unpretentiousness. All are quiet virtues; none of the readings demand proclamation or the raised voice.

Deliver these lines from Hebrews in a friendly mode, with frequent pauses, and with as much eye contact with your hearers as you can manage. It is a directly personal appeal to some dearly respected friends.

Luke 14:1, 7-14

General sense —

Jesus is not teaching etiquette here, but rather from good manners he draws two lessons about the Kingdom: first, we come there only by invitation from his Father; second, he invites those who recognize their lowliness and their need of salvation.

For your reading —

This is the third instruction today about the simple virtues. Once again Jesus enacts all the parts, so that your storytelling skills will be demanded here. No need to overact or exaggerate — just a small variation in your voice will convey the atmosphere Jesus intends.

Verse 11 is a direct address, as Jesus draws the moral of the story. Lift your head and make eye contact with your hearers as you deliver it.

The final three verses are a treatment of the same topic from another angle. They sound a note of warning and strike another image of Jesus' Father as the rewarder of kindness.

PROPER 18

Suggested theme for today's readings —

When we accept the responsibilities of the Christian life, we do so with trust in the Lord.

Deuteronomy 30:15-20

General sense —

God, through the lips of Moses, makes a covenant with his people. Blessing and curse were the ultimate sanctions. The heart of the encounter with the divine is, as always, salvation: the urgency of committing ourselves to a binding decision, today.

For your reading —

These are strong and earnest words, to be taken very seriously, and to be delivered by you in a tone which makes it clear and urgent to your hearers.

Pause after verse 16, as the contrast is drawn in verses 17 and 18. Verse 19 repeats and summarizes the choice; read it with special emphasis.

In verse 20, as you come to the conclusion, your voice softens and slows, as the Lord's generosity bursts forth, to end on a note of fidelity to his promise.

Philemon 1-20

General sense —

Paul appeals, not as an Apostle, not with authority, but simply "for love's sake," that Philemon take back a runaway slave who had apparently wronged his master.

It may seem odd that such a personal, non-pastoral letter would appear in the Canon of Scripture. But Paul's attitude toward slavery, even though in those days it would have been futile to try to change the system, besides his obvious affection for the slave, and his plea that Philemon treat him as a brother, teach an important human value: charity.

For your reading —

This brief note is so warmly human, so personal, that it needs no more special emphasis than the changes of voice demanded by its content.

Verses 17, 18 and 19 are the climax of the request, and should be read somewhat more slowly.

Luke 14:25-33

General sense —

Acceptance of responsibility is a keynote of all three readings today. Here in the Gospel, Jesus adds a warning: we must give ourselves not on impulse, but after careful consideration.

For your reading —

A great multitude bursts open this scene, and Jesus is quick to take advantage of it. Speak his opening words, in verses 25 through 27, in a somewhat raised voice. Jesus is saying, in effect, "Be sure you know why you are following me."

At verse 28 Jesus begins to speak more calmly, and you will be able to deliver the rest of the passage more evenly.

Make the final verse, 33, emphatic enough to justify its character as a summary of Jesus' remarks.

PROPER 19

Suggested theme for today's readings —
Awareness of our sinfulness makes us true children of God.

Exodus 32:1, 7-14

General sense —
The people, impatient for Moses' descent from Mount Sinai, fashion for themselves an idol made from their women's jewelry. God, in the primitive theology of the time, becomes angry, referring to them, as he speaks to Moses, as "your people," instead of the usual "my people."

Moses, however, invoking the Lord's promises and his honor, plays the role of mediator and, according to the authors, makes God "repent of the evil."

For your reading —
This ancient episode is so removed from our present-day experience that it would be well for you to render it on its own terms, leaving it as a warning to an unlettered, nomadic tribe to remain faithful to their divine benefactor.

A slight pause before verse 14 will set off that final verse as a predictable conclusion and a return to their status quo.

1 Timothy 1:12-17

General sense —
Timothy, head of the Church at Ephesus, one of the major Seven Churches of Asia, was one of Paul's most loyal companions and trusted workers. The Apostle's two letters to him, from which we will read today and for the next six Sundays, are instructional documents on the direction of the local community.

For your reading —
Paul, after the usual salutations and comparisons of old and new Laws, here sets down a sort of disclaimer, lest anyone think his Gospel is his own, or wonder if vanity moves him.

Except for a pause after verse 16 to set off the final doxology in verse 17, you need not place any special emphasis on the text. It was written humbly, and ought to be read in the same mode.

Luke 15:1-10

General sense —
Repentance for sin moved Moses in our first reading, as it did Paul when he wrote to Timothy. Here Jesus tells two parables of repentance, likening us to lost sheep or to a mislaid coin. Each of us is equally important to God, especially when we are aware of our sinfulness.

For your reading —
The point of these parables, the remarks which stirred Jesus

to make these comparisons, occurs in verse 2. It deserves special emphasis because it sets the scene.

As he does so often, Jesus acts out all the parts in the story, challenging you, as you read, to act them out as well. Use your storytelling skills to modulate your voice as the dialogues demand. Then raise your head and make eye contact with your hearers for the final direct address of Jesus to the people in verse 10.

PROPER 20

Suggested theme for today's readings —
Personal wealth and the pressures of business place great temptations in the path of Christian discipleship.

Amos 8:4-7

General sense —

Amos, the traditionalist, is fighting to bring back the good old days and the good old ways, when the people were steeped in the Law of Moses. Typically in the prosperous and peaceful time when he writes, the rich are oppressing the poor, and, in verse 4, can hardly wait for the end of the holy days so they can get back to business.

For your reading —

The traders' cheating practises are described in detail here, so that the point of the reading lies in the more generally applied first and last verses.

Lean on these two verses, 4 and 7, since they are ideas which still hold today.

1 Timothy 2:1-8

General sense —

Paul continues his advice to Timothy, developing the notion of the universal saving will of God. All Christians should pray for all people, because the Lord wants everyone to be saved, which means to come to the knowledge of the truth.

For your reading —

This is a key lesson in the practise of living our Christian faith — the reaching out beyond our own community interests. Read it without particular emphasis, since it is an extension of one idea.

Wherever you see the word "men," you may wish to substitute "people" for it, to avoid an obvious sexism.

Luke 16:1-13

General sense —

Luke records, in this section of his Gospel, two parables about riches. We read one today and the other next Sunday.

Jesus draws three moral lessons from today's story, in verses 8, 10 and 13. We are to be careful about the power of wealth to lead us to dishonesty.

For your reading —
Discipline the tones of your voice here to enact the roles in this little vignette of Oriental life. The conversational modulations are what will make the lessons come alive for your hearers.

Pause before verse 9, in which Jesus begins to address his audience directly. Then maintain this direct address, striving for frequent eye contact with your audience, to the end of the instruction.

PROPER 21

Suggested theme for today's readings —
Our wealth was given to us by God to be used for the benefit of others.

Amos 6:1-7

General sense —
Amos has but one theme: railing against the bad lot of the poor and the greed of the rich. He draws here a picture of the indolence and luxury of the rulers of Judah and of Israel, who, he predicts, will be punished by exile.

For your reading —
It would be somewhat unrealistic to deliver these lines in the passionate mode in which they were first written. But they do deserve a kind of emphasis, when we remember how often we hear working people who make it a point to complain about life among the "big shots." We can identify with that.

The final verse seems to say that all riches eventually turn to dust. It makes an apt conclusion, and one to be read a bit more strongly.

1 Timothy 6:11-19

General sense —
The incompatibility of wealth with a holy life deeply disturbed the prophet Amos in our first reading today. How much the advent of Christianity softened that view and kept wealth in perspective is evident here. Paul urges Timothy to respect the wealthy and to expect much good of them.

For your reading —
The first six verses of this passage are intensely direct and affectionate, as they recall Timothy's baptism and encourage him to fidelity. Read them as if Paul, in your imagination, had grasped the hand of his protege in greeting and had spoken earnestly looking into his eyes, without releasing his handshake.

Verses 17 through 19 are more reflective, as if the two men

had begun to enjoy a short walk together while continuing their conversation. Keep the note of informality as you read these verses in a slightly less animated tone.

In verse 16, feel free to substitute "no one" for "no man."

Luke 16:19-31

General sense —

Like the dishonest manager we read about last week, the rich man today also seems successful, but is unaware of his mishandling of wealth. He never realizes his mistake until after his death.

For your reading —

You are the storyteller here. Call forth that ability to draw this picture for your hearers, with its violent contrasts on earth in verse 19, and its grim view of the afterlife in the drama which follows.

At verse 24, raise your voice when the rich man begs for mercy, as also in verses 27 and 30, where he continues his pleading. The voice of Abraham, serenely at peace in the heavenly realm, will be read in a lower and calmer voice, so that the two figures in the dialogue will be clearly differentiated.

PROPER 22

Suggested theme for today's readings —
Good Christians base all their actions on the faith by which they live.

Habakkuk 1:1-6, 12-13; 2:1-4

General sense —

Like Job, and many other thoughtful people through the ages, Habakkuk is preoccupied by the problem of evil. Why is God silent in the face of injustice? The prophet is told to write down God's answer, so that all may read it. And that answer has never changed, to this day: the just person lives by faith.

For your reading —

Begin verse 2 in an urgent mode, and maintain that insistency through verse 4. Then pause for a moment.

Verses 5 and 6 are delivered after that pause, as God's answer, in a lower voice.

Verses 12 and 13 resume the prophet's questioning. Then in the final four verses, 1 through 4, occurs the resolution of the conflict. Read these verses on a positive note, reassuring your hearers of the unchangeability of God's ways with all of us.

2 Timothy 1:6-14

General sense —

The months between Pentecost and the advent of the new

year in the Church are times of general instruction in the Christian life. We move now to Paul's second letter to Timothy, as we continue his word to the Church at Ephesus. And we reprise the same pattern: be faithful to your lofty calling.

For your reading —
Paul writes as he must have spoken to this dear friend and co-worker for the Gospel. Read this passage in a calm way, yet, as in verse 12, seasoned with a typically Pauline flash of pride. Mark that with emphasis as you read.

Luke 17:5-10

General sense —
Two basic lessons surface here: 1. It is not the quantity of our faith, as the disciples expressed it, that needs help, but its quality. In verse 6, Jesus' sense suggests that the very boldness of our faith can be anticipated by fulfillment; 2. We can never stop and rest on our laurels. We have never done enough — indeed, we have only done what we were supposed to do. As in our first two readings today, we are alive in Christ principally by our faith.

For your reading —
Except for the disciples' cry in verse 5, no particular stress is indicated in any verse of this brief passage. Read it as the lesson it is intended to be, and conclude strongly as Jesus ends it with the moral.

PROPER 23
Suggested theme for today's readings —
Our family loyalties reflect our devotion to God's fidelity.

Ruth 1:8-19a

General sense —
The story of Ruth, aglow with family loyalty, solid citizens, and a beautiful romance, has two levels. Underneath the action of the drama appears the Lord's plan to preserve the line of succession from Abraham, to whom he had promised that succession, down to David and the dynasty which contained the seed of the Messiah. It is one of many Old Testament stories of a divine preservation which defies every obstacle — almost all of those stories featuring women as doers of good deeds.

For your reading —
In a touching tale of intimacy many of us have experienced in our own families, Ruth decides to stay with her mother-in-law Naomi, rather than to go home and find another husband.

This is not an easy reading. Emotions, pleas, life decisions — all serve to enhance the drama. Each must be transmitted clearly, especially the poetic final decision of Ruth in verses 16 and 17.

If you read, for background, the entire story from verse 1, you will have a good sense of what transpires, making your delivery of this affecting incident as moving as the author intended it to be.

2 Timothy 2:8-15

General sense —
Timothy, writes his mentor Paul, must be a model of fidelity, as was Ruth in our first reading, an example to his flock of devotion to the mission of Jesus Christ.

For your reading —
Lean on the recital of the old hymn which Paul quotes in verse 11. It is the climax of this reading, and should be read with particular pointedness, pausing before and after it.

Luke 17:11-19

General sense —
Today's theme of fidelity continues, in the well-known story of the ten lepers. How ironic, and how typical of this Gospel's literary excellence, that in one of the lepers being a Samaritan, Luke notices the great leveling power of misery among all of us. A hated Samaritan and the proud Jew have no trouble mingling with each other. Leprosy has erased their differences.

Lepers, here and elsewhere in the Gospels, do not ask to be cured, but cleansed. The affliction of leprosy was not so much the disease as it was the lonely despair of being excluded from the community, with its relationships and its assemblies.

For your reading —
In verse 13, raise your voice as the band of lepers calls out for mercy. Verses 17 and 18 tell us of Jesus' very human perplexity that all ten did not return, not to thank him personally but to praise God. Exemplify this wonderment in your voice as you read these lines.

Accent the word "faith" in the final verse, because it marks our own contribution to the healings in our lives, and is therefore important.

PROPER 24

Suggested theme for today's readings —
The Lord always invites our perseverance by his constant availability to us.

Genesis 32:3-8, 22-30

General sense —
The story of Jacob, the reluctant convert, rings with the truth of our human weaknesses. A schemer in his youth, his gradual

growth to maturity is the golden thread of one of the most touching biographies in the Bible.

Today's passage climaxes that grace-filled process we know as conversion. Jacob goes to be reconciled with his estranged brother Esau, but finds that he must first face himself.

For your reading —

This is storytelling at its best. Read it with the variation of tones demanded by the conversations. The climax of Jacob's acceptance of life in the second segment, verses 22 through 30, should be read a bit more slowly, as the Lord's angel appears and Jacob comes finally to face his destiny as a servant of God.

2 Timothy 3:14 – 4:5

General sense —

The useful lessons drawn for Timothy continue today, in the sixth of our seven readings from Paul's letter to the head of the Church at Ephesus.

Our current passage includes one of the Bible's most quoted phrases, in verse 16. This clear reference to the divine origin of the Scriptures grounds the Bible's authority in God as the principal teacher of humanity's behavioral norms.

For your reading —

As we have remarked, this is a teaching passage, requiring a delivery full of strength, clarity, and above all, confidence. Enunciate every admonition clearly, never speedily, since each lesson bears its own importance.

There is no particular point of emphasis, except for the final verse 5, which applies to all of us, and which it would be well for you to read as you make eye contact with your hearers.

Luke 18:1-8a .

General sense —

The lesson appears well here. Jacob persevered, Timothy is urged to do likewise. But this teaching on perseverance is a mysterious one indeed. Told only by Luke among the Evangelists, Jesus seems, incredibly, to be comparing his Father to a lazy, unreligious judge, whose response to perseverance is motivated only by a desire to be rid of the petitioner.

For your reading —

This is a brief reading; you will have but a moment or two at the lectern. So your delivery, full of conversational interest and with an unusual message, must be unmistakeably clear, devoid of any special point of emphasis but evenly paced throughout.

PROPER 25

Suggested theme for today's readings —
Our humble prayers to the Lord always find a loving heart.

Jeremiah 14:7-10, 19-22

General sense —

The prophet, describing the effects of a severe drought, attributes it to the "backsliding" of an unfaithful people, as the ancients always treated natural disasters.

But he never loses hope; he knows whence relief will come and whence it will not, and so turns despair into a hymn of praise.

For your reading —

This reading has two segments. Similar in mood, they are to be read with an evident pause after the Lord has spoken, in verse 10.

The whole passage takes the form of a prayer (except, of course, verse 10), and its reader should pay careful attention to using a tone which calls out to the Lord. It utters a plea, an urgent cry for mercy, a confession of sin and weakness.

Pause not only after verse 10 but after verse 9 as well, to set off the Lord's words by themselves.

Pause after verse 19, as the prayer becomes more insistently contrite, and after verse 22a, to emphasize the last petition of hope and praise.

2 Thessalonians 4:6-8, 16-18

General sense —

Paul contemplates his death, as we end our readings from his letter to Timothy. He refers to life as a race and a fight, and is proud of having kept the faith he was given. He forgives all who have not supported him and he recommends his life to the Lord.

For your reading —

This faith-filled last will and testament is read smoothly and calmly, without particular emphasis. If you catch a sense of the joy of the Apostle that he feels he is on the threshold of victory over the world, your voice will also reflect that sense of peace and happy anticipation of a heavenly crown.

Luke 18:9-14

General sense —

This familiar parable of pride and humility has graced many a sermon and retreat conference. Luke introduces the story himself as a showcase for the spirit of his Gospel. The failure of the Law alone to justify, the evil of pride, the mercy of God and the universality of salvation are exemplified here.

For your reading —
The life of this short reading is in your hands as a storyteller. Be sure to animate the action by your conversational voice modulations, as well as by a pause after verse 13, as Jesus draws the moral of the story.

PROPER 26

Suggested theme for today's readings —
God's absolute forgiveness always seems to surprise us.

Isaiah 1:10-20

General sense —
This passage sounds like a sermon; most think it might have been delivered before a crowd at a public festival.

God appears as both plaintiff and judge, then suddenly opens the hand of mercy, as Isaiah strikes the keynote of his whole ministry: accusation of evil and assurance of divine forgiveness.

For your reading —
We are to deliver strong words today, as the prophet rails against insincere worship for six long verses. God, in typical ancient expression, is pictured in anger and frustration. Let that spirit show as you raise your voice in protest.

Verses 16 and 17 reduce the tone, in the positive and constructive warnings for better living.

Finally, the last three verses reveal the God of love and prodigal forgiveness. Read them gently but insistently, as you conclude on this note of hope.

2 Thessalonians 1:1-5, 10-12

General sense —
Paul's first letter to the Church at Thessaly in northern Greece shone with optimism and gentle affection. A few months later he wrote this second letter, from which we will read for the next three Sundays.

Here, the Apostle comforts the people in persecution, praising and encouraging their steadfast faith.

For your reading —
This passage amounts to a friendly greeting, and is to be rendered with the loving appreciation of good friends and faithful co-workers which on occasion we hear even today.

It is a reading full of smiles, designed to comfort your hearers who are sharing the same faith, each in their own circumstances and difficulties.

Luke 19:1-10

General sense —
Zaccheus' spirit of curiosity and adventure literally propels

him off the ground. He puts forth much effort to win over the Lord. His resume on the tip of his tongue (verse 8), he thinks he is the searcher. But it is Jesus who is the eternal Searcher. "The son of man came to seek and save the lost (verse 10)."

For your reading —

Here is a story full of surprises. Fast-moving, it never wastes a movement or a gesture. Salvation comes in a whirlwind of conversion, as two kindred spirits meet and fall in together, with complete mutual understanding.

Keep your voice upbeat and animated throughout, passing along to your hearers the joy of this happy experience.

PROPER 27

Suggested theme for today's readings —
Our perseverance is the dawning of God's eternal life in us.

Job 19:23-27a

General sense —

The Book of Job is a dialogue between Job and his friends on the mystery of the suffering which comes to good people. Each speech of a friend is followed by a response from Job. The longest ancient Hebrew poem in the Bible, the book is unquestionably the work of a spiritual genius.

Our reading today is part of the so-called Fifth Response of Job, expressing his hope of the vision of God.

For your reading —

Job, in these dramatic and inspired lines, resists the gloomy pronouncements of his companions, thrusting a radiant sword of faith through their despair.

The lines you have been assigned to read ring out like a single shout of praise, from the depths of Job's abandonment by family, friends, and, apparently, God.

Raise your voice, reading so that your own faith rises up within you, placing special emphasis on verse 25, the act of trust which Job wants engraved in stone.

2 Thessalonians 2:13 – 3:5

General sense—

The Apostle Paul's personal reflections and recommendations draw this letter toward its close. He speaks of his gratitude for the people's faith, which will result in their glory; he urges their perseverance, and asks prayers for himself and the work of the Gospel.

For your reading —

Job's cry of faith in our first reading finds an echo here; faith is what Paul loves and respects most in his people.

Your reading should be of one tone: positive, earnest, affectionate. Except for a pause after verse 17, to mark the beginning of the writer's final advice, there is no special point of emphasis.

Luke 20:27, 34-38

General sense —

Since the resurrection of the body was not in the text of the Torah, or Law, the Sadducees denied this doctrine. (As the ancient joke goes, that is why they were sad, you see.)

The Sadducees were the party of the priestly aristocracy, conservative enough even to accept the Roman rule of Palestine. Luke could not have written of a group more alien to the teachings of Jesus than these people.

For your reading —

The Sadducees propose what they think will be a "trick question," seeking to confuse or to upset Jesus.

Your assigned reading unfortunately skips over the question itself; perhaps the answer was considered more important.

The reading's only climax comes in verse 38, as Jesus applies the resurrection to everyone alive right now in the Church. Read this closing verse slowly and somewhat emphatically.

PROPER 28

Suggested theme for today's readings —
Vigilance is a key part of our service of the Lord.

Malachi 3:13 – 4:2a, 5-6

General sense —

Dating from the middle of the fifth century B.C., this is the sixth oracle, or speech, called by some commentators "burden," of this prophet, who, like all the prophets, railed against the evils of the day.

Our reading compares the destiny of those who serve with the destiny of those who do not, and ends with the announcement of the coming of the great Elijah.

For your reading —

Read these lines with something of the feeling of this minor prophet for the suffering of the just and the prosperity of the unjust. There seem to be no other points of emphasis which express thoughts relevant to our world today.

2 Thessalonians 3:6-13

General sense —

The fate of those who serve and those who do not echoes our first reading. As the Church year winds to a close, Paul leaves us with the admonition that we mind our own business and carry our share of life's burdens with the rest of our community.

For your reading —
Some of these ideas sound a note of familiarity even today; the drones will always be among us.

Read, then, with the calm self-assurance Paul must have felt as he wrote. Make each sentence count, as you deliver his words not hastily but with deep conviction.

Luke 21:5-19

General sense —
Where Matthew writes that "Jesus left the temple and was going away," and Mark has, "as he came out of the temple," Luke places the Savior inside, as he watches the widow give her mite, in verses 1 and 2. Jesus is seen, therefore, to discuss the fall of Jerusalem publicly, as if to warn the whole Jewish nation of its coming tragedy.

For your reading —
Jesus speaks ominously and gravely here, prophesying the doom of his beloved city. Read verse 6 in this frame of mind. He ignores the request for signs, and stresses personal vigilance and a steadfast faith.

This tone of seriousness is to be maintained through verse 17. Then, as Jesus reveals his Father's unremitting love in verses 18 and 19, soften your voice and deliver these final lines in a tone of consolation and encouragement.

PROPER 29

Suggested theme for today's readings —
Our perseverance is the Lord's own guarantee of our heavenly destiny.

Jeremiah 23:1-6

General sense —
On the last Sunday of the Church year, our liturgy opens with this promise of great things for our future.

Jeremiah predicts the restoration of David's dynasty, not so much on political grounds as on a religious and moral level. Jesus was the new David who accomplished this hope.

For your reading —
This passage consists entirely of the words of the Lord, so that it becomes rather a proclamation, to be read as such, in a somewhat raised voice.

In order to avoid finishing on this tense note, read the final verse, 6, in a gentler tone, to reflect the goodness of the Lord and the happiness of our destiny.

Colossians 1:11-20

General sense —
As did Jeremiah in our first reading today, Paul speaks of our destiny as children of God. He concludes the passage with a hymn to the Christ who is all in all, the divine peacemaker of creation.

For your reading —
There is no reading of these lines in a matter-of-fact tone, as if they were simply greetings in a letter. They are rather words of divine praise, a fervent tribute to the divinity which graces our universe and our lives.

Let your voice echo this hymn-like quality, as you read with unmistakeable reverence and adoration.

Verses 19 and 20 are the climax of the passage; let them stand out with particular stress.

Luke 23:35-43

General sense —
One of the anchors of hope for all of us sinners, the story of the good thief speaks to us of our destiny on this last Sunday of the year.

Luke's Jesus exercises his ministry of forgiveness to the last, in a crucifixion scene free of the shadows and gloom remembered by Matthew and Mark.

For your reading —
Drop your voice after "watching" in verse 35. Luke wants the two classes of spectators at the Cross carefully distinguished. And slide over "saying" in the same verse. The important word here is "scoffed."

The same principle holds for "vinegar" in verse 36, "railed at him" in verse 39, and "rebuked" in verse 40. All those words are far more important than the word "saying," which merely connects them to what was uttered.

This is a solemn passage indeed, read in a tone of some gravity. Verse 43, however, bears the never-failing forgiveness of the Lord, and should close your reading on a note of gentleness and trust.